Making
Knowledge
Visible

Making Knowledge Visible

Elizabeth Orna

Communicating
Knowledge through
Information Products

GOWER

Published by   Gower Publishing Limited
Gower House, Croft Road
Aldershot, Hants
GU11 3HR
England

Gower Publishing Company
Suite 420,
101 Cherry Street, Burlington,
VT 05401-4405
USA

Elizabeth Orna has asserted her rights under the
Copyright, Designs and Patent Act 1988 to be identified
as the author of this work.

British Library
Cataloguing in Publication Data
Orna, Elizabeth
Making knowledge visible: communicating knowledge
through information products
1. Knowledge management
I. Title
658.4'038

ISBN   0 566 08562 3 (Hardback)
0 566 08563 1 (Paperback)

Library of Congress Control Number: 2004116730

Printed and bound in Great Britain by MPG Books
Limited, Bodmin

Design, typesetting, page make-up and drawings by
Graham Stevens. Typesetting and page make-up in
QuarkXpress; drawings in Freehand; text typeface Thesis
sans and Thesis sans mono designed by Luc(as) de Groot
and completed in 1994

Contents

Foreword

Liz Orna has produced another book based on research that is both so deep and broad that it puts to shame many of the more partial contributions to the field.

Firstly it takes an integrating perspective, thinking across boundaries of convenience or territorialism such as delineate or indeed divide information management, knowledge management and information technology.

Secondly, it is a reflective work, not driven by the need to commercialize a particular individualistic fad or fashion, and indeed both willing and able to recognize the incremental and cumulative contributions of many predecessors which underpin her work.

Thirdly, it serves as a constant reminder how the pursuit of information technology implementation, with its massive budgets and demanding vendors, has repeatedly tended to drive out consideration of the underlying purpose of information technology, namely the exploitation of information and knowledge to business advantage.

The book contains a wealth of case studies. Again, when in the more conventional IT and knowledge management fields there is often a tired re-working of case studies frankly past their sell-by date, Liz continues to provide us with a range of original cases from across the world, and across both public and private sectors.

Liz also has some wonderfully compelling turns of phrase such as:
'I gave up being surprised a long time ago by how often those essential products look as if they have been designed to repel all boarders, drive users to distraction, dissuade potential customers from purchase of goods or services, and impede staff in their work.'

Not everyone will be happy with the advocacy of yet another term, 'information products', but I feel on balance this is justified, and indeed has merit. These are the 'products'... through which information is presented for use. They embody the results of the transformation of knowledge into information ... and are an integral blend of content and container.'

The very intangibility of much information and knowledge makes it particularly useful to conceive of the importance of what physical manifestation that does exist. One of the problems 'down to earth' managers feel in dealing with information is precisely this intangibility. By seeing information through the more tangible lens of a product, this removes at least one common barrier to the effective exploitation of information.

Despite the excellence of its underlying research, the book sets out to be a practical text for readers, and in the final part of the book, Liz advocates the use of Information Auditing in addressing the management of information products.

This is not a book which advocates a simplistic quick fix solution to achieving value from the investments in information and knowledge. But its clear style and consistent messages mean that it has utility both for those already expert in the field, as well as those starting out on the search for achieving value.

CLIVE HOLTHAM
Professor of Information Management, Cass Business School, City of London

Acknowledgements

This book could not have been written without the organizations and individuals who were willing to tell me the stories which are strung throughout its length as illustrations of its themes. Visits and exchanges with them were a treat which kept me going, and it is a pleasure to acknowledge the enlightenment and entertainment they provided. Some had already been the subject of case studies over the five years of research on which the book is partly based, and I appreciate their generosity and fortitude in being willing to put up with yet more of my questions.

City University
The Department of Information Science for allowing me to extend the scope of information science in a rather eccentric direction, and for letting me use the University itself as a case study in my PhD research. David Bawden for his wise supervision, and Wendy Clifton-Sprigg for helping to bring the story up to date

The Cochrane Collaboration
Sir Iain Chalmers (James Lind Library),
Mike Clarke (UK Cochrane Centre),
Jini Hetherington (The Cochrane Collaboration),
Mark Starr (Update Software Ltd)

The Co-operative Bank
Chris Smith and Gayle Ramouz

The Department of Health
Linda Wishart

The Department of Trade and Industry
Liz MacLachlan

Essex County Council
Heather Leverett, Jane Jennings, Judith Sweetman and the members of the governors information audit team and steering committee

FreePint
William Hann

Inland Revenue
Gwenda Sippings and Jenny Coombes

Local e-Government National Customer Relations Management Programme
Danny Budzak

mda (the Museum Documentation Association)
Alex Dawson

The NHS Centre for Reviews and Dissemination
Julie Glanville

Premier Farnell
Chas Ewen

The National Archives (ex Public Record Office)
David Ryan

Tate (formerly the Tate Gallery)
Simon Grant

The Victoria and Albert Museum
Frances Lloyd-Baynes, Gail Durbin, Sarah Medlam, Alan Seal

I am greatly indebted to Professor Philip McPherson, who helped my thinking about the value of information products by guiding me through an experimental application of his Integrated Value Manager (IVM) methodology to information products in the course of my research.

My thanks also to other individuals who contributed stories from their experience: Claire Fahy, Sharon Hayward and Caroline Mann; to Andrew Booth, Alice Grant, Peter Griffiths and many others who answered my questions and told me useful things – and to Derek Ward who asked if dances could be information products.

I am grateful to the institutions and organizations who invited me to give workshops on information products, to colleagues who helped set them up, and to the participants who allowed me to learn from their experience as expressed in the maps they built:

KIMNET (Aslib Knowledge and Information Management Network)
The committee and members

Australian Library and Information Association, Queensland Continuing Professional Development Group
Gill Hallam and Karen Nelson

TFPL (London)

The University of Technology Sydney
Sue Burgess, Maureen Henninger, Jan Houghton, and Hilary Yerbury

If the book could not have been written without the co-operation of so many institutions and individuals, it would not even have been thought of had I not encountered information design and designers at about the time when I was starting out in information management. More than three decades of work with Graham Stevens have made the connections between the disciplines of information design and information management visible to me, and so have shaped the course of my working life. I am greatly indebted to him for that insight, as well as for the design of this book and of all its predecessors.

Many other members of the information design community have contributed thoughts and experience: I am grateful to all of them, in particular to Gill Scott, David Sless and Conrad Taylor, and to Saul Carliner, Judy Gregory and other members of the InfoD-Cafe.

Finally it is a pleasure to thank Suzie Duke, commissioning editor of Gower, for her thoughtful comments on the text.

Basic ideas

part 1

Welcome to the world of information products!
The two introductory chapters which follow set
the scene for this book. They define the concepts
which underlie everything in it, explain why it
had to be written, and present an overview of
the argument it advances.

Now read on...

Before we begin

In this chapter

This introductory chapter is written on the assumption that readers prefer, as I myself do, to be told at the start what they are in for, so that they can orient themselves.

Definitions of key terms used in this book

There are many definitions of some of these terms, but as this is a practical book I give here just the pragmatic definitions which I have found useful both for thinking about the ideas involved and acting on them.

For those who are interested, they do have a respectable information-science ancestry, based on a line of thinking developed in particular by Brookes (1980a and b), which relates to how human minds transform external information into internal knowledge, and internal knowledge into information, which can in turn be put into the outside world for others to transform again into knowledge which becomes their property.

To begin with, here are definitions of knowledge, information, and transformation, because the definition of information products depends on those concepts.

Knowledge and Information
Knowledge is the organized results of experience, which we use to guide our actions and our interactions with the outside world. We all store our knowledge in our minds in a highly structured form, which is directly accessible only to us. When we want to communicate what we know to others who need to use it for their own purposes, we have to transform it and make it visible or audible to the outside world.

The result of the transformation is *Information*: knowledge which has been put into the outside world and made visible and accessible through a series of transformations.

From the point of view of the user, information is what we seek and pay attention to in our outside world when we need to add to or enrich our knowledge in order to act upon it. One of the commonest ways of getting information is by using information products – which are so named because they contain information and have been produced, as a result of decisions by human beings, for specific users and use. (We also get information by knowledgeable observation – a geologist looking at landscape, a doctor examining a patient, a skilled technician observing processes – which leads to application of existing knowledge, either without the use of information products, or supported by them, as in looking up relevant research literature.)

So we can usefully think of information as the food of knowledge because we need information and communication to nourish and maintain our knowledge and keep it in good shape for what we have to do in the world. Without the food of information, knowledge becomes enfeebled and unfit for action.

Knowledge and information are, therefore, distinct, but interdependent, and they are the subject of transformations by human minds (*see* Figure 1.1 opposite).

Transformations

Information products are the end result of the series of transformations of knowledge into information; they also become the starting point of transformation in the other direction on the part of their users, who seek to transform what they require of the information contained in the products into knowledge, and to integrate it into their existing knowledge structure so as to make it fitter for whatever they need to do.

These transformations, of information into knowledge and knowledge into information, form the basis for all human learning and communication; they allow ideas to spread across space and time, and link past and present in a network that embraces generations and cultures over millennia (*see* Figure 1.2 on p15). By virtue of those qualities, they are also fundamental to the working of organizations of all kinds.

Information products[1]

The products, print on paper or electronic, through which information is presented for use. They embody the results of the transformation of knowledge into information – which accounts for the title of this book – and are an integral blend of content and container.[2] Knowledge can be made 'visible' (that is, accessible to the senses of others) in many different forms of container and in many media: not just text, but also speech, graphics, moving images, and action (dance, mime, sign language). Although the association today tends to be with digital media, information products have an ancient

1 McCain (2004) links information products ('information goods') and information services in this definition, given in an economics context: '...information goods and services share these properties:
a) An information product is a collection of symbols.
b) Its utility depends on the arrangement of the symbols, not on the material form they take...
We may extend this definition of information products by observing that information services are services that provide or involve the manipulation of information products.

Information products cannot be bought or sold alone. While it is the arrangement of symbols that gives utility, the symbols have to be recorded or expressed in some material form.'

2 'Content is what gives meaning to things and makes them unique. It is the driving force that determines how structure, form and behavior find expression in all things.' (Heidrich, 2002). The term 'container' covers bibliographic form, physical form, and medium in which products are presented. McCain (2004) 'Information products cannot be bought, sold, given away or even preserved except in conjunction with some medium.'

Making knowledge visible

Outside world

Information = knowledge transformed and
put out into the world, where it becomes visible
and available to others, to feed their knowledge

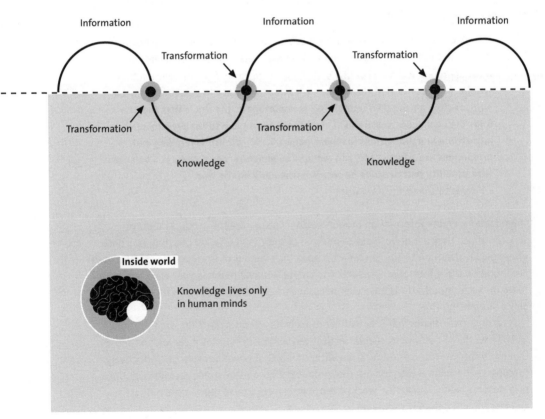

Information   Information   Information

Transformation   Transformation

Transformation   Transformation

Knowledge   Knowledge

Inside world

Knowledge lives only
in human minds

Figure 1.1 Knowledge and information: distinct but interdependent

lineage, extending back more than 5000 years to Sumerian clay tablets and Egyptian papyrus rolls (McArthur's *Worlds of Reference*, 1986, gives an illuminating account of the history of information products created for purposes of reference).

Today's most familiar digital products – websites and intranets – occupy a special place: information products in their own right, they act also as containers for other products; we might call them 'meta-information products'. And the technology that makes them possible is, as we shall see, a potential catalyst for upgrading the role that information products play in organizations.

The metaphor of the 'container' covers not only physically rigid, permanent, and static containers such as books, but also the fluid, flexible and mutable ones made possible by web technology. We should also remember that, despite their physical rigidity, traditional containers, as well as digital ones, can provide guides to navigation through them.

In my definition, the range of information products stops short of advertising. But there is a continuum between 'telling' and 'selling', and no sharp boundary between the two; the guiding principle in this book in defining information products is that they should be towards the 'telling' end of the scale, and embody substantial information content which aims to allow users to do something they need/want to do, rather than to evoke feelings and to persuade – in other words, the user has an active rather than a passive role.

The distinction is exemplified by this explanation from a company which has a worldwide business in selling electronic products; the company treats its 'Product Presentation Channel' (its information products) as a distinct stream, separate from transactions, sales, and marketing:

> **Our objective is to ensure that our goods and services are available via Product Presentation Channels in a manner that allows users to select the easiest and most appropriate channel or blend of channels, to easily find the solution they require. Please note that this concept tries not to confuse the established need with creating a need (marketing). This is important as the risk is that the user finds the catalogue/website/eCat etc difficult to use due to the prevalence of advertising and promotions (banners, page ads etc). Whilst advertising and promotions are a fact of life, and required to generate 'need', there is a balance with usability that needs to be struck, particularly on the web.**
> e-business Manager, Premier Farnell

Organizations create information products either to support the products and/ or services which they are in business to offer, or as their main market offering. This book gives special attention to the former – because they need it most; if you depend for your livelihood on the information products you create, survival requires your close attention to them. Such organizations have useful lessons for those whose information products play a supporting role.

A second main distinction is between products directed towards the organization's 'outside world' of customers, clients, institutions and communities it serves, and those that carry the internal communication without which it could not function effectively. (Despite that essential role, the internal products all too often don't get the attention they deserve, and so make the work of those who have to use them more difficult and less effective than it should be.)

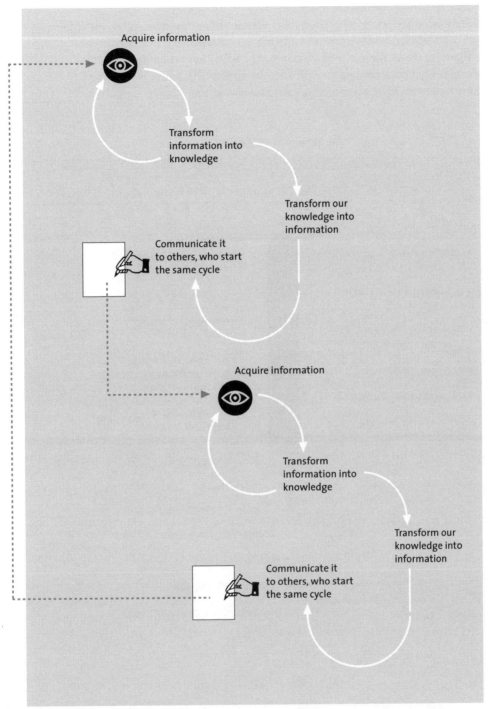

Figure 1.2 Transforming information into knowledge and knowledge into information – the chain of human communication

Reproduced from Orna, E and Stevens, G (1995), *Managing Information for Research*, Open University Press, with kind permission of the Open University Press/McGraw-Hill Publishing Company

Information and knowledge management

Just as knowledge and information are distinct but mutually dependent, so too with the domains of knowledge management and information management; they are distinct, but, as Figure 1.3 shows, there is territory common to both. They are not commonly thought of as having any connection with information products, but, as we shall see, the connection needs to be acknowledged and established.

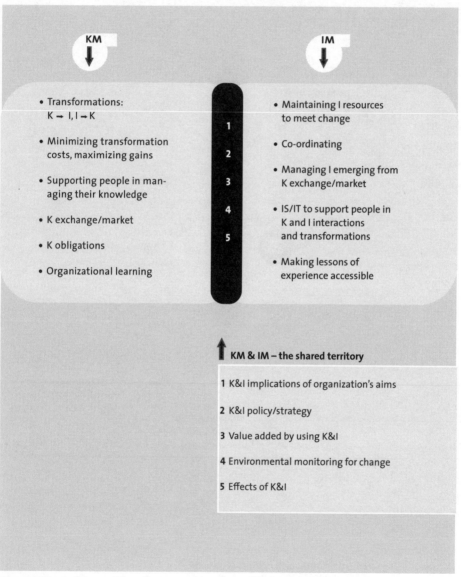

The domains of KM and IM

KM

- Transformations:
  $K \rightarrow I, I \rightarrow K$

- Minimizing transformation costs, maximizing gains

- Supporting people in managing their knowledge

- K exchange/market

- K obligations

- Organizational learning

IM

- Maintaining I resources to meet change

- Co-ordinating

- Managing I emerging from K exchange/market

- IS/IT to support people in K and I interactions and transformations

- Making lessons of experience accessible

KM & IM – the shared territory

1 K&I implications of organization's aims

2 K&I policy/strategy

3 Value added by using K&I

4 Environmental monitoring for change

5 Effects of K&I

Figure 1.3 The domains and shared terrritory of knowledge management and information management. Reproduced by permission of the publisher from Orna (2004)

Information design
Can be broadly defined as everything we do to make visible our knowledge and ideas (which by the definition used here live invisible inside individual human minds, and have to be put into the outside world before others can gain access to them), so that those who need them can enter into them and use what they learn from them for their own purposes.

And, as the definition of information products given earlier makes clear, what the users want to to do must come first; they have an active rather than a passive role; and the information designer's first responsibility is to them.

So the business of information design includes:

- The conceptual structure of information products
- Sequence of presentation
- Choice of medium and format
- Decisions about how the content is expressed (eg text, graphics, numbers, and combinations of all these)
- Management of the relevant technologies
- Writing
- Illustration
- Typography.

On this definition, many different skills and specialisms have a contribution to make to the processes of transformation that have been described above.3 The relationship between information designers and users of information products is to a large extent 'user-driven' in that 'there is a known body of users who desire certain knowledge'; and 'it is the cognitive aspects of the user that are of most significance, though feelings related to the user's need for knowledge are also taken into account'. (Orna & Stevens, 1991)

Why information products deserve a book

If we accept the definitions of knowledge and information given above, then it is evident that knowledge can't get into the outside world and reach others until it's been transformed into information and embodied in information products.

That means they are the essential carriers by which knowledge gets from one human mind to another; the process can't happen without them – knowledge can't travel directly between minds (we haven't yet got the hang of telepathy), so in order to pass it on, we have to transform it into information products in various media and put it outside our heads and into the world.

Yet – perhaps because information products are so universal – organizations have so far nearly always taken them for granted; their potential for adding (or subtracting) value has gone unrecognized, they have not captured the attention of top management, their creation and production has been fairly chaotically managed, if managed at all, and they have not been integrated into business strategies, let alone into information

3 Macdonald-Ross and Waller (1976) introduced the idea of the information designer as 'transformer' in a pioneering article, which is still worth reading today.

strategies. Even professional information managers have been reluctant to consider them as a concern of information management. At a meeting of experienced information professionals, a few days before I began writing this chapter, while there was general agreement with the idea that in making knowledge 'explicit' we turn it into information, nobody seemed to have considered that the final stage of this process was putting the information into appropriate containers in the form of information products, or that information products were what information managers manage.[4] Figure 1.4 opposite summarizes the reasons for the invisibility of IPs.

Indeed little has been written about information products in the context of the organizations for which they are created, and still less about any possible link between them and organizational information strategies and information management. It is particularly noticeable that among the vast quantity of advice on how to design websites, there are very few attempts to relate the topic to the organizational context.

While there has been much research on information products from the standpoint of information design, little of it, with some honourable exceptions, such as the Communication Research Institute of Australia (http://www.communication.org.au), has paid much heed to how and why information content gets into the containers, how decisions are made, who makes them, and how the products are related to the other things the originating organizations do in pursuit of their goals.[5]

Research in the field of information management too has showed little interest in the creation of information products as an aspect of information management. As Meyer and Zack remarked in 1996, 'Despite the economic importance and the rapid pace of innovation in this industry, [the creation of products based on 'data, information and knowledge'] no previous research has examined the design and development of information products.'

Since then, there has been little if any mention, in the copious literature about using information and knowledge for competitive advantage and related gains, of the mediating role of information products in achieving them. The recent excellent books by Marchand and his co-authors (2001a, 2001b), for example, about their research on the relation between business performance and 'Information Orientation' (the integration of the 'three key capabilities that influence information use in companies – people's behaviors and values, information management practices and IT practices.'), make no reference to the products that are the medium of information use.

And while Mahon and Gilchrist (2003) made an excellent argument for information architecture, taxonomies, metadata, thesauri etc as a proper concern of information management, as well as of information systems and software, in a preview of their book on information architecture (Gilchrist and Mahon, 2004)[6], they did not mention the

4 McCain (2004) has a relevant observation here too '… information services are services that provide or involve the manipulation of information products'

5 This was one of my reasons for undertaking the research which was part of the basis for this book (*see* p7).

6 The book itself contains just one chapter (an excellent one by Catherine Leloup on 'Document, information, data, content') which actually refers to the publishing process and to the need to integrate the management of information content and its publication in forms appropriate for a range of audiences. (The French definition of 'document' which she cites – 'a physical support and the information it contains' – is close to the 'integral blend of content and container' which I have used in this chapter as a description of IPs.)

Making knowledge visible

actual products by which information gets around. Yet 'architecture' in terms of a 'structure concerned with meeting the needs of individuals and groups' as they put it, is the essence of IPs, manifested from their earliest beginnings. They have structure in the form of sub-divisions, pointers to their content and aids to navigation. So they should be taken into account in developing organizational information architecture, and they should make use of it, for example in their structure, their use of terminology, their placing in organizational taxonomy, and the metadata attached to them.

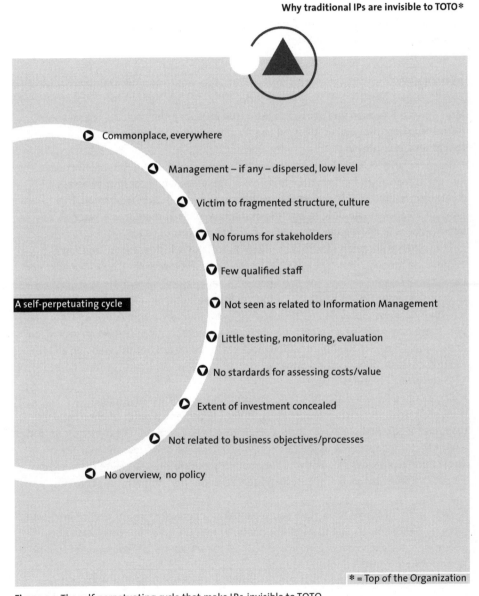

Why traditional IPs are invisible to TOTO*

- Commonplace, everywhere
- Management – if any – dispersed, low level
- Victim to fragmented structure, culture
- No forums for stakeholders
- Few qualified staff
- Not seen as related to Information Management
- Little testing, monitoring, evaluation
- No stardards for assessing costs/value
- Extent of investment concealed
- Not related to business objectives/processes
- No overview, no policy

A self-perpetuating cycle

*** = Top of the Organization**

Figure 1.4 The self-perpetuating cycle that make IPs invisible to TOTO

An irreplaceable role

Information products are actually a key asset, without which no organization could function. As discussed in the next chapter, they are representations of organizational values and knowledge, agents in transformation and diffusion of knowledge, and embodiments of organizational memory.

Value: added and subtracted

Because organizations aren't in the habit of looking at their information products as an entity, they have little conception of their actual or potential overall costs and value. Yet as we shall see, the total resources that go into creating them are large, and so are the effects – positive and negative.

Why now?

Most of what has been said above has been true for a long time; what's special about the present time that makes it a good one for this book?
Four main factors favour it.
1 The popularity of 'knowledge management' shows no signs of declining, nor does interest in the value of information and knowledge assets and how best to assess it – and there are signs that the concepts are becoming rather better understood. That makes it an appropriate time to put information products in their proper place, as key intermediaries in knowledge management, and as creators of value.
2 The universal adoption of web technology as a major vehicle for more and more information products: it is highly visible, receives massive investment, is fashionable, and for all those reasons receives top management's eager attention. And there is practical evidence of organizations using it as a tool for integrating their information products into their business processes and their strategies for managing knowledge and informa-tion. There may never be a better time to encourage organizations to take an overall look at the whole range of their information products in the context of the web and all the electronic transactions it makes possible.
3 The growing pressures towards:
● Encouraging (or constraining) users to accept online information products
● 'Multi-format, single-source' publishing of IPs – ie deriving a range of information products for different audiences from a single resource of content. The content is held in a form that is independent of the forms in which it will be delivered, and in a device- and vendor-independent format; it is automatically transformed to create the desired output (*see* www.tso.co.uk for a useful presentation on 'The multiformat publishing challenge').
4 The current demands for a more equitable balance between the interests of intellectual property rights-holders and users of information products, made by world-wide non-governmental stakeholder organizations such as the International Federation of Library Associations and Institutions (IFLA, 2004).

   All these factors can have good or bad outcomes – and which we get depends on whether the providers of IPs take initiatives to understand what users need to do; draw them into the process of designing IPs; develop new kinds of expertise (including information and knowledge management); and keep up with the technology and push it further so that it can deliver information content in IPs that really help users.

The pressures in this direction create an urgent need to find a fair balance between the interests of the originating organization and the end users. They also provide a great opportunity for linking management of information resources and creation of IPs, through the appropriate use of content-management systems and single-source publishing.

These are all strong reasons why this book is needed. They require a lot of thinking about unfamiliar ideas at all levels, and unfamiliar collaborations in doing it. They offer potential for great gains, and comparable losses, all round.

Dear Reader

This book is written for four groups of people who are actual and potential stakeholders in organizational information products.

1 The professionals in:
- Information and knowledge management
- Information systems and IT
- Web and intranet development and management
- Information design – visual and verbal – for printed and electronic products.
2 Students of the relevant professional disciplines.
3 Anyone else whose job includes responsibilities for creation and production of their organization's information products.
4 Senior managers who have overall responsibility for:
- Information and knowledge management
- Corporate communications
- Information systems and technology.

A transaction between author and readers

Any book that aims to give practical help implies a co-operative effort between author and readers; both have to contribute their knowledge if it's to do what it sets out to do. This is the transaction that I propose between us.
As author I undertake to present:
- An exposition of the basic ideas on information products and their proper role in how organizations use knowledge and information to achieve whatever they are in business for.
- Practical proposals for action to find out how well the products currently fulfill that role, and then to upgrade their performance, with examples from real organizations.

The readers' side of the transaction is:
- To bring their knowledge of their own work context to bear on that offering
- To reflect on the ideas
- To consider how they might apply them to take practical action on information products that will benefit the performance of their own organization.

How the book is organized

Part 1, consisting of this chapter and the next, is the exposition-of-ideas bit. This chapter has provided the basic definitions and orientation. Chapter 2 looks at what IPs (this is how they will usually be referred to from now on) can and should do for organizations, and proposes the context in which we should consider them. It acts as an introduction to the second part of the book, which looks at information products in the organizational context: Chapter 3 deals with factors in the business of organizations which are critical for their IPs; Chapter 4 considers the tangible and intangible value that IPs can add to (or subtract from) the organization's performance; and Chapter 5 looks at the stakeholders: the people who need to be concerned in creating them, the tasks that go to the process, and the often-neglected users of the end products.

The third part of the book – Chapters 6 to 8 – is devoted to the support which IPs need from the combined skills of information management, information systems and IT, and information design.

In the final part, we move from analysis to ideas for practical action, based on examples from real-life organizations. Chapters 9 to 12 propose an approach based on the well-established practice of information auditing (Chapter 9), which entails first (Chapter 10) working out what IPs should be doing for your organization, and then (Chapter 11) finding out what they are doing in reality. The last chapter demonstrates how to use the results to get increased value from IPs, by integrating them within an organizational strategy for using information to achieve whatever the organization is in business for.

'Architectural features'

I suggested earlier (p19) that information products have their own 'information architecture'. The present product has, of necessity, quite a complex structure; to help readers know where they are in it, some of its architectural features are marked with distinguishing symbols. They are:

    example material

    verbatim quotations from interviews and
from contributions to email discussions

References

BROOKES, B C (1980a)
'Informatics as the fundamental social science'
In P Taylor (ed) *New Trends in Documentation
and Information,* Proceedings of the 30th FID
Congress, University of Edinburgh, September 1978
London: Aslib

... (1980b)
'The foundations of information science. Part 1.
Philosophical aspects', *Journal of Information
Science,* 2, 125–133

GILCHRIST, A & MAHON, B (2004)
*Information Architecture: designing information
environments for purpose,* London: Facet Publishing

HEIDRICH, W (2002)
From unpublished work on *The Art of Visual
Interface Design*

IFLA (2004)
The IFLA Position on the Geneva Declaration
on the Future of WIPO
http://www.ifla.org/III/clm/CLM-
GenevaDeclaration2004.html *See* also Geneva
Declaration on the Future of WIPO (2004),
Managing Information 11 (9) 51–54

MCARTHUR, T (1986)
Worlds of Reference, Cambridge: Cambridge
University Press

McCAIN, R A (2004)
'Economics of Information Products' in *Essential
Principles of Economics: a Hypermedia Text*
http://william-king.www. drexel.edu/top/prin/
txt/EcoToC.html

MACDONALD-ROSS, M & WALLER, R (1976)
'The Transformer', London: *Penrose Annual,* 141–152
(Reprinted 2000, as 'The transformer
revisited', with a postscript, in *Information
design journal,* 9 (2&3), 177–193)

MAHON, B & GILCHRIST, A (2003)
'Information architecture, the logical way to
content management', *Library + Information
update,* 2(11) 38–39

MARCHAND, D A, KETTINGER, W J & ROLLINS,
J D (2001a)
*Making the invisible visible. How companies win
with the right information, people and IT,*
Chichester: John Wiley & Sons, Ltd

... (2001b)
*Information Orientation. The Link to Business
Performance,* Oxford: Oxford University Press

MEYER, M H & ZACK, M H (1996)
'The design and development of information
products', *Sloan Management Review,* Spring,
43–59

ORNA, E (2004)
Information strategy in practice, Aldershot: Gower,

ORNA, E & STEVENS, G (1991)
'Information design and information science:
a new alliance?', *Journal of Information Science,*
17, 197–208

No business without information products

In this chapter

This chapter presents the argument that I make in this book in compact and largely visual form. It acts as a bridge between the explanations of the last chapter, and the detailed look at information products in the context of the organizations that produce them which forms the subject of Part 2.

The argument

1 Organizations have no business without information products, because:
- Knowledge is created and lives invisible inside human minds
- It's made visible, communicated, and exchanged only when people transform it into Information, and put it into Information Products (*see* Figure 2.1 p26).

2 Information Products are therefore:
- Knowledge made visible
  and by virtue of that they are:
- Information Resources – which have to be managed,
  and
- the carriers by which Information gets around.

3 That being so, we should:
- Recognize them as essential elements in whatever the organization does
- Manage them as an essential element of Knowledge Management and Information Management
- Support their creation and use with appropriate infrastructure and human resources
- include them in the organization's strategies for Information and Information Systems (*see* Figure 2.2 p28).

Now let us expand a little on the elements of this argument.

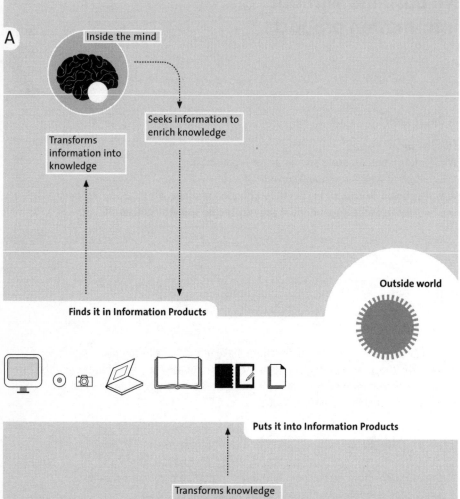

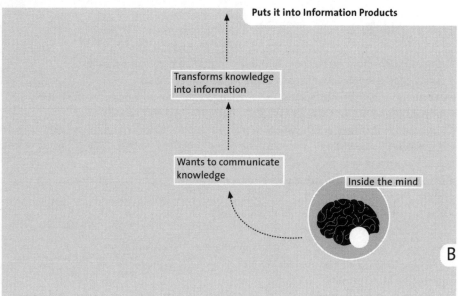

Figure 2.1 How information products support knowledge exchange

What information products should do for organizations

Information products should serve the organizations which create them by acting as:

1 Representations of their values and knowledge

All organizations need to understand 'their' outside world and to exchange information with it, and all need self-knowledge and internal exchanges of information. Information products are the vehicles by which their values and knowledge reach those outer and inner worlds, and by which internal and external exchanges of information and knowledge take place.

The Co-operative Bank

 This small retail bank – with a record of being highly successful and profitable, distinguished by its pioneering ethical policies, high level of customer satisfaction and staff commitment, and successful use of technology – provides a good example of IPs that perform this role. Particularly noteworthy are its Partnership Reports, detailed and sometimes self-critical accounts, produced by the Bank and externally audited, of how the bank has fulfilled its responsibilities to the 'partners' it identifies as involved in its activities or affected by them. It uses its IPs actively to present its ideas and to seek exchanges with customers and other 'partners', as the basis for informed action and innovation. (*see* Chapter 3, pp54 to 56) for a discussion of how the Bank's culture influences its information products).

2 Agents in transformation, diffusion and organizational learning

Constant transformation of knowledge to information and information to knowledge is vital for the progress of organizations. Information products are the medium for those transformations, and by virtue of that they are essential for communication, exchange and 'trade' of knowledge and information, inside the organization and between it and its outside world.

Information brought into organizations by their staff from their interactions with the outside world can become a source for organizational learning and the diffusion of new knowledge. But it can do so only if it gets embodied in information products and made accessible throughout the organization by means of well-managed information systems and stores.

The Office of Government Commerce

 This independent Office of the UK Treasury is responsible for providing guidance and expertise to support the successful delivery of procurement-based projects and other forms of commercial activity. As Figure 2.3 (p29) shows, the essence of its work is 'trade' in knowledge and information, and that trade depends on managing the knowledge and information brought into, and created inside, the organization as an accessible resource for learning and spreading knowledge. Information products are a critical element of the trade.

3 The repository of organizational memory

Information products, if properly managed, can be the repository of organizational memory, a resource of knowledge of what the organization did and thought in the past, the outcomes of its actions, the lessons of experience, the knowledge legacy of people who no longer work for it,

Experience from information audits, however, shows that many organizations lack appropriate information products to embody the results of projects, the lessons of failures as well as of successes, or the valuable knowledge of former staff. So a resource that could bring better return on investment, save repeating costly errors with the

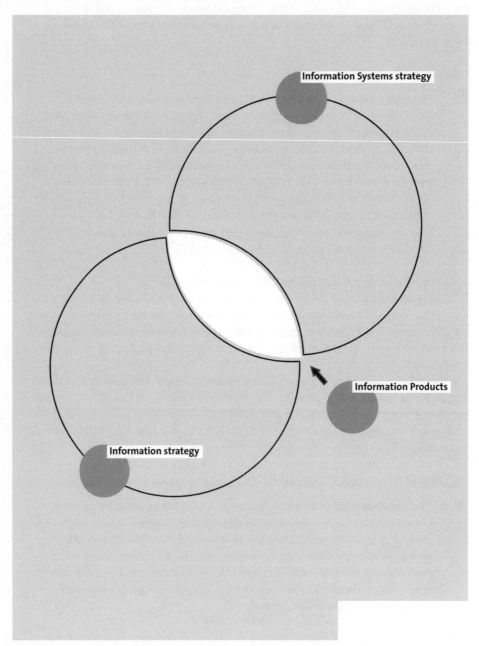

Figure 2.2 We should include information products within the organization's strategies for Information and Information Systems

Making knowledge visible

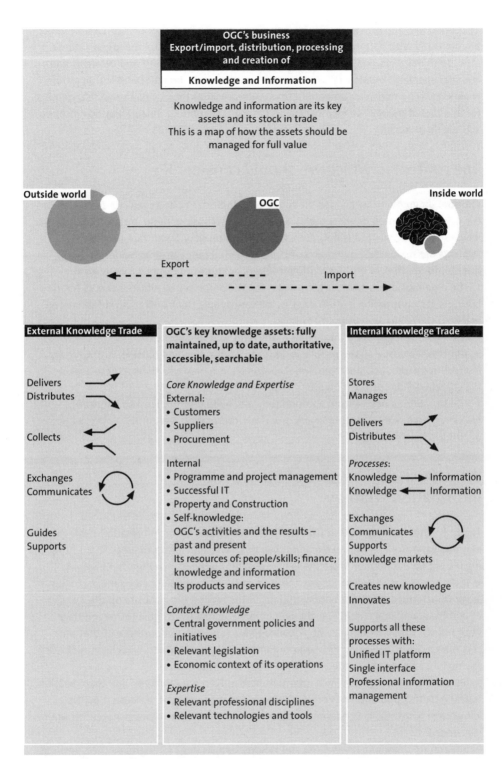

OGC's business
Export/import, distribution, processing and creation of
Knowledge and Information

Knowledge and information are its key assets and its stock in trade
This is a map of how the assets should be managed for full value

Outside world   **OGC**   **Inside world**

Export

Import

External Knowledge Trade	OGC's key knowledge assets: fully maintained, up to date, authoritative, accessible, searchabie	Internal Knowledge Trade

Delivers
Distributes
 	
Collects
 	
Exchanges
Communicates
 	
Guides
Supports
	Core Knowledge and Expertise
	External:
	• Customers
	• Suppliers
	• Procurement
	
	Internal
	• Programme and project management
	• Successful IT
	• Property and Construction
	• Self-knowledge:
	  OGC's activities and the results –
	  past and present
	  Its resources of: people/skills; finance;
	  knowledge and information
	  Its products and services
	
	Context Knowledge
	• Central government policies and
	  initiatives
	• Relevant legislation
	• Economic context of its operations
	
	Expertise
	• Relevant professional disciplines
	• Relevant technologies and tools
		Stores
		Manages
		
		Delivers
		Distributes
		
		Processes:
		Knowledge → Information
		Knowledge ← Information
		
		Exchanges
		Communicates
		Supports
		knowledge markets
		
		Creates new knowledge
		Innovates
		
		Supports all these
		processes with:
		Unified IT platform
		Single interface
		Professional information
		management

Figure 2.3 A picture of 'What Should Be' (reproduced by permission of the Office of Government Commerce)

associated risk, and prompt profitable new ideas, cannot be drawn on. The lack tends to be connected with patterns of information culture and behaviour – the organization's attitude to mistakes, and levels of confidence and trust among staff and between them and management. People who work in such organizations complain that learning from experience is hampered or downright impossible because there is no formal requirement for this kind of memory to be recorded and made accessible, or indeed that doing so is actively discouraged.

The context in which we should consider IPs

Information products are created on behalf of organizations, by people, for people, with the help of systems and technologies. So we need to consider them in that total context, which seems obvious, but is not often done; the originating organizations and their interests are seldom taken into account, nor is the full range of stakeholders in them. It is helpful to think of IPs in a fourfold context, as shown in Figure 2.4 on page 31:

1 The organization – what it is in business for, the processes by which it carries out its business, its 'information culture', that is, the way people think and about information, and how they behave in using it.

2 The value – tangible and intangible – which IPs add (or subtract).

3 The stakeholders – all the people, inside the organization and outside, who have an interest in the products and a potential contribution to make to them. (These aspects of the context are discussed in Chapters 3–5).

4 The support IPs need – from appropriately managed information and knowledge resources, from relevant technologies, and from information design. This is the subject of part 3 (Chapters 6–8).

Why IPs should be part of an overall information strategy

The basic argument states that IPs should be an element in the information strategies of organizations. Here, we can expand it like this. (We shall return to ideas about bringing IPs within information strategy, as part of a programme of change, in Chapter 12.)

• If IPs are, as they are described at the start of this chapter, the embodiment of knowledge transformed into information, then by virtue of that they operate on the frontier of information management – at the point where people meet the information they seek and start transforming it into knowledge for action. The importance of that process for success in achieving whatever organizations are in business to achieve is the key reason why they need a strategy for knowledge and information.

• IPs are the main objects which information management manages; and their creation is a culminating point in the process of knowledge management, because it makes knowledge accessible in the form of information, and allows it to travel around to where it's needed.

• Integrating them into knowledge and information strategy strengthens their position, and links them – like all other aspects of knowledge and information – with organizational strategy. That protects them from floating about in a void, at the mercy of territorial battles, vanity, or cost-cutting.

Making knowledge visible

- Integrating them in this way makes it possible to establish criteria for what they're supposed to achieve for the organization, and to evaluate how effectively they do it.
- And finally, as a principal means by which information gets around, they can make a link between communication and information, which in most organizations are separated by an unbridged gulf.[1]

1 Meyer and Zack (1996) advance some other original and convincing reasons for bringing IPs fully into organizational information strategy. They look at information products in the same way as physical ones, and liken their 'manufacture' to refining. The process consists of acquiring raw materials; refining them (activities to make products accessible to users, from indexing to analysing trends by means of appropriate software); storing and retrieving them; distribution; and presentation – 'ensuring ease of use and sufficient functionality is part and parcel of the information product itself'. To manage its information products successfully, an organization needs an appropriate technological infrastructure; knowledge about its own business; external knowledge about its current and emerging markets; and self-knowledge – understanding of how it organizes and manages itself. If it does that, it can create new information products very quickly and cheaply compared with the costs for physical products. And the authors believe that the greatest potential lies in the acquisition and refinement stages, rather than in the output-end technology.

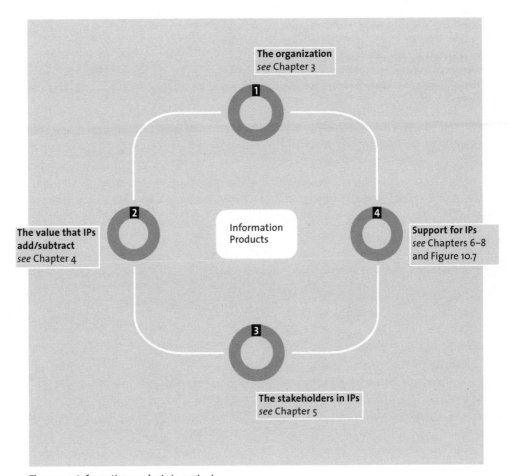

The organization
see Chapter 3

1

The value that IPs add/subtract
see Chapter 4

2

Information Products

Support for IPs
see Chapters 6–8 and Figure 10.7

4

The stakeholders in IPs
see Chapter 5

3

Figure 2.4 Information products in context

The final stage of the argument – if you want to do something about it ...

As this is a practical book, as well as arguing a case, it has to suggest how to act on it. The underlying argument at this point is that any change process should start by:

1 Asking and answering questions to establish what should be happening
2 Finding out what is actually happening at present
3 Comparing the two, in order to see where there are serious and important differences; these will be the focus for change.

Because if you don't have a reasonably accurate map of where you are starting from, you may well finish up some distance from where you intended to get to.

This approach, which is proposed in the final part of this book, is a well established one, usually called Information Auditing.

References

THE CO-OPERATIVE BANK (2003)
Sustainable development, Partnership report 2002,
Manchester: The Co-operative Bank www.
cooperativebank.co.uk/ethics/partnership2002

MEYER, M H & ZACK, H Z (1996)
'The design and development of information
products', *Sloan Management Review,* Spring,
43–59

Information products in the organizational context

The argument introduced in the last chapter is founded on the idea that information products develop in an organizational context, to do things the organization needs, and that they should therefore be consciously and explicitly related to that context, as part of an information strategy. Experience suggests that this does not often happen, but that when it does, IPs contribute more fully and productively to achieving the organization's goals.

The next chapters examine the three key elements in the organizational context: the organization's business (Chapter 3), the value that IPs add (Chapter 4), the stakeholders and their interests (Chapter 5).

The business of the organization

In this chapter

Three critical elements

This chapter is devoted to the three critical elements of the organizational context for IPs. Two main factors should, as shown in Figure 3.1 (p36), determine what kind of IPs the organization needs, and the appropriate content, medium and form for them (it does not always happen in practice!):

1 Its objectives – how the organization itself defines what it's in business to achieve, what it views as most critical for its survival and success.

2 Its business processes – the way it works to achieve its objectives, how it does what it's in business to do. The most productive way of looking at them is as 'an interlocking series of activities devoted to creating outputs, instead of a set of functional departments within the bounds of which self-contained activities take place – the metaphor is a river, rather than a stack of boxes' (Orna, 1999, p11).[1]

A third factor has a decisive influence on how IPs are managed, and how effective they are:

3 The way the people in the organization think about information and behave in using it – its 'information culture'. The effects can, as we shall see later, be positive or negative; and it takes a long time to change information culture and behaviour.

---

1 Davenport (1993), suggests that the flow of documents can often define the flow of business processes. I would argue from this that if documents have that defining role, and play so essential a part, then it's important to look closely at processes, and the documents by which they're carried, together, in relation to one another, especially at the points where processes cross interfaces between different parts of the organization, and between the organization and its outside world

Objectives and business processes

It is of course obvious that the nature of organizations' business requires them to create certain information products, for both the outside world they depend on, and the inner world of those who work for them. If you sell equipment of any kind, you need instructions to tell purchasers how to use it; if you offer goods or services, you need to describe them to potential customers or clients; pharmaceutical companies need to provide dosage and safety advice for their products; membership organizations need handbooks for their members. And whatever the kind of organization, the people who run it need a range of information products to help them do their jobs, from internal directories to statements of the organization's policies and procedures.

I gave up being surprised a long time ago by how often those essential products look as if they have been designed to repel all boarders, drive users to distraction, dissuade potential customers from purchase of goods or services, and impede staff in their work. My 'black museum' of examples goes back to the 1970s, and the supply has not dried up with the coming of the web; far from it.

The reason for the poor showing is probably that IPs usually develop piecemeal over time to meet emerging needs, and so organizations seldom pause to consider the whole range of their products in the light of their current objectives and future plans, let alone draw up a clear statement of the contribution that IPs should make to achieving them.

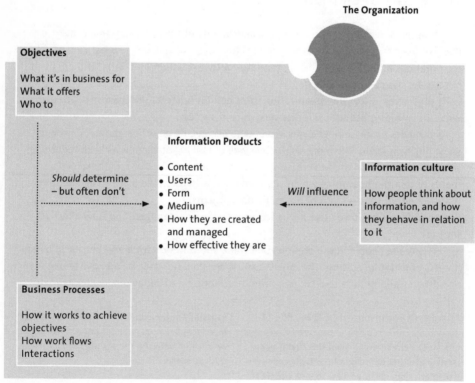

Figure 3.1 The organization: factors that should determine, and do influence, information products

And, as mentioned in Chapter 1 (*see* p17), there's little encouragement from the top of most organizations to do so.

Fortunately there are encouraging examples of organizations that have made a conscious effort to relate their IPs to their changing objectives and evolving business processes, and that are aware of the benefits they have gained by doing so. The rest of this section is devoted to them.

Premier Farnell

 This is an example of a business which recognizes that its IPs are central to its objectives and business processes, and must develop as they evolve, because the connection between its IPs and its business performance is so clear.

Farnell has been selling industrial, mechanical and electronic products worldwide by mail order for over 60 years; today it sells more than 150,000 lines of products in the European region. Its printed catalogue, developed over the years, has gained an excellent reputation with customers. The company has always realized it was the critical element in its business ('If you can't find it, you can't buy it!') and has always put more effort than its competitors into making it easy for users to get quickly to what they wanted.

They made a well-planned move to complementing print with web-based IPs in 1994/95, guided by the objective of providing business services to all customers by creating the most helpful mix of channels for whatever they needed to do, whether catalogue browsing, searching for specific items, or for topics as they themselves defined them. Premier Farnell's IPs constitute a distinct business stream – the 'Find and Select channel', separate from transactions, sales and marketing.

They are very well aware of the 'selling–telling' distinction, between products whose main function is to advertise and those intended to meet users' self-defined needs for information.[2] As their e-business Development Manager, who is responsible for the Find and Select channel, puts it: 'We try not to confuse the established need with creating a need (marketing). This is important, as the risk is that the user finds the catalogue/website/eCat etc difficult to use due to the prevalence of advertising and promotions – whilst [these] are a fact of life, and required to generate 'need', there is a balance with usability that needs to be struck, particularly on the web.'

And while Premier Farnell is committed to developing e-business, it is no part of its objectives to drive customers away from paper to electronic media; instead, it anticipates that the blend of media will change over time, and aims to manage that change in a way that maintains its high reputation with customers, as well as its competitive position. (This has entailed an unusual degree of thinking from first

---

2 I have to confess that I find this approach to its customers, from a successful business, more respectful of the users of information products than the thinking which appears to underlie much current 'Customer Relations Management' material. This example, from an academic institution, advertising its 'Service Quality Toolbox', suggests a more commonplace view of users as a passive audience whose feelings are to be worked over: 'It is this total experience that influences the customer's perceptions of value and service quality, and which consequently affects customer loyalty.'

principles about content management, taxonomy and terminology, technology, use of human resources, and organizational structure – *see* pp116 and 143–144.

Recognition of the Find and Select channel as a distinct stream, governed and owned by Product Management, and managed by the e-business Development Manager allows its contribution to all business processes – transactions, sales, and marketing – to be clearly defined and efficiently carried out. The move into web-based presentation has intensified this – eCatalogues are loaded into Procurement systems, and into Marketplaces, Portals etc.

mda (formerly the Museum Documentation Association)

This is a case where an organization had to find new ways of fulfilling its objectives in response to the changed economic environment of the museums who are its members and its 'clients'. It decided that developing a portal was the key to the solution. The process led to a creative interaction between portal development, how the organization defines its objectives, and how it carries out its business processes.

The objectives with which mda started more than 30 years ago were to provide support, advice, and training for museums in managing the documentation relating to their collections. The organization grew from the activities of the Information Retrieval Group of the Museums Association (IRGMA) in the late 1960s – a pioneering body interested in the application of computers to handling museum records). Initially as the Museum Documentation Advisory Unit, it provided standards and procedures for preparing records of objects, and information products to help museum staff to do the job of putting information based on their knowledge of their collections into records.

IPs have always had an important role in the service that mda offers, and they have come a long way since the beginning. Initially, what was on offer wasn't overhelpful, and some of the first IPs probably didn't do much to further objectives. '… computing being the esoteric specialism that it then was, they [MDAU computer specialists] were effectively set apart from most of their colleagues in the museum profession … minds were not so much meeting as going straight past each other in opposite directions … and … the early publications in which the MDA and its predecessors sought to explain themselves were pretty stern stuff…' (Orna & Pettitt, 1998).

Despite the interest in computer applications, the real situation in most museums meant that the most useful IPs were for many years the record cards for various types of museum object, which were distributed in quantity to many museums, and helped enormously to upgrade the quality of records and facilitate information management. At the same time, the Association took a lead in developing software specifically for museum documentation – initially for large-scale use (GOS) and later for use with micro-computers (MODES).

Over time, the range of the IPs, both printed and electronic, increased, and their quality was enhanced. A notable example is mda's UK Museum Documentation Standard, first published in 1994, and known as SPECTRUM. It was created by the kind of collaboration between the organization and practising museum professionals that is now typical of mda, with results that have made it an invaluable product.

Making knowledge visible

The first edition, and its successors, in both printed and electronic form, are notable for clear presentation, both visual and textual, which reflects a sound conceptual structure, based on solid thinking.

Although mda has travelled a long way from its technology-oriented origins, helping museums to make productive use of appropriate IT has remained an important part of its activity. This aspect of its work enabled it to make good use of web technology in responding to the situation created by the changed economic and political situation in which museums and mda found they had to operate from the late 90s.

That situation can be summarized like this: the top-level sources of funding and the regulatory framework for institutions mda existed to serve had changed; a new body – Resource (now MLA – Museums, Libraries, Archives) – had been established to replace the previous Museums and Galleries Commission, with the remit of strategic oversight of both museums and libraries; they were under pressure to manage 'strategically', and to act more commercially and even competitively.

mda's thinking about how to respond to these changes led it to the decision that a new portal was the key to a solution. To begin with, the thinking was that a portal could simply substitute for its 'outreach' activities of promoting ideas of best practice, and training to give people the skills and resources they needed to implement the ideas. That was soon replaced by the realization that it had to use the technology to complement and support new kinds of interchange with museums, act as a pointer to resources of information and knowledge, and advise on managing information. The project for portal development caused mda to look at how it delivered its services and at the needs of collection-holders for support. In-house discussion, and consultation with stakeholders, revealed that, while resources were too limited to go on providing a direct personal advice service through outreach, people must still continue to be a vital factor in delivering service through the portal.

It also led to an enriched view of the organization's objectives, towards advising not just on documentation, but on managing all the kinds of information related to the management of collections. Thinking has now developed to the point where mda envisages achieving its objectives through a combination of three elements:
1 Making information content available from mda's existing resources, and from new content resources arising from the new means it now has of giving training and advice (through the 'Providers' described below).
2 Providing training and advice through partnerships with external independent trainers and consultants working in the museum field; these 'Providers' would work to mda standards and use mda information products, while retaining their freedom to negotiate with the purchasers of training (eg universities and large museums). And they would contribute content from their experience to the portal.
3 The portal, with the role of being a 'meta-IP', containing IPs to help all mda stakeholders, supporting mda's interactions with them, and constantly enhanced by new IPs resulting from its work.

This has a clear impact on mda's business processes, and the information products required for carrying them out. The aims of the portal project are now defined as:

- Enabling everyone to update information for which they are responsible on the portal
- Providing for direct input from in-house and remote mda staff
- Developing the range of content to offer new IPs within the portal – eg real-life 'stories' to embody advice and experience on common problems and basic standard clear explanations of content, which are treated as IPs in their own right and catalogued so that they come up first in the results of any relevant subject search.

So the development of new processes, the development of IPs and the development of the technology to make them accessible have moved forward together, interactively, and with considerable effects also on mda's information resources and how they are managed (*see* Chapter 6, p117).

The portal project has yielded valuable lessons, which mda is currently applying to further development of the portal with its own content; it hopes that in due course funding will allow it to go on developing the other aspects described above.

mda's approach is a good example of what Detlor (2000) advocates for portal design; he says that portals should provide organizations with 'a rich and complex shared information work space for the creation, exchange, retention, and reuse of knowledge' (p93). As a 'communication space' they can 'provide rich information channels that help users engage in conversations and negotiations ... so that shared interpretations can be made. In this way, new perspectives and innovation can result and be stored back into the portal's knowledge base for later reuse.' (p94). Taylor (1986) whom Detlor quotes on the 'information use environment', advocates looking 'at the user and the uses of information, and the contexts within which those users make choices' about what information is useful to them at particular times. These choices are based, not only on subject matter, but on other elements of the context within which a user lives and works. And Davenport (1997) writes on 'information ecology', which places emphasis on 'how people create, distribute, understand, and use information'. These concepts are deeply relevant to the information products in which information is embodied, and essential in thinking about their creation and design.

Tate (formerly The Tate Gallery, London)

Another example from the museum and galleries area, of holistic thinking that relates information products, information systems and information management, and brings them all into the context of the institution's strategic objectives and key business processes.

In the course of research on how organizations manage their information products I had the opportunity to observe developments at the Gallery over a period of five years; and I have been fortunate enough to be able to keep in touch with them since. The change over the past ten years has been remarkable in many respects. In 1994, when my case study began, the Gallery's information products were managed in a fragmented way; there was no meeting ground for the people with responsibility for them, and there were consequent misunderstandings and antagonisms; the potential for using valuable reference material in the collection records was not fully exploited, and could not be with the existing technology; and attempts to develop policies and strategies for information appeared to have run into the sands of organizational culture. Altogether a rather disheartening prospect.

The perseverance and insight of the staff concerned began to bear fruit around 1998, with the establishment of the Gallery's website (*see* Chapter 7, pp128–129). Over the seven years since then, Tate has built a world-class online documented source of art collections information, which is now used as a central resource for a range of information products and services, for both in-house and external users. Image digitization and subject indexing of the entire Tate Collection have been carried through. The Concise Catalogue has been published online since 1998, and Tate has developed systems that support collation, management and publication of Collections information in electronic form.

Much of the investment for these developments has come from such external sources as the Heritage Lottery Fund and commercial sponsorship. Tate is now moving towards gaining maximum benefit from its astute use of these opportunities, by putting what it has gained from them into the context of its strategic objectives of:
- Strengthening and extending the range of its collections, and enhanced online access to them
- Expanding display and exhibition programmes
- Extending research and dissemination
- Developing services for visitors and the wider audience
- Improving internal efficiency and increasing revenue.

Key topics for discussion on this theme by the gallery's Information Group relate to:
- The level of core information that should be published on the Collections, and the resources necessary to manage it
- The case for integrating the Collections databases with the Library and Archive information, and the value that could be gained from 'cross relating and delivering information products that relate to material from both areas', accessible to users through same interface
- Developing an electronic publication policy 'responsive to the varied needs of both audience and originators of products and services' which takes account of the vast scope for electronic publishing and the need for it to be within a strategic framework
- The possibilities for integrating this aspect of publishing with Tate Publishing (Tate's commercial publishing initiatives), and using the content management tools recently introduced into the Gallery to support its business processes (*see* Chapter 7 p126 for more on this).

It seems likely that one outcome will be an overall publishing strategy which will form part of an integrated strategy for managing Tate's information resources. (*See* also Chapter 7 p126 for other aspects of Tate's integrated approach to information products.)

FreePint

 This is an example of a business whose main offering is a range of associated electronic information products, and those products are the principal means of achieving its objectives.

Established in 1997, initially as a newsletter designed to promote founder William Hann's own information consultancy business, it developed into the current set of products for 'people who use the Web in their work': a fortnightly newsletter; email 'Bars' for information professionals and students, where users can ask questions, post answers, and exchange ideas; three-times-a-week Bar digests; and a well-indexed archive.3 FreePint is a free offering because it is funded through sponsorship and advertising, and through the revenue it earns from list hosting, job-vacancy listings, etc. Its primary role is not a selling one, though it has to pay its way as a business, which it has done from the beginning.

FreePint's objectives are to demonstrate to the wider business community the knowledge and skills which information professionals have to offer, and to provide a forum for exchange of knowledge about quality on the World-wide Web. They have determined the character of the information products which constitute its offering, and there is a close fit between them. The founder saw a user-led enterprise as the best means of realizing them, and FreePint is characterised by lively and purposeful interaction – among the contributors, between them and the editorial team, and between FreePint and the business community it aims to educate.

The rapid rate of growth in subscriber numbers (63,000 by 2003 – an increase of 14,000 over 2002), the high level of retention, and the quality and relevance of the contributions to both newsletter and the Bar, certainly suggest that it is achieving its objective as a useful forum for its target audience.4

Department of Health – CHIP

 The Department of Health's Comprehensive Information Portfolio (CHIP) is an electronic IP with very high policy value at the top of the organization.

Its origins go back to the point when, after the Labour victory in the 1997 general election, the new Secretary of State for Health requested the Excalibur database used by the Labour Party during the election campaign. His intention was that it should be used in this new context as a database of key policies and related facts to support ministerial briefing.

The objective was to provide a single authoritative resource on policies and facts for ministers and policy officials, accessible to them 24 hours a day and seven days a week. This shaped the development of CHIP; and led to close involvement not only of IT specialists but also of information managers, who now coordinate and manage CHIP for a wide range of stakeholders.

3 Other elements in the FreePint model include its sister company, Willco Limited, which provides the technology to FreePint and some 50 other publishers, and VIP, a paid-for subscription service for business information professionals.

4 A useful source on email newsletters as a form of publishing: http://www.epsg.org.uk/meetings/email2004/ (British Computer Society Electronic Publishing Specialist Group).

Making knowledge visible

The database was built into Lotus Notes, which was already in use in the Department, and soon expanded to include, besides policies, relevant Hansard extracts, and factual material of value to ministers – to whom it was available full-time on their laptops – and policy officials. An intranet version, containing just the policy documents, was made available to all DoH staff. Today, besides policies and briefings, CHIP contains primary-care-track factsheets on NHS Trusts, Hansard links, statistics, press releases, key ministerial speeches, and a link to the Knowledge Network on the government-wide intranet.

CHIP is also vital in facilitating the business processes of the DoH, which involve multiple interfaces between the department and its outside world: intra-government, at various levels from ministerial down; Parliamentary; health service; other institutions; the public; the press; international.

Its success has led to diffusion and replication; it has enhanced the reputation of the department where it originated, and the UK government Knowledge Network, which it inspired, is the recipient of a government computing award for innovation.

Essex County Council Education Service

 This is an example of work over a long period which has led to high-quality information products, and a management process for them which supports the relations between the Council's Education Service and schools, governors, teachers, and parents. It is also a potential model for the publishing process throughout the County Council. And it delivers information products that support Essex County Council's objectives for communicating with the whole community which it serves.

The initiative was taken more then ten years ago by an information professional working for ECC. Her experience in supplying information content for a book being published by the Council led her to critical observation of the publishing process as then carried out, and so to making a case to management for coordinated publishing activity, which was accepted.

A representative group with members from each area of the education service was set up with the objective of ensuring that all material for publication met agreed standards. The group set up a system, initiated a house style, established production procedures, and developed a complete catalogue of the Council's education publications. It is still working today, as a forum 'embedded in senior managers' psyche'; its continuity has been maintained, the initiator of the developments is still involved, as the person responsible for those IPs which are called 'statutory documents' (such as Key Stage 2 performance tables and admission criteria), which local education authorities have a legal obligation to publish. The Education Services publishing programme now has a range of priced publications, which carry an ISBN, and the normal standards and practices of a publishing house, with its own e-shop on the Council's website. And in the process, close working relations have developed between the Publishing Unit, Information Services, Communications, and the rest of the Council's Education Service.

The publishing process established for the Education Service is now ready to extend to the whole Council, and the current move to electronic communication and publication throughout the Council creates a unique opportunity.

In effect, what has taken place here is the creation of a business process that did not exist before, centred on information products, which has not only led to vast improvement in the quality of the IPs, together with significant revenue generation, but has also provided a model that could be extended to the whole of the Council's publishing, where it could have similar effects.

Information culture and behaviour

By now there is a large body of opinion, based on observation and experience, that links the overall culture of organizations to the way they deal with information and knowledge, and to the effects which that has on their business performance

Skryme (1992), for example, on the basis of experience of Digital Equipment Corporation's attempts to develop knowledge networking, identifies these features of organizational culture as favourable to knowledge networking:
- Openness of communications; willingness to share information
- A belief that coordinating expertise from different people is better than going it alone
- A network of individuals with shared visions and goals
- A strong sense of responsibility to co-workers
- Self-regulation of the network.

Davenport and Prusak (1998) have put forward the idea of knowledge markets as a realistic way of achieving the benefits that are presumably covered by the common aspiration to 'knowledge sharing' (a hopelessly vague term if ever there was one!). In an organizational knowledge market, people can play the roles of buyers, sellers and brokers. The deals arrived at by negotiation over information can offer various rewards (both parties get something of comparable value; one party gets information of value and the other enhanced reputation; or one gets something of value and the other no immediate return other than gratitude, but the possibility of reciprocal help in the future). They depend on mutual trust, and that can't exist unless there are visible rewards, trust prevails everywhere, and it starts from the top. Managements must recognize the value of talking, and provide real physical places for knowledge markets, and time to 'shop' for knowledge there; and the technology should provide an infrastructure to support the activities of the marketplace

Of course, how well such markets can work depends, as the authors point out, on the culture and political realities of the organization. Nothing as civilized as an information market or knowledge networking is likely to happen in organizations which have such features as:
- Poor provision for induction, job handover, knowledge transfer when people move on
- A human resources policy dedicated to keeping people in their proper boxes, where the only kind of 'flexibility' encouraged is acceptance of imposed change without consultation or question
- Sharp boundaries between different levels, and cooperative endeavour between them discouraged

Making knowledge visible

- Commitment to openness in mission or vision statements, but the opposite in practice
- Lack of an ethical policy governing the use of information
- The main direction of information flow is top down; upward flow takes place only when required from the top, and no reciprocal information comes back when the required information has been provided – it disappears into the clouds around the summit and is heard of no more.
- Functions and departments keep themselves to themselves, protect their knowledge against outsiders; they value their own kind of knowledge highly, but don't reckon much to what other people know, and they certainly don't want to understand what they actually do.

Recent work by Marchand et al. (2001) suggests why it is so difficult to develop the kind of information behaviour in which people willingly take information initiatives because they see them as of benefit to themselves as well as others. They observe that this area has not been the object of structured and measurable management activities; nor yet has improving people's behaviours and values as regards information use been seen as part of either the IT or the information management functions. They also remark that it is not easy, because it depends on other interdependent information behaviours and values:

- Integrity: guaranteeing that information is truthful, accurate and without bias, it sets 'appropriate boundaries for ethical information behavior' and influences directly 'the formal use of information within an organization.' (Marchand et al. p102)
- Giving first place to formal rather than informal information sources
- Linking individual performance to organizational performance, which could 'directly motivate employees, creating proactive information behaviors for improved information effectiveness.' (Marchand et al. p103)
- Treating 'errors, mistakes, failures, and surprises as constructive learning opportunities' (Marchand et al. p103).

Their discussion of information culture and behaviour comes in the context of a research project which started with the question: 'Is there a comprehensive measure of effective information use that predicts business performance?' They concluded, after studying the thinking of a large international sample of over 1000 top-level managers on these topics, that they had, for the first time, established the nature of the relationship between information use and business performance, and that they had been able to create a comprehensive measure.

The research indicates that business performance depends whether and how effectively the organization interlocks IT practices, information management practices, and information behaviour and values (sometimes described as organizational information culture), to form an integrated 'Information Orientation' relevant to its business goals.

They stress that organizations 'must achieve competence and synergy across all three information capabilities … as a precondition to achieving superior business performance' – it is not enough to be good at each element in isolation; they have to work together and support one another in achieving organizational goals, as shown in Figure 3.2.

So it seems there is good evidence to suggest that the organization's overall culture influences its information culture and behaviour; and its 'Information Orientation', of which information culture is one part (along with its IT and information management practices), influences its business performance.

Links between information culture and information products

And what of the connections between all that and IPs? That is something which has seldom been researched, or discussed in print or spoken of by information professionals (which perhaps explains why it's possible to find organizations which combine a good information culture with unawareness of the role of IPs, and so allow their information products to undermine the value of what they do with information).

These are some specific features of information culture which I have learned from first-hand experience to be bad news for IPs:

- The full range of stakeholders in the products is not recognized, because of fragmented organizational structure, and the resulting fragmented rather than holistic view of the organization
- The users and context of use of IPs are not seen as important
- It is not part of the culture to think it necessary to understand what other groups do and know about

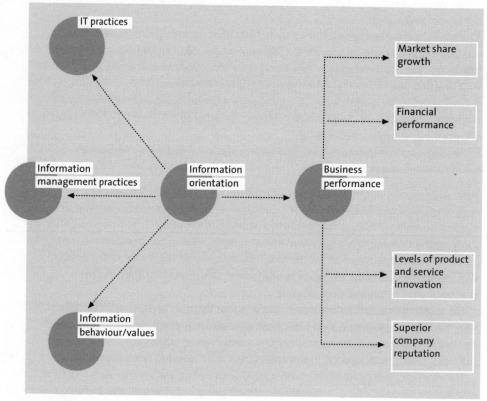

Figure 3.2 The way organizations manage information and IT, and their information behaviour/values, exert a combined effect through 'Information Orientation' on business performance. Based on Marchand et al. (2001) *Information Orientation: the link to Business Performance.* By permission of Oxford University Press

- Low status is given to people who do key jobs relating to IPs, including supervising contractors; and the relevant skills (especially of design) are little esteemed
- There is no communication between the staff responsible for 'communications' (including printed products) and those who deal with web-based IPs
- Only prestige IPs for the outside world are seen as significant; the effects of everyday internal ones on the quality and efficiency of work are not understood
- Testing and evaluation of IPs is considered an unjustifiable expense
- Corporate ID dominates design concerns, at the expense of standards covering the whole range of IPs in all media
- The role of IT is over-emphasized, and the significance of information content and information management undervalued
- No-one is responsible for an overview of all IPs in relation to organizational objectives and strategies.

Fortunately there is evidence to show that projects which involve creating new information products or upgrading the way they are managed, as part of strategic development, can bring about changes for the better. Here are three examples from experience, based on case studies of real organizations.

UK Department of Trade and Industry

 An extended case study of the DTI was part of the research mentioned earlier (*see* p7). In the early stages, the organization displayed some of the features on the list above, which were undoubtedly influencing the quality of its IPs and their management.

The organizational culture showed traditional civil service features, in particular a concentration of information flow within functional hierarchies and an accompanying reluctance to countenance horizontal flow between different hierarchies. The autonomy of individual divisions could be energetically guarded; there was a tendency to believe that no other part of the organization could have anything useful to impart; a reluctance (possibly well founded) to rely on others for any support or service, or to learn from them; readiness to undertake everything from within; and a certain distrust of central functions.

The traditional features were compounded by what is described as 'very fast decentralization' in the early 1990s, by failure to accompany the decentralization with identification of common ground, and by 'lack of imagination' on the part of the central functions. Examples abounded of duplicate initiatives, for example in relation to the Internet; information managers had an uphill task in trying to promote co-operative working between those with related interests. The Department as a whole was said to lack awareness of the significance of information resources and information management; and information technology specialists were reported as seeing themselves as the repository of all that needed to be known about information and its use. Central advisory functions – including those relating to information products – were sometimes seen, where they were known of, as at best a hindrance to getting on with the job.

A process of change, centred on the creation and management of the Department's IPs, was, however, already beginning. In the early 1990s concern about the efficiency and cost-effectiveness of this large and complex area led to the commissioning of consultants to look at how the Department assessed what it should publish and how it managed production, storage, stock control and distribution.

One of the first tasks was to establish how many titles there were and the size of print runs, because there was no complete central record; even the Information and Library Service, which was reported as trying valiantly, could not keep up. The 1700 or so publications for external consumption ranged in scale from print runs of over a million down to as few as 150. The vast range of internal material – notices, newsletters, leaflets, guidance notes and instruction manuals – was noted as having increased in diversity with the devolution of management responsibilities to individual Directorates.

It proved difficult to identify the full cost of producing, storing and distributing the Department's publications, because of variations in how costs were allocated and the ways in which publications were funded. The input of professional skills to products for external distribution varied from Directorate to Directorate, with the result that some products were considered to 'work against its aims'. Similar variations prevailed in relation to information content; some publications were actually found to contradict agreed departmental policy.

While most staff were found to be aware of some aspects of consistency of presentation, such as the logo, there was very little understanding of the effect of presentation on how others perceive the DTI. It was difficult for the Information Directorate to enforce standards, even though they had someone with responsibility for this. Examples were found of publications for high-profile audiences where the quality of presentation was poor, and of others produced to a more expensive level than necessary. Staff 'need to attach a value to what they produce before they can actually decide on the quality of the product... what they may consider to be an expensive product may, in fact, provide value for money...'

Problems of attaining and maintaining standards of presentation also arose from devolved budgeting: people were said to think they were saving money, whereas in fact they were getting poor performance out of their products; the report commented in this connection on the 'conflict between freedom of choice and maintaining standards.'

Most concern was caused by 'inefficient and sometimes ill-considered' methods of storage and distribution; external publications were found to be distributed from 270 different points, with the inevitable results of wastage, duplication, and inefficiency. The originators of external publications often lacked information on which to base their decisions on print runs; in some cases they knew something about likely demand on which to base an order, but in others they had no information to go on. While print runs for internal products were supposed to be set by the number of staff in the target audience, the information on this which the existing system provided had proved very unreliable.

Recommendations for improvement included:
● Creating a Publications Unit within the Information and Library service, to provide advice and guidance on standards, value for money and cost-effective options for producing publications.

- Asking managers responsible for publications to make an investment appraisal for every product, itemizing costs and proposed benefits as the basis for assessing its value-for-money potential, and deciding on the best options for the various stages of producing it.
- Establishing a database of publications with information on all titles.
- Rationalizing storage and distribution.
- Defining the roles of the in-house professional resources for information design and graphics.
- Identifying expenditure on publications, and considering how internal providers of design and production advice could compete with external agencies.

Action was taken on the recommendations; in particular the Publications Unit was set up within the Information and Library Service and a database of publications established within it, and an external contractor became responsible for storage and distribution. In the final stages of the study, the Unit formed part of the Public Services Unit within the Information Management and Technology Directorate (created in 1996) and was primarily managed by professional librarians.

Although in the course of the research there were still complaints of the difficulties arising from the conflict between traditional vertical hierarchies and coordination of work across different hierarchies, by the time the case study reached its final stage, there were noticeable, if gradual, changes in many respects. People were now more prepared to give information if others asked for it, though there was still a problem in getting them to do so without knowing how it was to be used. Some of the information difficulties created by decentralization were coming home to roost – especially that of regaining critical information, such as that on health and safety, which was dispersed in the process of decentralizing.

The 1996 merging of the Library with Information Technology to form Information Management and Technology was said to have given positive results; library and information services had a higher profile, and were well respected for their know-ledge of external online sources.

Significant development of the Department's use of web technology for IPs also took place during the period of the case study. The DTI intranet was launched in 1997, under the guidance of an Intranet Strategy Management Board. The Board worked on the principle that 'if we can do the thinking right at the beginning, IT will be the easy part', and saw part of its task as developing the future role for information managers towards being largely concerned with promoting informa-tion interactions among people.

Revisiting the situation, four years after the completion of the original case study, showed encouraging developments. The DTI is now looking at its information activities – including those associated with its IPs – in the context of a unified information architecture, which will form the framework within which all its information resources are integrated and managed.[5]

5 For an exceptionally lucid account from the inside of the process of establishing and using an information architecture, *see* MacLachlan (2004).

Its approach to developing the information architecture depends on bringing together: acceptance of information management as being part of the job responsibilities of all staff; the human and cultural aspects of the information behaviour necessary to achieve this; and using the technology to support that behaviour. (The concepts underlying the DTI's information architecture, and their implications for information products, are discussed in Chapter 6, pp111–112.)

Two examples of the approach relate to information products: the electronic records and document management programme; and intranet developments. Both give due heed to the cultural aspects. Hyams (2002) quotes the Director of Electronic Records and Document Management, an information professional with long experience and great authority in the Department, who is convinced that the key to success, and the main challenge, for both electronic records and document management and the wider information architecture project '...is to embed a different attitude to information management in the staff, from the most junior to the most senior, and to raise the level of information management skills'.

As described above (*see* p49), a good start was made on the intranet, but then things were allowed to stagnate – in particular no real editorial control was established for the intranet and other web-based IPs; and the technological tools were not developed to make it easy for people to contribute products and maintain the integrity of the original system. The predictable result was that people found the procedures for loading information were too cumbersome, in the absence of proper controls 'went off and did their own thing', and internal websites sprang up all over the place. The situation is now being tackled through an information management policy, with a clearly defined editorial role to maintain quality and standards.

It is encouraging to find an approach to information products that, on the basis of long experience, pays due heed to communicating and interacting with people, to supportive training, and to the feelings that human beings have about that most precious possession – what they know.

The British Galleries, Victoria and Albert Museum, London

 This is the largest re-display project the V&A has ever undertaken; the British Galleries, which opened in 2001, show British design and art from 1500 to 1900, drawing on every variety of material in the national collection. The seven-year project, whose total cost was £31m, began in 1994. It was an enormous undertaking, which required information inputs from all the museum's resources – the archive, the National Art Library, the Picture Library, the collections management system and departmental records – and collaboration among curators, educators, documentation managers, researchers, and IT and multimedia specialists and consultants, both in-house and external.

The full integration of information products, especially but not exclusively interactive ones, with the presentation of objects was a central and innovative feature of the project, and that makes it an instructive story for our purposes from many points of view, not least the cultural. The role of all the IPs in the British Galleries is to present context information, which embodies material from the whole range of the museum's resources, in forms which allow various degrees of user initiative in pursuing their own interests.

Large museums like the V&A tend to have a culture in which the many different groups of professionals who run them have very high levels of knowledge and know-how, which they rightly prize. It is, however, not usually part of the overall culture to think it necessary to understand and appreciate what other groups know and do; the point of reference lies within one's own professional group, inside the museum and in the outside world. This has traditionally been the case in the V&A, and it created problems on a project which required input from and cooperation among many different groups and specialisms. Fortunately there was awareness from the start of the British Galleries project of the nature of the culture; and those responsible sought to use the project to build on its positive aspects and overcome the negatives.

Probably only the Concept team who were in the central place from the very beginning had anything like full appreciation of obstacles to be overcome.

The composition of this essential group was a balance between senior staff members who acted as advocates of the curatorial and of the educational role, and of the interests of visitors. Its four members were the Chief Curator of Furniture and Woodwork (now the department of Furniture, Textiles and Fashion), who was designated Project Curator, the Deputy Keeper of the same department, the Head of Gallery Interpretation (now Head of the Online Museum, and Deputy Head of Learning and Interpretation), and the Head of the V&A/Royal College of Art MA programme (responsible for the initial development of the themes of the galleries). One member observed that the 'psychological balance of the complementary roles on the team took time to develop; it probably took nine months for us to understand each other', during an initial period of travelling together and with the designers.

For many others involved, there were some shocks and surprises. There were for example different ideas:
● Among people responsible for providing content and writing for the interactive IPs, about nature of the content, and the way it should be presented
● Between multimedia IT specialists and educators; educators and curators; museum staff and writers and others from outside, about users and how to present information to them
● Between various specialist groups who had to cooperate, about one another's knowledge and skills
● Between IT specialists and educators about the desirable nature of the interaction between users and IPs, the one seeing it as more or less 'cut and dried', and the other wanting it to be open-ended, allowing for user initiative.

The extracts from interviews set out below are examples of how some of the people most closely involved now look back on these cultural conflicts and the ultimate outcome.

The mediator between various interests

The Deputy Keeper, Furniture and Woodwork (now Deputy Keeper, Furniture, Textiles and Fashion) – a member of the Concept Team from the start – was responsible for an overview of the whole period, the overall balance of content, management of the content team, and collaboration with designers and historic consultants on the period rooms. She described her role as that of 'Mediator between the outside experts and the demands of educators and designers, holding the academic balance.'

Project management as overseen by the Concept team was by three team leaders. In a departure from usual hierarchical practice, each team had a relatively junior coordinator supported by two senior subject specialists. The coordinators were said to have found it 'a bit uncomfortable to start with', but then it started to work well (and the coordinators found in their subsequent work that they had benefited from the experience of doing this job). The Concept team and the coordinators met regularly, so there was shared responsibility and authority. Each team also had an educator and a curatorial assistant. Later on young historians recruited from outside for their historical knowledge were appointed as research assistants; this gave rise to yet another cultural tension. Their background meant that they tended to think about historical concepts first; in contrast to curators' faith in the preeminence of the object as evidence, their orientation was towards documents and theoretical thinking, and they had to learn the skill of interpreting such concepts through the display of objects, rather than by means of text and argument. While this was described as having caused some management difficulties, 'it was probably a useful stimulant/irritant'.

The educator/visitor advocate

This member of the Concept Team (the Head of the Online Museum, and Deputy Head of Learning and Interpretation) had interesting reflections on the collaboration with the multimedia specialists from the firm commissioned to implement the interactive products.

She described meetings which 'discussed learning styles and audiences over several sessions', at which she tried 'to get them thinking about the project in the same terms as the Concept Team, given that they lacked experience of educational projects.' It was hard, and not entirely successful, work to achieve mutual understanding between different cultures and ways of working. The 'reluctance of people from the technical side to work on paper while developing ideas, their habit of going straight to the computer meant that ideas and structures got too fixed too early, and there was not enough allowance for change' and that was to the ultimate detriment of the outcome. 'It would have been better to spend more time talking and thinking; over-emphasis on getting forward and settling things can have economic costs, and result in less effective end products.'

Looking back, she considered that the interactives which allow users to design something for themselves, for example Design a Coat of Arms or Design a Book Plate, in particular, came out as 'too closed, the activity paths are too set; the number of possible variants is huge but there is no opportunity outside the selection process for users to bring their own contribution of intuitive thinking, and pursue their own self-education through them. ... On another occasion it would be good to try to think of ways of making better use of the creativity of the visitors.' She, like the Content Manager, whose observations are given below, found that some of the database entries provided by the large group of staff who created content were inappropriate for the purpose – 'There were texts that failed to tell users what objects were for and how they were used, or to explain unfamiliar terms.' And insufficient time for reviewing the drafts meant that these problems could not be fully solved within the schedule for the project.

The Content Manager

The Documentation Manager and Head of Records Section was seconded to oversee overall content development. The system designers' project team brought in the content manager very late in the project. By that time, the system designers had established processes that worked less well than they should have done, and time was lost on manual working to compensate for system shortcomings. This was a case where a lack of full understanding of other people's specialisms meant that advice which would have facilitated delivery of the project's IP outputs was not sought.

Other cultural problems in the content area arose from the use of more than 70 authors to provide text. The resulting material was of variable quality, and at times failed to meet agreed content guidelines. Some of it showed evidence of a lack of understanding of users; some writers found it impossible to put their own knowledge into appropriate language, perhaps because of difficulty in appreciating the general user's perspective. Some authors who were used to writing of other kinds found it hard to create the brief texts required for multimedia presentation. Although project educators were involved in reviewing content, the time was too short to deal with all the issues raised during the project, but the Museum has since addressed them in creating content for other information products.

Here are some of the views of people closely involved, all with long experience in the museum, of how the culture changed as a result of the work on IPs, two years after completion of the British Galleries project.

The Head of Records and Collection Services

" The British Galleries project contributed to a gradual building of consensus after a few false starts and some blind alleys; we are moving towards sensible approval rather than imposing ways of working on people. We have to try to trade off between quick gains and the long-term value put into documentation, and it's hard to resist pressure for quick gains. Curators now realize the value that comes from the effort put into the core system … The whole museum contributed, other projects held fire in favour of the British Galleries project. It proved it can be done; cross-organizational hurdles can be overcome if you have enough clout!

The education member of the Concept Team

" Experience of the British Galleries project brought more commitment to the idea of interpretive devices, which became embedded; the people involved invested something of themselves in them; new ways of thinking became internalized. … It was a new departure for V&A to

have interpretation in galleries. The emphasis in the interpretation approach was on what would happen in the gallery, what would
be built in as part of experiencing it, rather than on separate
'extraneous' leaflets. Initially there was some opposition, it was
seen as threatening, but halfway through the period of the project
attitudes changed, under the influence of the educational requirements of Heritage Lottery Fund.

The mediator among different interests

" Projects like this need someone in a bridge/translator/mediator
role, to deal with the difficulties of human interactions, communication, and the exercise of authority.

The necessity of cooperation in a project that every one recognized as important,
gave priority to, and wanted to succeed, led to some cultural changes over time,
expressed in widening of professional horizons, and appreciation of the knowledge
and skills of others. The pre-existing culture influenced the quality of the IPs created,
but the necessity of cooperating on creating them, and the experience of doing so,
has influenced the culture and the lessons learned will benefit both the management and the outputs of the next ventures in this line.

The Co-operative Bank

 The Bank was briefly mentioned in Chapter 2 (*see* p27) as an example of an organization whose information products serve it well. Its information culture makes
a strong contribution to that happy state of affairs.

The Co-operative Bank was founded in 1872, as the Loan and Deposit Department
of the Co-operative Wholesale Society (today known as The Co-operative Group),
initially to support local retail cooperative societies with banking facilities. Over
the years, it extended its services to personal customers, and in 1975 it joined the
Committee of London Clearing Banks. In 2002 the Bank and the Co-operative
Insurance Society (CIS) came under common leadership as Co-operative Financial
Services Limited, an Industrial and Provident Society.

One of the smaller high-street banks, with a market share of 2.5 per cent, it currently
employs 4000 staff and has 133 outlets and 119 Handybanks. Its results show a
consistent rise over the years in such indicators as profit before tax (up 14 per cent
in 2002 over the preceding year), operating income (6.1 per cent up), and customer
satisfaction (97 per cent very satisfied or fairly satisfied – which makes it top of
the list of high-street banks surveyed by MORI, at 8 percentage points above the
average rating for banks).

In spite of its small size, it enjoys a high degree of public recognition, primarily
because of its well-known ethical policy; it is the only bank with such a policy and
this was given as the reason by over one third of the customers for moving their
accounts to the Co-operative Bank from another institution (1993 Annual Report).

The Bank has invested extensively in information technology, with very successful
results. Its highly efficient telephone banking service handled more than 13 million

Making knowledge visible

calls in 2002. It has made large investments in improving internal processing efficiency, centralized account maintenance, telephone banking, and network distribution.
In 1998 it became the first major UK bank to offer a full on-line Internet service to
personal customers. Today its internet bank, Smile, is an award winner for its website, credit card, online current account and savings account, and 80 per cent of its
customers are very satisfied with its service.

The research case study which I made over the period between 1994 and 1999
showed the Bank's organizational culture to be very different from that of other
banks – strongly bound to its ethical stance, and to the traditions of the cooperative
movement. Many staff have a family tradition of strong links to the cooperative
movement, and many are involved in community affairs because of it. The organizational climate tends to be informal and non-hierarchical, and the Bank promotes
open communication. It is probably significant that the organization chart of the
Co-operative Bank Group Structure puts 'Actual and Potential Customers' in the place
normally occupied by the Chief Executive or Managing Director, and shows the CE
and the Executive Directors of the different divisions at the bottom, rather than the
top. The organizational structure has been a very flat one for many years, with only
five layers of management; and a lot of work on projects is done by cross-functional
teams, whose members are free of the need to constantly refer decisions upwards.

The *Partnership Reports* which the Bank began publishing in 1998 after the first year
of operation of its Partnership Approach[6], throw interesting light on the organization's culture as seen from the inside by staff. The 2002 staff survey drew a response
rate of 61 per cent (compared with the 30 per cent of a similar survey four years
earlier); figures from the 2002 *Partnership Report* show that:
● 80 per cent of respondents think they have developed valuable skills and behaviours while working for the Bank (though only 36 per cent agree that they are provided with appropriate opportunities for career progression).
● 93 per cent say they enjoy good working relations with colleagues
● 76 per cent believe that the Bank maintains job security to the best of its ability
● 60 per cent agree that they are kept up to date about organizational changes
● 88 per cent understand the Bank's ethical policy, its ecological mission statement,
and its cooperative values
● 60 per cent believe that the Bank behaves fairly to them.

In the course of the research case study of the Bank, it was noticeable that the
longer people had worked for the Bank, the stronger was their feeling of pride in
it. Most of the people interviewed in the case study because of their management
responsibility for information products showed high job satisfaction; some of
them had come in at a modest level up to 20 years earlier, and had been given the

6 The Bank identifies seven partners in its
'Partnership Approach': shareholders, customers,
staff and their families, suppliers, local communities, national and international society, and past
and future generations of Co-operators. 'The bank
seeks to deliver value (as defined by the Partner,
not the bank) to all Partners in a socially responsible and ecologically sustainable manner.'

It acknowledges that 'conflicts of interest can
arise: situations where giving to one Partner
will mean taking away from another', and so
'alongside "profitability" which is absolutely vital
to the bank's continued existence, the pursuit
of "balance" is a key concept within the Partnership Approach.'

opportunity of 'growing with the job' and being trained to do so. Those who had worked on the *Partnership Report* itself particularly valued the non-hierarchical team approach to the project, which included working with the Chief Executive and inter-facing at director level.

The Bank has a long history of creating outstanding information products, both printed and electronic, which have gained a high reputation. There is an evident connection between the culture as described above and such features as:
• The very good relations between Bank staff and the design groups, copywriters, and website contractors they work with
• The attention devoted to preparing briefs for outside writers and designers and maintaining interaction with them over the long term. The quality of the best of the end products can certainly be attributed in part to this
• The readiness to be self-critical and to present critical comments of staff and others in its own information products, notably the Partnership Reports.

The effect of the overall culture on ideas about information behaviour must also contribute to some of the distinctive characteristics of the Bank's information products:
• The rich information content of everything the Bank produces over the whole range from advertising to purely informative products. The mission statement in particular is stronger in content than is general with such documents, and the policies and strategies which have been progressively developed from it are also rich in content and form the basis for unusual information products, such as the statements of ethical policy and the *Partnership Report*.
• Serious pre-publication testing of products by finding out how actual users manage in using them for the purposes they were designed for, and the range of steps that have been taken for post-publication monitoring and evaluation.
• The high quality of information products intended to extend knowledge of the Bank's policies, and to reach particular groups of customers and potential customers; and of some of the information products which have been developed for staff.

The lessons from the case studies in this chapter are drawn on in Part 4, which suggests how organizations can examine the implications of their own objectives, business processes, and culture for what their information products should be and do.

Summary

- The organization's objectives (how it defines what it's in business to achieve, what it views as most critical for its survival and success) and its business processes (how it does what it's in business to do) should together determine what kinds of IPs it needs, and the appropriate content, medium and form for them.
- Information products should help achieve the objectives, and support the business processes.
- The information culture in organizations has a decisive influence on how IPs are managed, and how effective they are. So its influence on the creation, dissemination and use of information products should be studied and learned from; and the results may lead to action to modify information behaviour and get better value from information products.

References

THE CO-OPERATIVE BANK (2003)
Sustainable development, Partnership report 2002, Manchester: The Co-operative Bank www.cooperativebank.co.uk/ethics/partnership2002

DAVENPORT, T H (1993)
Process Innovation. Boston, MA: Harvard Business School Press

... (1997)
Information Ecology: mastering the information and knowledge environment. New York: Oxford University Press

DAVENPORT, T H & PRUSAK, L (1998)
Working Knowledge, Boston MA: Harvard Business School Press

DETLOR, B (2000)
'The corporate portal as information infrastructure: towards a framework for portal design, *International Journal of Information Management,* 20, 91–101

HYAMS, E (2002)
'All change at the DTI', *Information + Library Update,* 1 (9) 46–47

MACLACHLAN, L (2004)
'From architecture to construction. The electronic records management programme at the DTI'. In A Gilchrist and B Mahon (Eds), *Information Architecture: designing information environments for purpose,* London: Facet Publishing

MARCHAND, D A, KETTINGER, W J, & ROLLINS, J D (2001)
Information Orientation. The Link to Business Performance,. Oxford: Oxford University Press

ORNA, E (1999)
Practical Information Policies Ed2, Aldershot: Gower

ORNA, E & PETTITT, C (1998)
Information Management in Museums, Aldershot: Gower

SKRYME (1992)
'Knowledge networking – creating wealth through people and technology', *The Intelligent Enterprise,* 1 (11, 12) 9–15

TAYLOR, R S (1986)
Value-added Processes in Information Systems, Norwood, NJ: Ablex Publishing

The value that IPs add (add subtract)

In this chapter

Introduction

The first two chapters made the case that IPs are:

- The essential carrier by which knowledge travels from one human mind to another, and without which it couldn't get around
- A key asset, without which no organization could function, because they represent their values and knowledge, are agents in the transformation and diffusion of knowledge, and embodiments of organizational memory

and that by virtue of all the roles they play, they are
- Vital information resources

and that therefore they should be
- Recognized as essential supports for whatever the organization does
- Managed as a key element of knowledge management and information management
- Supported, in their creation and use, with appropriate infrastructure and human resources
- Included in the organization's strategies for information and information systems.

If those arguments are accepted, then the value that IPs can add, or subtract, deserves a lot more attention than it gets at present. As yet, most organizations, not being in the habit of looking at their information products in this light, or considering them as an entity, have no realistic conception of their overall value.

This chapter examines what the true nature of IPs means in terms of their value – positive or negative – to the organizations that create them.

The peculiar value characteristics of information and knowledge

Information and knowledge, as I have written elsewhere (Orna, 2004) differ from material resources when it comes to value:

1   Information, on the definition used in this book (*see* pp11–12) has no inbuilt value. It acquires value only when human minds have transformed it into the knowledge which they need in order to act successfully, and without which nothing of tangible value can be created or exchanged.

2   If information and knowledge are exchanged and traded, the value from using them can increase for all parties to the transaction.

3   The potential value of information is not reduced by use; it can be transformed into knowledge and used many times by many users to add value to many activities and outputs. As Itami and Roehl (1987) put it, 'The essence of invisible assets is information, and it is this characteristic, which is not shared by other resources, that makes a free ride possible. Only information-based assets can be used in multiple ways at the same time ...'. And information 'can be used simultaneously, it does not wear out from over use, and bits of it can be combined to yield even more information.'

4   Information doesn't just sit around in 'information repositories' which constitute 'information assets'; it also, and more significantly, enters into all business activities of all organizations – it is, as Davenport (1993, p140) calls it, a diffused resource.

Those characteristics of information and knowledge point to the essential fact that their value for organizations (which may be positive or negative) comes from people transforming information into knowledge and acting on the knowledge to do something. This is why concentrating on 'intellectual capital' and 'information assets', popular in the 1990s, hasn't got anywhere much. There's not much hope of getting a nice tidy 'bottom line' value for them because:

● Assets are static, but knowledge and information are dynamic

● The only 'assets' you can see and count are 'containers' of information

● That misses how people use the information content; and worse still, it misses the effects of using it and what they imply for the future

● Using information content means transforming it into knowledge and acting on it

● And it's only from the effects of that process that you can judge the value that information adds to or subtracts from other assets.

Valuing information and knowledge is not an objective exercise

The other important fact to remember is that no valuing of anything, including information, can take place without human judgement about the relative value of different things in relation to what the people doing the judging want to achieve. Of course human judgement can't be anything but 'subjective' – but organizations hire people, particularly for 'knowledge work' and for high-level management posts, precisely for their ability and experience in exercising professional judgement on their behalf. So what's the objection to applying that kind of judgement to the value of the knowledge and information they need to use in their work?

Recent research on the value of information (Oppenheim et al., 2002a and 2002b, and Marchand et al., 2001a and 2001b) takes this line of reasoning, and makes short work of the objection to 'non-objective' methods of ascertaining the business value of knowledge and information.[1] Oppenheim and his colleagues at Loughborough concluded from their study of the attributes of information as an asset, and its role in enhancing organizational effectiveness:

> To put it bluntly, arriving at a value of information or knowledge is not an objective exercise. Different stakeholders (customers, employees, managers, owners and investors) will employ different methods depending on their various perspectives. Their evaluations will be subjective. Attempts to value information and place it on the balance sheet of organizations does have benefits in that it positions information within an area of financial management with which all senior managers are concerned. However, an objective value of information is not possible in our view. Information value by its very nature is subjective, dependent on the interpretation of the individual or team members who employ information in particular situations for particular purposes. Objective measures are also often far less reliable than they at first appear. Recently, accounting has been high-lighted as an area where organizations can present seemingly objective and audited financial statements, e.g., Enron, which have in fact little to do with their real underlying financial position. (Oppenheim et al., 2002a)

And they state plainly in the final report on the research that:

> Attempting to place a value on information which was dynamic and subject to the changing perceptions of users was seen as an impossible task ... Almost all of the senior managers interviewed saw a role for information assets in enhancing the effectiveness of their organizations. They also saw a role for information assets in improving communication and decision-making in their organizations. However, the practical application of information assets to these issues may be more dependent on how people use and apply information in everyday situations. ... there is a link, tentative as it may be, between information assets and organizational effectiveness. Any organization which is concerned with achieving effectiveness must also be concerned with the management of its information assets ... The leveraging of information assets requires more than technological solutions. It also requires attention to the long-term building of assets for future economic benefit. (Oppenheim et al., 2002b)

The link between information orientation and business performance

Those conclusions, from a small though thoroughly researched sample of UK organizations and their managers, receive strong support from the work of Marchand and his colleagues (2001a, 2001b) with a large international sample of senior managers in a

1 The British Library has recently made a study of the economic value it contributes to the British economy through its services (Pung & Patten, 2004). The research, using contingent valuation methodology, studied through user surveys the value they set on the information the BL provides to them, and then transformed their qualitative assessment into money terms.

variety of businesses. They present a method for measuring the link between mature 'information orientation' and good business performance. When they began their research, it appeared that 'there has been no significant progress, until now, for establishing a practical business metric of effective information use that was causally linked to business performance improvement.' (Marchand et al. 2001b, p248). As it proceeded, they found that, while managers in many companies have learned how to integrate people, information and IT to achieve superior business performance, 'they have had no clear metric' for evaluating the interactive effects of these factors on business performance.

In trying to develop such a metric, the researchers first looked for an 'objective' measure that would be valid across the different countries and different types of business in their sample. But the wide variations they found between the reporting requirements in different countries on company performance, and between what privately and publicly held firms divulge about performance, made them conclude that '...use of "objective" measures of performance was not possible nor advisable, given these quality constraints.' They chose instead to use qualitative, but statistically reliable, methods, depending on the evaluation of knowledgeable people in the population they were looking at: 'a perceived multi-indicator of business performance that has been considered superior in previous management research under these circumstances, rather than "objective" or secondary measures.'

The indicator was senior managers' perceptions of their own company's business performance (a 'subjective' judgement, but one likely to be pretty accurate), as given by their answers to these questions:

> **Relative to our competitors:**
> 1 **Our market share growth has been ...**
> 2 **Our financial performance has been ...**
> 3 **Our level of product and service innovation has been ...**
> 4 **Our ability to achieve a superior company reputation has been ...** (op cit p147)

Their final conclusion was that 'effective information use does lead to better business performance but the link is through I (nformation) O (rientation)' that is, through combining effective management of information, IT, and organizational behaviour in relation to information and knowledge; IO 'predicts business performance much more powerfully than the three capabilities independently.' (op cit p149). They also concluded that people are fundamental to getting better business performance via IO, because:

> **organizations involve relationships among people, and how people choose to contribute their knowledge to achieve organizational purposes. People are constantly balancing their own interests against the group and organization's interests, in deciding whether and how to contribute their personal expertise, skills, and experience to the welfare of the group or organization. The organization defines a relevant context to continuously convert human knowledge and learning into creative ideas and innovations of value to achieving organizational success in the future, rather than for today alone.** (p150)

To summarize where we've got to so far, in the matter of value information and knowledge are unusual compared with other commodities:
- Transactions in them among people can benefit all parties

Making knowledge visible

- They don't wear out from use
- Information can be used in multiple ways by many people simultaneously.

The value of information and knowledge indeed comes from the use to which human beings put them, and in order to use them we have to carry out transformations.

- We have to transform information from the outside world into knowledge in the mind, which we then act on to achieve something of value – to ourselves personally and/or to the organization we work for.
- And to make knowledge in our minds accessible to other people, we have to transform it into information and put it outside into the world, where they can find it and transform it into knowledge for themselves.

Human judgment and human feelings enter into all valuing, including that of information and knowledge, and there's nothing wrong with that, especially as humans carry out the essential transformations which alone allow information and knowledge to contribute value for individuals and organizations.

And to facilitate and get the best out of those transformations, organizations need to combine information management, information technology and information behaviour effectively.

Applying this value approach to IPs

If we are agreed that:
- Information products are what we put our knowledge into when we transform it into information and put it out into the world, and that
- They are therefore the means by which people access the information they need, so that they can transform it into knowledge and act on it
– then any attempt to value knowledge and information must take them into account.

Not many authors have contemplated doing so – neither of the groups of researchers just quoted, for example, mentions the information products in which the information with which they are concerned is embodied.

McCain (2004), who has written in an illuminating way about the economics of information, includes an interesting chapter on 'The economics of information products' in his hypermedia text on 'Essential Principles of Economics' (his definition of IPs has been quoted in Chapter 1, *see* p12). This being an economics text, he considers the subject from the point of view of 'supply, demand, monopoly and competition and the role of government in markets'. He concludes that in certain aspects IPs are 'quasi-public goods', and as such, left to the market alone, they could tend to be under-produced. There might, however, be opposite tendencies in a purely market-based approach. To determine where 'an active government policy of adjusting the production of information' would be appropriate, 'each particular information-producing industry would have to be investigated and evaluated on the details of its operations.' McCain steps aside at this point; whether this is a feasible solution is 'really beyond the scope of economics' to answer.

Other authors, approaching the subject from the point of view of information science and information systems, have had interesting things to say about the value implications of IPs, in at least one case going back over more than 20 years.

Taylor (1982) describes IPs as tangible formal communications which organizations 'consciously design and issue in some form' (p341) whose value lies in the judgments of the users about the usefulness of the information they contain for what they want to do; the fundamental question then becomes 'How much initiative and effort must a user invest (Cost) in order to get useful information (Benefit)?' (p345).

Sless (1995) draws particular attention to the costs to the end user of the complexity in information transactions as embodied in information products; governments and businesses 'outsource costs' by passing them on, but this can lead to loss of the value of customer goodwill. He also (1994) refers to the dangers that organizations, especially those in information-intensive industries, court when they 'hit out at paper work and try to control printing and design costs' by handing responsibility for design as well as printing to a printer, a practice on which he comments:

> **Printing companies have no primary interest in good design, their primary interest is in volume printing. Asking a printer to look after both your design and printing needs, without the advice of a professional intermediary, is like asking a drug company to supply all your medication needs, without a doctor acting as a professional intermediary.**

Penman (1996) makes a similar point in discussing the distinction between corporate identity (on which organizations often spend a lot) and corporate reputation, where they often fail to see the potential of information products for adding value. van Wegen and De Hoog (1996) argue that:

> **The value of information cannot be determined independently from the medium that encapsulates and processes it ... though information of course acquires its value from its role in decision making, the information product as a whole also adds values to other activities in information processing.** (p248)

The work of Meyer and Zack (1996), which has been discussed earlier (*see* pp18 and 31) is unusual in looking at how information management can identify resources with the potential for transformation into products that will support the organization's aims, improve its competitive position, or add value in other ways.

How IPs add and subtract value

Information products are capable of both adding and subtracting value for the organizations they serve. As we shall see, the subtracting can be dramatic and even tragic – they can lead to irreparable harm, and wreck the reputation of those who offer them; on the other hand well-managed IPs bring commercial advantage and enhance reputation. And the positive or negative effects of IPs are strongly related to how effectively the organizations that create them manage their information resources and support them with IT.

Tangible and intangible values

IPs contribute to both tangible and intangible value, positively and negatively, as Figure 4.1 shows.

Figure 4.1 is a summary of how value can be lost or added at the point where people meet information. If the products that are the meeting point don't support the users in finding the information they need and transforming it into knowledge to do what they want to do, then the inputs that have gone into making them have been wasted, and the desired outputs will not happen.

The stories from real life that follow show how this can come about, and the consequences, ranging from financial loss, through reputation damage, to human tragedy.

The input from the stakeholders in the organization's information products (to be described in Chapter 5) is critical for what happens – and most critical is that from the three groups considered in Chapters 6–8: information managers, information systems/ IT managers, and information designers. The positive or negative value of IPs in the stories which follow is always related to and dependent on the quality of information management, information technology and information design, and to the information culture of the organizations responsible. Because examples of information products that subtract value are unfortunately a good deal commoner than cases of the opposite process, I don't apologise for starting with cautionary tales. Awareness of the terrible costs that lack of attention to information products can bring may be the best incentive to investing appropriately in them.

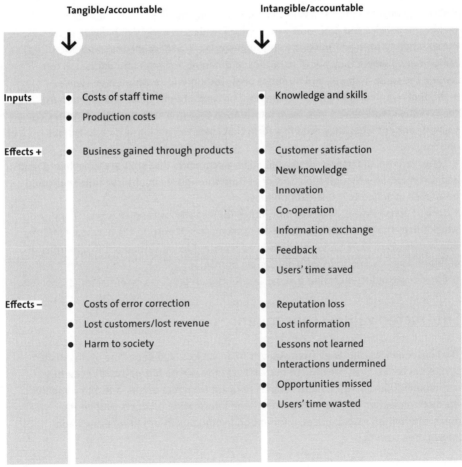

Figure 4.1 The potential of IPs for adding (and subtracting) business value

Subtracted value – some causes

It is everyday experience to find people in organizations complaining of:
- Internal products that repel users and impose high costs in staff time, especially badly organized intranets without information professionals to manage them, and with no inputs from the people who manage and design the organization's printed products.
- Websites with similar defects, like the one in a government agency, where staff complain that they are unable to refer customers to pages where they will find the information they need, because they themselves can't find their way round their own site. It's not just government either: early in 2002 a report on leading companies in the UK claimed that they were 'woefully inadequate at providing corporate information on their sites'– share prices weren't given, the nature of their business was not explained on the home page, and search facilities were poor. And a report (SOCTIM, 2003) on the information presented on a variety of sites reveals great variation and many unhelpful features. The researchers used test questions based on typical inquiries dealt with by Citizens Advice Bureaux on benefits, housing, health, debt, legal proceedings, consumer complaints and relationship breakdown. They found little to raise enthusiasm – using everyday language in searches often led to inappropriate pages, availability of forms online varied greatly, and alas, the government's own signpost to e-government services, UK Online, was 'disappointing'.
- Over-reliance on email as a vehicle for distributing important new information, updates of policies and procedures, etc – which leads to a variety of individual outcomes, ranging from just missing it, through storing it as best they can and not remembering where they put it, to dozens of different non-standard databases containing the same material, and no single organization-wide authoritative source.
- Products created by originators who have no contact with those who need to use them in their work, which give them information they don't want, omit what they do want, or present what they need in a form that costs them a lot of time to extract and use.
- Long, verbose and poorly signposted policy documents that staff are expected to read and comment on – though the effort of getting through them absorbs time that could be applied in action to implement policies.
- Lack of authoritative guides to procedures for jobs whose essence is procedural, which forces the job-holders to devise their own ways of getting the necessary information, and leads to work tasks that should be standard being carried out in a number of different ways – sometimes with deplorable outcomes.
- Inadequate induction training in using information products essential for job-holders.

Subtracted value – consequences

The consequences can range from straight financial loss, and departure of dissatisfied customers to the most dreadful of human tragedies whose horror dwarfs their huge consequent financial costs. All the stories here are from real events, and all exemplify the interconnection between on the one hand information products, and on the other information management, information technology, information design and information culture.

Costs of bad management of information products: the DTI

 The survey of the Department of Trade and Industry publications described in Chapter 3 (*see* pp47–50) revealed large and unnecessary publication costs incurred because of lack of standards and control at all points in the process – from initial decision-making and funding, through production, to distribution and storage. That took place more than a decade ago; the DTI learned lessons and took action.

Reports of losses from similar causes in companies in the UK and Europe continue to appear. The internal IPs produced in organizations' own print services are responsible for much of the waste from what one vendor of document workflow products describes as 'Documess'. According to the company Danka Europe, the annual wastage in the UK from poor control of the production end alone is over 1.8bn euros (Danka, 2003).

Costs of error correction and of lost customers

Examples of the negative financial value which information products can bring to organizations if they fail to invest in appropriate quality are comparatively rare – probably because there are not many situations where it is possible to put a direct monetary cost on the results – but those that exist are telling ones.

 Herget (1995) makes the straightforward point that when any product is defective, 'the buyer incurs additional costs' and when those costs are too high to be borne, purchasers vote with their feet and stop buying the product. He cites a case which illustrates this principle, drawn from a company which provides customers with tailor-made compilations of reviews from technical magazines worldwide. Losses that could have been avoided by attending to quality before delivering the products amounted to:

Lost clients (40/year at 5000 Ecu each) of which 50 per cent due to quality failure	100,000 Ecu
Quality inspection	16,000
Editing costs	20,000
Feedback	10,000
'Defensive' client visits	25,000
Internal firefighting	25,000
Internal administration	10,000
Total cost of 'non-quality'	**206,000** Ecu

I found a comparable situation in a consultancy assignment some years ago (Orna, 1990, pp281–288). An organization which depended on a single information product was losing customers as fast as it gained them mainly because its management had not recognized that the quality of the product depended on high-level indexing skills, and was using people with keyboard skills for the task. The losses were compounded by poor information flows inside the company and between it and its customers, and by lack of quality control at all points in the production process.

 Fisher and Sless (1990) present an extensive account of an information design project by the Communication Research Institute of Australia in a large Australian insurance company, to improve the quality of its forms and establish standards for them. The existing ones were the result of piecemeal changes and of computer system interfaces which had not been designed to suit the ways in which data was collected and presented. Interviews with people in various situations in the company revealed that policy proposal forms which customers completed created the greatest problems for both sales and processing staff, each of whom blamed the other for the design of the forms. Analysis of a sample of 200 forms revealed that 100 per cent of them contained errors, with a total of 1,560 for the whole sample, and that turnaround to acceptance of proposals ranged from 1 to 167 days. The authors estimated the staff time needed to repair each category of error found, and worked out the cost for each category and the approximate total cost to the company. At a conservative estimate the total number of errors per year exceeded 320,000, requiring over 53,000 hours to repair, at a salary cost for the people making the repairs in excess of $A551,000. (Similar work on the cost of errors in forms for the UK Department of Health and Social Security was reported by Coopers & Lybrand in 1986 – Kempson and Moore, 1994 – though the actual costs are not quoted.)

Development of a new design which would help to bring down these costs by making it easier to fill in the form correctly depended strongly on understanding organizational politics, involving the stakeholders in the associated processes closely in the development while formalizing the points at which they made decisions, and allowing a lot of project time for negotiations (though this still proved to be an underestimate). Acceptance of the new design depended critically on the significant reduction of error rates it delivered: only 15 per cent of the new forms contained errors as against the previous 100 per cent; turnaround times were significantly reduced; there were only 44 errors in a sample of 200 new forms as against the previous 1,560, a reduction of 97 per cent. Savings in the cost of time spent on repairing the errors were over $A500,000 or five times the cost of the whole project. As the authors point out, the kind of costs measured by this project have not usually been taken into account, and the traditional data-processing costings of information systems are misleading. 'Organisations would do well to revise their thinking on such matters, particularly if their objective is to improve productivity.'

Loss of client goodwill

 An information product delivered as the final output from a project can undo much of the good from previous stages, as illustrated by this true story.

A consultancy assignment had gone well; but when the first version of the report was presented to the client, a good deal of warmth went out of the relationship, because the report didn't take the intended readers into account. In the first place, it used a lot of technical terms associated with IT, without explaining them – and that immediately created difficulties for some of the senior managers to whom it was addressed. Changes to the IT infrastructure were indeed an essential part of the solution to their problem, but that problem had arisen for the very reason that they lacked experience of the technology. To compound their difficulties, the draft report was arranged quite differently from the schedule that had been used in gathering information, and under different headings from those they had become familiar with. Finally it contained a lot of large and distinctly unrefined tables, which, while easily understandable to the compilers, were anything but to the recipients. The effect was as might have been expected. When people find themselves at sea in

Making knowledge visible

something that is difficult to understand, outside their experience, and different from what they expect to receive, they are liable to become anxious, and that is what happened in this case. A lot of time had to be spent on revising the report and trying to undo the harm, but the loss of trust was such that some of the most important recommendations were rejected, and no further assignment resulted.

Reduced job satisfaction from poor IPs

People in organizations, as I have observed in the course of information audits or case studies, often complain of the information products they are expected to use in the course of their work. Sometimes, indeed, you might think the products had been specially designed to hinder rather than help the unfortunate users.

 That everyday observation gets some scientific support from a study by Joshi and Rai (2000) of a sample of over 360 participants, working in a range of jobs (senior and middle management, supervisory, professional, and clerical), in a number of large organizations in the mid-West of the USA, including manufacturing firms, governmental agencies and educational institutions.

The researchers based their work on a model drawn from earlier research on the technical and social effects of information systems and IT at work. They looked at both the direct and indirect effects of the quality of the information products delivered by information systems, on the job satisfaction of the users. They asked users about their confidence in the systems that delivered the products, and about quality of the products in terms of: timeliness, currency, reliability, relevance, volume, accuracy, precision and completeness; and about factors associated with how at ease they were with their work situation.

The results showed that there was indeed a positive relation between the quality of information products and job satisfaction, and that it was via the factors of 'role conflict and role ambiguity', rather than direct. Those concepts cover the extent to which conflicting work demands are placed on people, and to which they lack adequate information for carrying out tasks or understanding the nature of the job they're supposed to be doing. The effects of high role conflict and ambiguity are to make them dissatisfied with the job, and so to lack self-confidence and motivation; and that in turn can have costs to their employers, ranging from absenteeism, staff turnover, and poor performance, to loss of customers and investors. Poor quality IPs were found to have a 'substantial indirect effect' on both role conflict and ambiguity, and through that on job satisfaction. The authors recommend that organizations should have a policy of refining system requirements and modifying systems on the basis of users' experience of using them, to ensure that the quality of the information products offered matches the work environment of the users.

Misinformed pensioners; losses all round

 Government misinformation to pensioners about legislation which would reduce the proportion of the State Earnings-Related Pension (SERPS) that can be inherited from a husband or wife created a 'mis-selling scandal' in 2000. The guidance which government issued for pensioners, about how they might be affected by changes in social security legislation which were due to come into effect in 2000, was inaccurate and misleading.

The Parliamentary Commissioner for Administration (2000) found the Department of Social Security and the Benefits Agency were guilty of maladministration because they had provided 'misleading and inadequate' information about the changes; and a report by the National Audit Office (2000) examined how the failure to provide 'correct and timely information' would result in the National Insurance Fund losing 'billions of pounds' of anticipated savings, together with the costs of redress packages (available only for those who could prove they were 'actively misled') and putting right the blunder.

Criminal records – IPs with maximum risk potential

Records dealing with people are a particularly sensitive and critical form of information product, because they are the meeting point between the holders of information and those who have the duty of using it in many contexts to ensure compliance with the law, justice, access to rights, security, and safety. Bad management of the most critical of records – those dealing with criminal intelligence – can bring the most terrible consequences of all.

e As a curtain-raiser to this theme, here is the tale of how, in 2002, the Criminal Records Bureau failed in its obligation to process details of teachers in time for the start of the school year. The firm which holds the government contract for the job explained that it had not anticipated that 70 per cent of the applications it had to deal with would be submitted on paper rather than electronically; nor apparently had it expected that 30 per cent would contain errors. History does not record why the contractor, or those who prepared the brief for the work, didn't investigate in advance the medium which applicants would be most likely to use. The effects were still persisting two years later, but, in the words of one report (*Guardian*, 07 09 02), the government contracts that the firm concerned had lined up were so many and so large that it could 'afford to soak up the criticism'. Its prospects suffered no ill-effects – unlike those of many of the teachers affected by the delay.

e The name of Soham, a small quiet Cambridgeshire town, will for many years be associated with an appalling series of events that led to the murder of two children by a school caretaker. At every point along the way, a fatal combination of systems flaws (both electronic and paper-based), poor information management and disastrous human resources management all compounded one another. The result – with a dreadful and haunting inevitability – was that critical information products, in the form of essential records, were not available to be used as they should and could have been, and so Ian Huntley was able to get the job that allowed him to murder two young girls.

The tangled tale started on Humberside, where Huntley lived before taking up the Soham job. At the time of his trial, in December 2003, the Chief Constable of Humberside claimed in a press statement that his force had deleted information about Huntley from its records because of the requirements of the Data Protection Act. The information so lost contained sex allegations against Huntley in the 1990s including four suspected rapes. The Chief Constable's claim led to what proved to be something of a red herring: the 1995 Guidelines for police on the Act, drawn up by the Association of Chief Police Officers. A Home Office working group was immediately convened to review the current guidelines, which had been issued with the approval of the Information Commissioner.

In due course it turned out that the deletion was from quite other causes. The intelligence reports on Huntley in Humberside were in fact lost by a combination of systems cock-up and human error. As the *Guardian Unlimited* reported on 04 03 04, a 'catalogue of faults with [Humberside] computer systems' has since emerged. An internal report from 2002 by the then director of intelligence at Humberside, which was put before the Bichard inquiry into how Huntley was able to get the job, spoke of the 'hasty, under-researched and under-funded introduction' of the force's main intelligence system in 1999, which led to the loss of a lot of potentially important information. Changes made to the system – 'CIS Nominals 11' – in late 1999, to counter the threat of the millennium bug, resulted in general intelligence notes being removed from one third – around 20,000 – of the force's records. Thus the system did not 'fulfil its role as the central, reliable, storehouse of all available intelligence', and its shortcomings were compounded by the 'alarming ignorance' of basic intelligence matters among Humberside police officers.

Sir Michael Bichard's report on his inquiry into the factors which led to the murders for which Huntley was convicted (Bichard, 2004) highlighted the failings of Humberside Police:

The process of creating records on their main local intelligence system – called CIS Nominals – was fundamentally flawed throughout the relevant period. Police officers at various levels were alarmingly ignorant of how records were created and how the system worked. The guidance and training available were inadequate and this fed the confusion which surrounded the review and deletion of records once they had been created. ... there was not even a common understanding of what was meant by 'weeding', 'reviewing' and 'deletion'.

The main recommendations for action included (very unusually for such reports) 'A new Code of Practice on information management':

8 A Code of Practice should be produced covering record creation, review, retention, deletion and information sharing. This should be made under the Police Reform Act 2002 and needs to be clear, concise and practical. It should supersede existing guidance.

9 The Code of Practice must clearly set out the key principles of good information management (capture, review, retention, deletion and sharing), having regard to policing purposes, the rights of the individual and the law.

10 The Code of Practice must set out the standards to be met in terms of systems (including IT), accountability, training, resources and audit.

How poor manuals for social workers contributed to a child's murder

This is another harrowing tale of a short life and dreadful death that could have been prevented. In this case, the information products that played a major part were the various manuals and handbooks that were meant to give social workers guidance on their responsibilities for child protection under the law, and the procedures they had to follow. The lack of standard texts, and the free-for-all which apparently prevailed, allowed different local authorities to produce their own – often hopelessly inadequate and out of date – versions. The effects were compounded by disastrous human-resources management, and more or less non-existent information management in this critical area of work.

In 2003, Lord Laming published the report of his inquiry into how the eight-year-old Victoria Climbie met a terrible death at the hands of her great aunt, who had brought her to England with the promise to her parents that she would care for her and give her the chance of education.

In the months of abuse before her death, social workers in four local authorities in London had had responsibility for Victoria. They were ill-equipped to carry out their task, and poorly supported by their employers and managers. Her social worker in the authority where her life ended 'never consulted her social services department's child protection handbook in the seven months she was responsible for Victoria' (*Guardian*, 23 01 2003). But if she had, 'the advice might have proved useless because local authorities have not kept pace with government reforms.' A report for the Metropolitan police in 2002 found that in many councils social workers were having to work from 'unforgivably poor and out-of-date child protection policies'. The Laming report (Department of Health/Home Department, 2003) cites a variety of inaccurate, out-of-date, and confusingly presented manuals and handbooks in the four local authorities that dealt with Victoria. In one:

social workers had little by way of up to date manuals to guide them in their day to day practice. The field-work manual 'current' in early 2000 which dealt with matters other than child protection [and was therefore relevant to Victoria at the time she made contact with the borough's Social Services], amazingly predated the Children Act 1989. … New child protection procedures were implemented in February 1999 and the eligibility criteria for children's services were being developed, but a manual of child protection practice guidelines, which should have been finalised in April 2000, was marked 'interim'. Significantly, it was to retain that status through to at least the end of the Phase One hearings of this Inquiry, in February 2002. (Laming Report, para 4.16)

The Social Services department in another of the boroughs concerned offered its social workers procedures and policies that were so long and complex that they 'were of limited help'. Witnesses described them as voluminous and daunting, and unfriendly to the users, and the Social Services Inspectorate had three years earlier found them 'inadequate and in need of a major revision' – which did not happen. (Laming Report, para 6.63)

A third had 'several sets of guidance' for social workers undertaking investigative and assessment work. They included undated Child Protection Guidelines (rewritten in 1997), and procedures 'intended to operate as a pocketbook enabling social workers to be clear about their duties at a glance', which had been devised locally by a district office manager. While one witness said she was aware of these procedures, another reported that 'social workers were never directed to it and practices developed which were separate to the practice manual. There was a lot of confusion about what the relevant procedures were.' (Laming Report, para 6.59)

Making knowledge visible

And to complete the tally of confused guidance in a miscellany of information products, the fourth Social Services department had a 'profusion of guidance in various documents relating to the different agencies', which 'made it very unclear what was expected of front-line staff.' (Laming Report, para 8.)

It is small wonder that Lord Laming recommended:

Directors of social services must ensure that staff working with vulnerable children and families are provided with up-to-date procedures, protocols and guidance. Such practice guidance must be located in a single-source document. The work should be monitored so as to ensure procedures are followed.

Perhaps the worst reflection from this case is that it is just the most recent of a line stretching back many years. The continuing combination of poor guidance for social workers, and poor information and communications management has undermined the interactions that are essential for child protection, and prevented lessons from being learned.

Added value from IPs

Added value from information products yields less dramatic stories than those I have just related. The examples quoted below from some of the organizations and businesses whose stories have been told so far, do, however, show how well-managed IPs contribute to their high-level information orientation, and add value to their overall offering.

The Co-operative Bank

 Outstanding information products are recognized as contributing to the high profile of this very successful small bank (*see* pp54–56). The unusual high level of public recognition it enjoys is mainly on account of its ethical policy, presented in a range of effective information products, especially its *Partnership Reports* (*see* p55) and its award-winning website. The Bank uses its IPs actively, in winning and retaining customers and in conducting exchanges with them, as the basis for informed action and innovation. The products and the exchanges are supported by a sound IT infrastructure, an appropriate mix of electronic and traditional media – including highly reliable telephone and Internet banking systems – excellent design, and out-standing collaborative input from in-house stakeholders.

mda

 As described earlier (*see* Chapter 3, pp38–40) the membership of museums which mda serves faced a change in their funding and regulatory arrangements, which in turn affected the resources available to mda for delivering its services. The process of developing its portal represents a well-thought-out solution to the changed situation, going far beyond the mere introduction of technological changes.

It led to far-reaching and productive developments in mda's objectives, in its business processes for delivering training and advice to members, and in its information management. The interactive development of new processes, IPs and the technology to make them accessible through the portal resulted in new thinking about mda's information resources and their management. The process of cataloguing them led to new ideas for using them to create IPs for the portal, and for treating users' contributions as the source for new products. That resulted in an initial content management policy for the portal, which in turn will contribute to a future publishing policy and an information strategy.

So changes that could have threatened the quality of mda's service to museums, and its value to members, have actually been the stimulus to creative development centred on information products, which offers new benefits to museums, and also brings mda closer to an information strategy which includes information products.

Essex County Council publications

 The long-term work in Essex County Council's Education Service (described in Chapter 3, *see* pp43–44) to establish a publishing process, with a group forum responsible for setting and maintaining standards, has added value in two ways. The Education Service itself, the staff responsible for its publications, and the authors, have over the years gained in reputation from product quality, and in the cost-effectiveness of the process; and the users benefit from publications that are designed with their needs in mind. Today the opportunity is open to add further value by extending this successful practice to the whole range of the Council's publishing, in line with a move to electronic communication and publication. If it is taken, there is potential to integrate the Council's information products into its existing excellent strategies for knowledge and information management, enhance the overall quality of its offerings to the customers it serves, and generate significant revenue.

The Cochrane Collaboration

 The story of the rapid and world-wide development of The Cochrane Collaboration, which is told in detail in Chapters 6 and 7 (pp114–115 and 130–131) shows the results of far-sighted thinking about electronic delivery of high-quality, evidence-based, up-to-date information products, which are of the highest value to health services and to the whole community. The reviews by the international groups of individuals who make up this global collaborative effort have become a key means of making rational and equitable use of NHS resources, and of spreading international knowledge of effective forms of health care.

Victoria & Albert Museum

 Multimedia information products have contributed to the business value added by the £31-million investment represented by the V&A's British Galleries (*see* Chapter 3, pp50–54). Developing them has been a valuable learning experience[2] which the Museum is now applying to further innovative management of the collections and their presentation. The information orientation of the Museum has benefited from the eight-year process, in terms of increased interdisciplinary understanding and interaction. Applied to future projects, this should bring enriched content provision, and enhanced value from collaboration with multimedia contractors, which should bear fruit in IPs that allow full play for the creativity of visitors.

2 Reports of the extensive research programme on visitor responses to the British Galleries and the multimedia IPs (V&A, 2003) can be downloaded from the museum's website.

Making knowledge visible

Tate (ex Tate Gallery)

 The success of its website – a pioneering venture proposed and created by communications managers and information systems managers (described in Chapter 7, *see* pp128–129) marked a turning-point for Tate. This major information product raised the public profile of the Gallery at a time of intensive development, when work on Tate Modern (opened in May 2000) was in progress. In addition, it had a positive effect on senior management's understanding of the importance of managing information about collections as the basis for the website, and so opened the way to the realization of a long-pursued but never yet attained information systems strategy.

As discussed in Chapter 3, the institution has now moved towards getting maximum value from these gains, and the outstanding Collections information system on which they are based, within the context of its overall strategic objectives.

Premier Farnell

 This business, with its high dependence on its information products for maintaining its competitive position, has devoted more thought than most to adding value through them by coordinated management of information and the associated technology (*see* Chapter 3, pp37–38).

A recent example of its value-oriented thinking relates to establishing which combinations of: medium for finding and selecting goods and services, transaction type, and order-fulfilment and payment methods, have most potential for cost-effectiveness. As Premier Farnell's e-business development manager points out, each variable on its own has an associated cost (process cost, and effect on returns), and the costs can vary greatly. It's possible to spot intuitively where savings should be possible, but not with sufficient certainty to justify investment based on achieving cost reduction rather than investment based on increased sales. To identify where major cost efficiencies could be gained, it is necessary to look at the options currently selected by different customer groups (large, medium and small enterprises). These give a clear indication of what savings would be achieved if, for instance, 50 per cent of large-enterprise customers used the web catalogue. This kind of analysis has potential for decision-making about allocating resources in order to achieve maximum cost-effective value from information products.

Added value through cost-saving

 One example has been given already in this chapter of the large cost savings, in terms of staff time released for more creative and productive use than dealing with customer errors in completing forms, that can be achieved by intelligent information design (*see* pp67–68). Others are quoted by Walker and Barratt (2004) in the information design section of the Design Council's website. Examples quoted include design work for The Environment Agency which reduced the number of forms for customers to complete from 1200 to under 250; redesign of phone bills for Cable & Wireless (subsequently sold to ntl) which reduced customer calls to its call centre by over 35 per cent; and redesign of documents which the Open University sends to new students, which led to a saving of 25 per cent on printing costs in the first year, and allowed redeployment of staff who had previously had to deal with problem cases, to more productive work.

Richards, too, (2000) in a study of how diagrams can be productively used in electronic user guides for products, quotes a case study of documentation overhaul for Dixon's, which led to a 60 per cent reduction in 'no fault found' call-outs.

Local IPs unlock value of ICT for rural poor

 A good many people today question the real value that the transfer of computer and telecommunications technology has brought to developing countries. Arunachalam (2002) argues, from his experience of the InformationVillage project in the Pondicherry area of southern India, that value, for recipients and donors, can come only when the technology is used to deliver locally created information products that local people actually need for their own use in their daily lives.

As he relates, 'We understood the need to develop "content" – the information needed to satisfy the communities' needs – and developed much of the content in collaboration with the local people.' The products created in this way for knowledge centres in the villages making up the project cover a range of databases, including rural yellow pages, and an entitlements database which gives access to the whole range of government programmes. All the knowledge centres are open to all villagers, regardless of age, sex, religion, caste or level of education; and local people – most of them women – are responsible both as operators and as providers of primary information.

A far cry from the other stories related here, but no bad example to end with.

Assessing the business-value potential of IPs

The argument of this chapter has been that IPs should make an optimal contribution to adding value to whatever the organization does, and should do it cost-effectively. The examples from a range of organizations show that IPs can add value in a variety of ways.

It follows that:

- Organizations should have appropriate criteria for evaluating the contribution their information products make to business value, which takes into account both tangible and intangible costs and value.
- They should apply them in the context of an organizational information and knowledge strategy, derived from their business objectives.
- They should use the results in allocating resources for creating and managing IPs.

They should also be aware of the various approaches and methodologies that have been developed and applied to assessing the value that information and knowledge contribute, some of which have been described above.

 In the course of the research which was one of the sources of this book (Orna, 1999), I had the opportunity of trying out one sophisticated methodology, the Integrated Value Manager (IVM – *see* McPherson, 1994, 1995, 1996) in one of the case-study organizations – an insurance company. A form of information auditing approach was

Making knowledge visible

used in a small-scale investigation[3] of how information and knowledge had contributed to creating a new investment product and its associated information products, and the results were applied as input to the IVM in order to assess:

1 The value the investment product had contributed in terms of money, achievement of business objectives reputation etc
2 The proportion of that value which came from applying information and knowledge
3 The proportion of the overall value contributed by associated IPs.

So far as the first was concerned, limitations on the amount of financial information that could be provided allowed no more than a minimal financial model; useful results, however, were gained about the value contributions of information and knowledge to both the investment product and its associated information products, and about the potentially critical effect of the information products on the value added by the investment product they supported.

A high overall proportion of the cost-effectiveness value of both kinds of product was contributed by intangible assets as compared with the monetary contribution; and interactions within the project team responsible for the investment product, about the associated information products turned out to be the most sensitive of information categories; improvement in their quality had most potential to add value, reduction to do most damage.

This very interesting methodology is still under development, and offers great potential. Like the 'information orientation' methodology of Marchand and colleagues (2001b) described above, the IVM depends on knowledgeable judgements by responsible decision-makers. Such methods demand a heavy investment of highly paid time, and hard individual thinking at detailed levels, together with negotiation, discussion, and resolution of contradictions; so applying them is no trivial matter, and that may act against their being taken up widely. Spending time on thinking is not much favoured in economies and businesses dedicated to short-term payback.

Even without going into this new territory, however, there is plenty of useful work for organizations to do in working out appropriate criteria for evaluating their own IPs. Some of them are set out below.

Some criteria for evaluating information products

These criteria are based on the arguments and examples set out in this chapter and the preceding ones:

- The importance of the organizational objectives to which the IPs contribute; and how effectively they support achieving them.
- The significance of the risks against which IPs should protect the organization and the users; how well the IPs perform in this respect; and how well they are integrated with other aspects of protection (eg training, information management, systems/IT, communications, human resources management).
- The extent to which information management, systems/IT and information design make an integrated contribution to creating, managing and disseminating information products.

3 Described in Orna (1999)

- How fully the range of stakeholders in the organization's information products are enabled to contribute to their development.
- How well the products match the characteristics of the users, and the ways in which they need to use the products.
- The extent to which they impose avoidable expenditure of time, intellectual effort and frustration on staff and on outside users (which can be quantified in terms of agreed cost/h of users' time, as in the Fisher & Sless example quoted on pp67–68).4
- How well the organization's information products support it in managing its relations with its outside world (usually called Customer Relations Management, but it's not an appropriate term because for many organizations the outside world doesn't consist exclusively of customers).
- How well the products work in combination: with one another; with related products/services; with related processes/transactions.

Summary

- Information and knowledge have unusual value characteristics.
- Their value for organizations, which may be positive or negative, comes from people transforming the information contained in information products into knowledge, and acting on the knowledge.
- Valuing information and knowledge is not an objective exercise; it depends on human judgment.
- Since information products are the means by which people access the information they need, so that they can transform it into knowledge and act on it, any attempt to value knowledge and information must take them into account.
- Information products can both add and subtract value – tangible and intangible.
- When they subtract value, the consequences can range from direct financial loss and loss of customers, to appalling human tragedies.
- Well-managed information products benefit from and contribute to a high level of information orientation in their organizations, and add value to their overall offering in a range of ways.
- Organizations need appropriate criteria for assessing the contribution their information products make to business value.

4 Ryan (2004) describes a method for determining the value of the information provided by an information unit which has some comparable features, though it starts from the opposite end. The method, which is in current use, depends on 'time-saved tariffs' agreed between the unit and its users – ie the time that the unit's services saved the users, converted to an agreed £/h figure.

References

ARUNACHALAM, S (2002)
'Reaching the unreached: how can we use information and communication technologies to empower the rural poor in the developing world through enhanced access to relevant information?', *Journal of Information Science*, 28 (6) 513–522

BICHARD, M (2004)
The Bichard Inquiry Report HC 653, London: The Stationery Office

DANKA EUROPE (2003)
Documess Research Report
http://www.danka.co.uk/DocumessResearch Report.pdf
(*see also Managing Information*, 10 (8) 19)

DAVENPORT, T H (1993)
Process Innovation, Boston, MA: Harvard Business School Press

DAVENPORT, T H & PRUSAK, L (1998)
Working Knowledge, Boston, MA: Harvard Business School Press

DEPARTMENT OF HEALTH/HOME DEPARTMENT (2003)
The Victoria Climbie Inquiry. Report of an Inquiry by Lord Laming. Presented to Parliament by the Secretary of State for Health and the Secretary of State for the Home Department, London: The Stationery Office

FISHER, P & SLESS, D (1990)
'Information design methods and productivity in the insurance industry', *Information Design Journal*, 6 (2) 103–159

HERGET, J (1995)
'The cost of (non-)quality: why it matters for information providers', *FID news Bulletin*, 45 (5) 156–159.

ITAMI, H with ROEHL, T, (1987)
Mobilizing Invisible Assets, Boston, MA: Harvard University Press

JOSHI, K & RAI, A (2000)
'Impact of the quality of information products on information system users' job satisfaction: an empirical investigation', *Information Systems Journal*, 10, 232–345

KEMPSON, E & MOORE, N (1994)
Designing public documents. A review of research, London: Policy Studies Institute

McCAIN, R A (2004)
'Economics of Information Products' in *Essential Principles of Economics: a Hypermedia Text*
http://william-king. www.drexel.edu/top/ prin/ txt/EcoToC.html

McPHERSON, P K (1994)
'Accounting for the value of information', *Aslib Proceedings*, 46 (9) 203–215

... (1995)
'Information mastery', *Managing Information*, 2 (6) 33–36

... (1996)
'The inclusive value of information', 48th Congress of the International Federation for Information and Documentation, Graz, Austria, 25–28 October

MARCHAND, D, KETTINGER, W & ROLLINS, J (2001a)
Making the invisible visible. How companies win with the right information, people and IT, Chichester: John Wiley & Sons Ltd

... (2001b)
Information Orientation. The link to business performance, Oxford: Oxford University Presss

MEYER, M H & ZACK, H Z (1996)
'The design and development of information products', *Sloan Management Review*, Spring, 43–59

National Audit Office (2000)
State Earnings-Related Pension Scheme: the failure to inform the public of reduced pensions rights for widows and widowers
London: TSO (House of Commons papers. Session 1999/2000; HC 320)

NICHOLAS, D et al. (2002)
'NHS Direct: its users and their concerns', *Journal of Information Science*, 28 (4) 305–319

OPPENHEIM, C, STENSON, J, & WILSON, R M S (2002a)
'A new approach to valuing information assets', *Proceedings of the 26th Online Information Conference*, Oxford: Learned Information, pp21–31

... (2002b)
The attributes of information as an asset, its measurement and role in enhancing organizational effectiveness. Unpublished Report to AHRB

ORNA, E (1990)
Practical Information Policies: how to manage information flow in organizations, Aldershot: Gower

... (1999)
The role of information products and presentation in organizations, Unpublished PhD thesis, London: City University

... (2004)
Information Strategy in Practice, Aldershot: Gower

PARLIAMENTARY COMMISSIONER FOR ADMINISTRATION (2000)
State Earnings-Related Pension Scheme (SERPS) Inheritance Provision, London: TSO (House of Commons papers. Session 1999/2000; HC 305)

PENMAN, R (1996)
'Corporate identity or corporate reputation?' *Communication News*, 9 (5/6)

PUNG, C AND PATTEN, L (2004)
'British Library worth £363 million a year to UK economy' (Interview with Caroline Pung, Head of Strategy and Planning at the BL, and Laurie Patten of Spectrum Strategy Consultants), *Managing Information* 11 (1) 4–6

RICHARDS, C (2000)
'Getting the picture: diagram design and the information revolution', *Information design journal*, 9 (2&3) 87–110

RYAN, F (2004)
'Information has no value unless it is used: a blueprint for valuing a library and information service' (Interview with P Matthews), *Managing Information*, 11 (5) 40–43

SLESS, D (1994)
'International best practice and the citizen', *Communication News*, 7 (2) 3–5

... (1995)
'The economics of information transaction complexity', *Communication News*, 8 (5/6) 14

SOCTIM (2003)
'Better connected: advice to citizens', *SOCTIM Insight* (Quoted in *Refer*, 20 (1) 2004, pp25–26)

TAYLOR, R S (1982)
'Organizational information environments', In G P Sweeney (ed) *Information and the transformation of society*, Amsterdam, Oxford: North-Holland

VAN WEGEN, B & DE HOOG, R (1996)
'Measuring the economic value of information systems', *Journal of Information Technology*, 11 247–260

V&A (2003)
Summative Evaluation of the British Galleries (Creative Research), and *Visitor responses to interactives in the V&A British Galleries* (Morris Hargreaves McIntyre) http://www.vam.ac.uk

WALKER, S & BARRATT, M (2004)
About: Information Design
http://www.designcouncil.org.uk/information design/

The stakeholders and their interests

In this chapter

Unrecognized stakeholders

Figure 5.1 on p82, shows the key groups of stakeholders in IPs. There are more of them than is usually recognized. Lack of recognition, and poor communication among the internal stakeholders, and between them and external specialists and suppliers of services, can and does lead to lack of attention to either the original brief or to what the users need, and so to wasted investment. And presenting people with inappropriate, inaccurate or unusable information products in turn creates risks and missed opportunities for the organization which does it (*see* Chapter 4 for examples).

Most of the stakeholder groups shown in the figure will be treated in this chapter; the exceptions are three groups whose specialist knowledge and skills are essential supports for IPs. They are dealt with in Chapters 6–8, their specialisms are:
- Information and knowledge management
- Information systems and technology
- Information design.

These domains are not often brought together for consideration, but I have found it productive to do so. The outcome of the rather rare occasions when they are able to work together on IPs in full understanding is a good one, and it's unfortunate that practitioners so often misunderstand one another's specialisms, and that there is even more misunderstanding on the part of senior management of what they know and do, and of the relative status of their disciplines. (For a full explanation of why I think they should be treated together, and why their cooperation is so essential, see the introduction to Part 3, pp106–108.)

The organization as overall stakeholder

The whole range of stakeholders is seldom taken into account, because it is not often recognized at the top that the business as a whole is a stakeholder in its information products, and no thought is given to how IPs should further its strategies. Therefore no one is made responsible for identifying all the other stakeholder groups and individuals. The business as a whole is in fact often either an absentee stakeholder, or one so confused by its own structure and/or politics that there is no overall view of IPs from the top. So it is small wonder that this is often a disorderly terrain, where territorial skirmishes rage, and disconsolate stakeholders complain that their interests are not considered, and their potential contributions are ignored (*see* Figure 5.1 below).

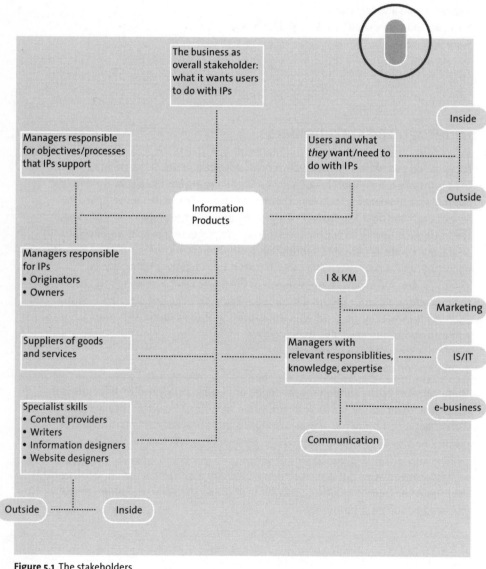

Figure 5.1 The stakeholders

e　　The situation at the Department of Trade and Industry in the early 90s, quoted in Chapter 3 (*see* pp47–50), is an example of the costs and inefficiencies incurred when no overall view is taken, stakeholders are not recognized, and there is no coordination among them.

The case of Essex County Council education service publications is another instance of a similar situation; when the work described in Chapter 3 began (*see* p43), there was no overall strategy for the education service publications, let alone for those of the whole Council; there were no professional inputs of editing, proofreading and design, no attempt at marketing, no pricing policy, and distribution procedures went no further than sending a free copy to each school.

On the other hand the organization benefits if the people who have a contribution to make to its IPs are clearly acknowledged, and are supported by:
● A clear and agreed definition of their contribution to IPs, and the people with whom they need to exchange information about it
● A forum where such exchanges can take place, and mutual understanding of roles can develop
● Processes and standards which allow all stakeholders to collaborate harmoniously.

The V&A British Galleries project

e　　As described in the last chapter (*see* pp50–54), the large investment in the British Galleries created a powerful imperative at the highest level to identify, and bring together in new forms of collaboration, all the stakeholders in the information products which were an essential part of the project. One of its outcomes was better mutual understanding among stakeholders, and an appreciation of how to make use of this, and develop it, in future projects involving integration of IPs.

The Co-operative Bank

e　　The Bank's Partnership Approach (*see* pp55–56) is another example of an organization taking a strategic decision to identify and work with the stakeholder groups whose interests it must recognize and respect, in this case: 'shareholders, customers, staff and their families, suppliers, local communities, national and international society, and past and future generations of Co-operators.' The introduction of the Partnership Approach gave explicit form to the Bank's existing ethos, and also provided the basis for applying a similar approach to the way it manages its information products.

City University

e　　A research case study which I made over the period 1994–1999 at City University in London (Orna, 1999), is a good example of the effect of website development on thinking at the top level about IPs. At the start of the study, the University presented a fairly classic example of the federal structure and territorial culture characteristic of seats of learning. This created both direct difficulties, and problems deriving from a lack of overall strategy, for the management of information products. The direct

problems arose from the fact that departmental autonomy led to variable awareness and use of the professional advice and services available. More seriously, the
absence of an overall institutional strategy, let alone a strategy for the use of
information, meant that there was no strategic framework in which information
products might find an established place.

In the course of the study significant changes were in progress, for which there
seem to have been two main catalysts: the arrival of a new Vice-Chancellor with a
strong interest in information; and the development of the University's website.[1]
The first lent support to a new corporate strategy, and development of the
University's information strategy, while the creation of the University's website
had quite a dramatic effect on breaking up log-jams and freeing channels for new
interactions and new ideas which had the potential to feed constructively into
both the development of strategies and the creation of information products.

The process started in 1997, when a WWW Working Group was set up, with a membership drawn from academics, teaching and learning interests, administration, and
library services. A Management Group for the University website, with a balance of
membership between information content and technology requirements, chaired
by the Director of Academic Services, reported to the Working Group. The University
funded a full-time post of Web Coordinator for the website (a joint appointment
between External Relations and Computing Services); management is shared by two
staff members, one from Computing Services Department, and the other from the
Academic Registrar's Department.

In the autumn of 1998 the WWW Working Group organized a University-wide
'Web Day' for staff users, with the aim of finding out what they wanted from the
site and how they wished to use it for their own purposes. Participants called for
the web to be seen as part of the University's overall strategy, and to be put into the
context of its information and marketing strategies (which were then under development) which should inform decisions about resource priorities. They said that the
cost- effectiveness of various courses of action should be considered (including costs
incurred by not investing in web development) and potential benefits from developing the site should be identified. In the meantime, short-term priorities and possibilities for progress with the website should be determined and acted on. Finally,
the participants emphasized that the development of the essential long-term policy
and strategy depended on a senior management 'buy-in'.

Early in 1999, as a follow-up to the Web Day, the Working Group presented a Web
Strategy to the University's Information Services Committee; it was accepted and the
necessary resources granted. By the end of the case study, greater integration of
printed and electronic products was under discussion.

1 Another motivation came from the 'Continuation
Audit' of the University which the Quality Assurance Agency for Higher Education was due to
make in 2000. Internal and external communications were one of the main areas to be scrutin-
ized. The outcome expressed 'general confidence'
in City's systems to assure academic standards.

Making knowledge visible

Managers responsible for objectives/ processes that IPs support

Managers who are responsible for the objectives and processes that IPs are intended to support should have a key role in deciding what IPs are needed, and what they should do for the organization. Often, however, they do not quite recognize the full implications of that role. Their decisions on what IPs are needed are not always informed by clear thinking in depth, nor are they accompanied by comprehensive briefs for the people who have to implement them. When decisions about IPs need to be taken or reviewed, they should take active initiatives in consulting all the other stakeholders, but experience suggests that often they haven't much idea that there are stakeholders, or of who they may be, and what their interests are.

My first experience of this kind of situation came when I began a job with an Industrial Training Board, which involved setting up a research publishing programme. It quickly became clear that the first thing I had to do was start educating managers about the relation between the Board's objectives and the information products that were needed to support them, and about the stakeholders in the products and their roles. Before I could get on with doing the actual job, some polite, and on occasion not so polite, exchanges had to take place, over such issues as:

- Discussion with decision-makers of the brief for IPs and the key objectives they were required to support
- The role of committees in the production process for IPs
- Print-buying for the information products – a responsibility hitherto exercised by a general purchasing department, innocent of any knowledge of printing and much cultivated by local printers on that account. (For more on this aspect, *see* pp96–97)
- Briefing and management of relations with external designers, and getting it established that professional design was essential (rather than leaving it to good offices of miscellaneous printers with some such injunction as 'Neat but not gaudy', or 'Not too much white space')
- The job of in-house editors and appropriate training for it
- Establishing and starting to enforce rational publishing procedures
- What the term 'house style' actually covers, and developing a real house style
- Defining series of publications and the criteria for selecting suppliers.

IPs in the context of the Freedom of Information Act

 This is the story of a very successful initiative involving information products, taken in the context of legal obligations which Essex County Council had to comply with. It shows managers responsible for some of the relevant objectives and processes taking action to raise awareness at the highest levels, to the benefit of the whole organization.

The FoIA requires all public authorities, including local government, to prepare and submit to the Information Commissioners schemes outlining their publishing programmes and the availability of all their publications (*see* Simpson, 2003, for a non-too-cheering report on how the websites and published information of some LAs deal with the Act). For the first time, schedules of published information must be produced, indicating where and how publications may be obtained. The objectives that the products need to meet are:

- To fulfil the Council's statutory obligation under the FoIA to make known the existence of its scheme
- In particular, to ensure that all the population of the Essex County Council area gets to know about it – including those groups which are especially difficult to reach.

The publication-scheme requirements of the Act mean that the Council has to create some new products, including:
- Information for the public
- Guidance for staff in the Council's services, including Data Protection, Information Security, etc
- A publications database available on the Council's website.

An ultimate product resulting from work done to meet the requirements of the Act is likely to be an 'Information Assets Register'.

The original initiative was taken by the Information and Knowledge Management Coordinator and the Acting Records Manager, who were both aware in good time of the need for action. They presented a report to the Council's Strategic Management Board, drawing attention to the implications of the FoIA.

Their report set out the requirements of the Act for a publications scheme, proposed an information audit to ascertain the actual situation, and requested nomination of a senior manager with FoI responsibility, a network of 'FoI champions' at Head-of-Service level, and an FoIA steering group, nominated by the champions, of practitioners in the different disciplines concerned (library, records management, information management, specialist information units with subject knowledge, member information, communications) together with the Council's IT strategic partner company.

The report was accepted and action taken as proposed; its authors were named joint project managers, working in a small team with specific FoIA responsibilities, along with a lawyer and a web services specialist. FoIA training coordinators were also nominated by the FoIA champions; their job was to identify key front-line staff in service groups who needed to know about publication schemes.

It had not previously been recognized that there is common ground between Communications staff and those responsible for content management, information management, and editorial management. A recent organizational change which brings together Information Services, Finance and Communications should help rectify this.

The proposed information audit of records for the FoIA publication scheme took place in 2002, and management approval was given for a follow-up corporate records audit which will meet the requirements of the Act for the year 2005 by showing who holds records, access arrangements, and permissions.

A new post of Information Sharing/Information Security (ISIS) Manager, reporting to the Knowledge Manager was created. The Council took this pioneering initiative because it became clear that it was essential to have someone with specific responsibility for understanding what information needs to be shared with whom, and what security requirements are involved, so as to get full benefits from information exchanges, and to safeguard against risks, on the one hand of not sharing, and on the other of endangering essential security. This is part of a new Essex County

Council governance structure for information-sharing and security, which consists of a powerful new Information Security Council, led by the Head of Information Services, and chaired by the Council's Strategic Partner, reporting to the Council's Strategic Management Board

So far as the 2005 FoIA compliance requirements are concerned, a recent report presented to the Strategic Management Board, its SMB cabinet, and the Corporate Management group, has pointed to wider organizational implications, including:

- Training needs
- IT implications
- Administrative procedures
- Request forms and other consequential information products
- Legal procedures needed under FoIA, including the public-interest test.

This has turned out to be an unprecedentedly large enterprise involving actions never taken before by the Council. It has brought benefits in the way of establishing procedures and organizational structures that can be applied to other initiatives, past and future; for example, it is now being retrospectively applied for Data Protection.

The initiative around the FoIA publication scheme has also led to new productive cross-service working, as with Communications, and to integrated approaches, for example to manual filing management – which was previously part of Assets Management (facilities, office services, registries) and not linked with Records Management or information and knowledge management. This link has now been made, and the Information and File Management working group includes people concerned with FoIA, so that there is the possibility of including manual files in the corporate records audit, and in an ultimate Corporate Records Management strategy.

This initiative has brought great satisfaction for all concerned in it, which arises especially from the growing understanding and cooperation with colleagues in other functions, and the professional development gained by the initiators, which one of them describes as 'the best experience in 20 years of professional work'. She also points to the advantages which experienced information managers have, because of their understanding of organizational structure and of how to push initiatives upwards for attention in the right quarters. Another interesting instance of what information professionals can contribute to strategies related to information products.

Managers and developers of IPs

Responsibility for IPs in organizations is usually distributed (scattered might be a better word in many cases) to an unclear pattern. It's very rare to find one manager with responsibility for coordinating the whole range of the organization's IPs. (It is not, however, unusual to find one person – the overseer of corporate identity – who wields organization-wide authority over a single aspect which takes no account of the role, content, users, or organizational context of IPs, but only of conformity to an ID which has usually been developed by outside consultants with little if any concern for any of these, but great attention to brand.)

Organizations need someone who has overall strategic responsibility for their IPs, supported by a representative management group (including those who have responsibility for particular groups of IPs or individual products), whose remit is to create the link between business objectives/processes, and all the stakeholders in IPs, in both the internal and outside worlds on which the organization depends. The job-holder could be located within various areas of the organization structure, eg communications, publishing, e-commerce, web and intranet management, information management. Wherever he/she is drawn from, these areas should be represented in the management group.

City University

 At the end of the case study described earlier in this chapter (*see* pp83–84) the University was moving towards unified management of electronic and printed products with representation of stakeholders and clear links to the top of the institution. The World Wide Web Working Group provided a forum of a new kind for the full range of key stakeholders, who have made good use of their opportunity to shape university policy on the 'meta-information product' which is the University's website.

mda

 The work by mda in developing its portal which was described in Chapter 3 (*see* pp 38–40) has led to a new approach to responsibility for IPs. The Advice Team, whose manager is responsible for the structure and content of the portal, supported by a cataloguer and content manager, now works in collaboration with the previously separate Communications Team which is responsible for printed publications. The activities of the two teams were initially seen as separate, and there was an effort to allocate different activities to each; experience has now led them to find more and more common ground, and to recognize a mutual need for collaboration.

Premier Farnell

 Premier Farnell, described in Chapter 3 as a business which recognizes that its IPs are central to its objectives and business processes, has a correspondingly clear and unified management structure for them, which allows for appropriate variety as well as overall standards. All the company's information products, both print and electronic, are governed and owned by the product management department; and the e-business Development Manager is responsible for ensuring the right overall structures. Staff from a number of stakeholder departments and functions, including the traditional publishing function, IT, the e-commerce department, and the product management team, have all been involved in creating systems and procedures to ensure that, as IPs are created, they can be delivered equitably and at high quality via all Find and Select channels. The final technical overlay is added by specialists of each channel, to ensure that the products are properly presented to users. A centralized model is run, where most of the Web Shop and eCat is created; it is managed divisionally and information products are then signed off and accepted by each business unit, which allows the addition of some local 'look and feel'.

Area of responsibility	They are stakeholders because
Information and knowledge management*	They manage resources of information and knowledge that IPs need to draw on
	They have responsibilities for the organization's information architecture, which should be reflected in its IPs
	Their professional knowledge should be drawn on to help users of IPs
Information systems and IT*	The organization's information infrastructure should support all the people and activities concerned with creating and using IPs
	The technology tools for which they are responsible should be explicitly considered and strategically used to integrate the organization's IPs and unite the stakeholders
e-Business, Marketing, Customer relations	They are concerned with delivery of IPs to users in the organization's outside world and have essential knowledge about them, which should contribute to the creation of IPs (*see* the Premier Farnell example on p88)
Communications/ Corporate communications	They are often responsible for internal communication of essential information to staff
	Their remit can also cover external relations
	They are often responsible for printed IPs, while excluded from contributing their specialist knowledge to the organization's IPs in other media (*see* the City University examples on pp83–84 and 90 and the mda example on p88)
	*I have chosen to treat the contribution of these managers in Chapters 6–8, along with that of the specialists in the design of information products; for reasons which are explained in the introduction to Part 3 (*see* pp106–108).

Table 5.1 Other managers with a stake in IPs

Other managers with a stake

As suggested above, there are other managers who are stakeholders – though often neither they nor anyone else realizes it. Table 5.1 above, shows who they are and why they are stakeholders; some of them have been referred to already in this chapter, others are considered in more detail below, and some will be treated in the next chapter.

Communications managers

The overall coordinating role mentioned above as necessary but not often recognized as such (*see* p82) could well be, and sometimes is, held by this function, or jointly them and a manager from the IS/IT area (especially web technology). Experience shows instances of lack of contact between the people responsible for corporate communications or print publishing for the outside world of the organization on the one hand, and those responsible for web-based IPs on the other. More encouragingly, there are cases where both parties realize that there is common ground between them, and set about cultivating it together. The valuable knowledge that the communications side has to contribute consists of: the organization's relations with its inner and outside worlds particularly via its printed IPs; it also often includes contacts with the suppliers of professional services, such as writers and designers; and links with the marketing and commercial functions.

City University

 The successful initiative centred on the University's website described above resulted from an alliance between the manager responsible for communications with the University's outside world via print (designated External Relations), and a manager from Computing Services with a particular concern for the website. At the start of the research case study described earlier, the remit of External Relations covered corporate communications, marketing and publicity, including publications (corporate and student recruitment publications in both print and electronic form), press and public relations, internal communications, advertising and events. The products for which it was responsible were the University's annual report, printed information on courses, and corporate information. It also had a quality-assurance role in relation to course material produced by departments, to ensure that it conformed to University policies on information for potential students, and ran a publication service, selling layout, design and print production to the rest of the University.

External Relations had also expressed its interest, in 1994, in investigating the use of the World-wide Web in promoting the University. ER and its manager came to play a key part in the WWW Working Group which was set up in July 1997, in the Web Day initiative described on pp83–84, and in subsequent developments.

Department of Trade and Industry

 The DTI recently appointed a manager with responsibility for internal communications, whose job entails close collaboration with information managers.[2] Communications and information management strategies mesh with one another, and the information strategy includes a welcome emphasis on the structure of communications, ie understanding how people need to be communicated with on particular topics, for example what should go on the intranet, what should be sent as email, and what requires print on paper. The communications management post requires an 'overall view of all information products' and their coordination. And it's not seen as a sinecure, because 'people find it difficult to think rationally about what information products are for, and about their responsibilities for communicating and receiving information.'

2 An example of an information manager in the lead role in developing a communications strategy for the Royal College of Nursing (Lord, 2003), is discussed in Chapter 6, p13

Making knowledge visible

Specialist skill and knowledge	Owners are users because …
Content provision	They have specialist knowledge from the nature of their work, which constitutes essential content for IPs (*see* examples below)
Writing and editing*	Their role is to provide text which is appropriate for the content of IPs, the users, and the ways in which they need to use the products
	The two skills are sometimes combined, more usually they are exercised by different specialists, with the editor in the role of 'reader's friend', ensuring that the final text does all that it should to help users do what they want/need to do
Design* *Includes* information design, typography, graphic design – as applied to products in all media, so it covers website design, graphical user interface design etc, as well as traditional print	The role of design is to complete the integration of 'content and container' which together make up IPs, and the matching of product to users and use
	Design is also involved in choosing appropriate technology tools for creating IPs and presenting them to users
	Its special skill is in reconciling different requirements to present an optimal solution
Quality assurance	The job of quality assurance is to ensure that IPs conform to essential internal and external standards, so that they do not mislead users and thus create risk for them, and for the originating organization
Supplier relationships	This specialist role as it relates to IPs is to ensure that all suppliers of products and services are appropriate for the requirement, and that they deliver appropriate quality
	*I have chosen to treat the contribution of these specialists in Chapter 8, for reasons which are explained in the introduction to Part 3 (*see* pp106–108).

Table 5.2 Specialist skills and knowledge whose owners are stakeholders in IPs

Specialist skills and knowledge

We come next to the professional skills and knowledge required for the creation of IPs, some traditional, some much more recent; which may be provided from in-house or bought in. They are very necessary, but are often entirely absent; and even if there is some attempt to provide for them, responsibility for them may be inappropriately assigned, or they are not brought in at the right time, or no adequate brief is given. Some of these specialisms will be considered in Chapters 6–8, others here. Table 5.2, above, indicates their role, and the fact that they are stakeholders with a special contribution.

Content providers

These stakeholders are the people with responsibility for acquiring, maintaining and managing, and supplying the information content that goes into particular IPs or parts of IPs, so that it is available when needed, accurate, up to date, and in the required format. They are usually specialist professional staff who are also 'incidental information managers', but everyone whose job involves adding to knowledge through their work, exchanging information with others inside and outside the organization, and transforming that knowledge into information which is made available in the organization's information resources, is a potential content provider for IPs.

All of them should be, but seldom are, part of a network of originators, creators and contributors (*see* Figure 5.2 below), managing interactions amongst themselves directed towards providing the right content in appropriate form. Identifying the appropriate content providers on given topics, and making them – and the originators of information products – aware of their responsibility in this direction is a difficult one

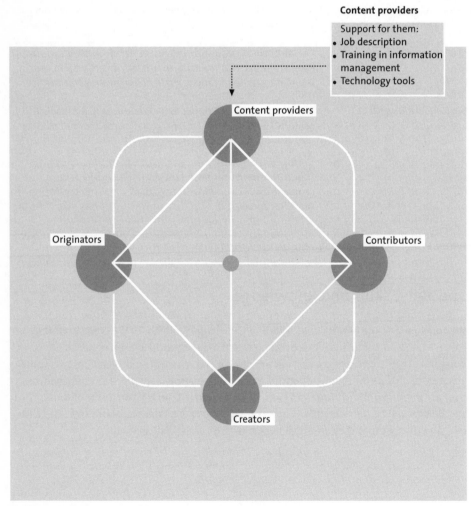

Figure 5.2 Content providers as part of a network of originators, creators and contributers

to get right. Information audits often reveal this as a problem, especially when content has to come from multiple sources and many people, for whom it may not have high priority. Yet if it isn't tackled, the organization can, in the worst case, risk loss of money or reputation by providing information products that contravene legal requirements; and at best it means that users get products that are misleading and/or in which they have justifiably low confidence. And the organization will suffer from inadequate access to knowledge and information essential for successful action and innovation.

One of the solutions is a clear statement in job descriptions that the holders of specified information content are responsible for providing it for given information products, and that they should interact with named job holders in this connection. Their need for support in this aspect of the job should be recognized (eg by training in managing information, help from technology tools in transforming new knowledge into information), and the organization's information resources should include details of the authoritative sources who should provide content on specific topics.

V&A

As we have already seen (Chapter 3, p53), curators at the Victoria and Albert Museum were the content providers – and writers – for the interactive IPs of the British Galleries. While their subject knowledge was extensive and impeccable, they experienced some difficulties in selecting and presenting information for the products and the intended users, partly because the briefing for the task may not have been sufficiently specific, partly because of unfamiliarity with providing content for this kind of IP. The work of the Documentation Manager, who was seconded to oversee overall content development, was made more difficult and less effective, because she was not brought into work on the project until too late a stage.

Premier Farnell

The company is learning the lesson from its move to web-based IPs that all content needs to be created and held at a 'very granular level before formatting and context is applied to allow it to be published to a given audience in a given medium'. Ultimate responsibility for providing the information content required for correct presentation of specific products rests with the Product Managers concerned. Their task now includes providing the appropriate taxonomy codification, and managing such digital assets as images and pdf data sheets relating to the products.

FreePint

As described in Chapter 3 (*see* p42) this is a case of a 'user-led' information product, whose subscribers are major content providers to the FreePint Bar. Their in-house collaborator and coordinator is the Moderator of the Bar, who exercises the editorial role of selecting and structuring content, assigning access keys to it in the form of subject headings to contributions, and managing the archive.

A large legal firm

In this major provincial legal firm, the partners now act as key content providers for essential information products, a development which has emerged in the context of a knowledge management initiative.

The information products in this instance are office standards and precedents, such as standard terms of agreements, letters of advice on specific topics, standard forms of wording, standard clauses, together with memoranda, seminar notes and presentations.

The collaboration between the information professional who proposed the knowledge management initiative and the firm's IT director has led both to technology developments (a document management system to control the IPs) and the promotion of interactions among stakeholders, including the providers of content. It was clear that procedures needed to be established to ensure that standard IPs were regularly updated, and that associated guidance was provided on the circumstances of use by staff without specialist background in the particular subject area. Hitherto, most teams in the business had maintained their own collections of such IPs, which was far from enough to ensure the required control and access. Today, as KM projects are set up with different teams in the firm, the standing representative KM committee is joined by ad hoc members who provide content expertise on particular topics.

Quality assurance

Quality assurance (QA) of IPs involves commissioning someone – in-house or from outside – who has not been involved in the development of a product to make a critical analysis of its fitness to meet its objectives.

A local-government Information Management Policy

 The context for this example of QA is the UK Local e-Government National Customer Relations Management Programme. In the course of work on the programme, it was agreed that an information management policy was an essential element in the business of customer relations management, and that a model 'off-the-shelf' Information Management Policy would help local authorities to develop and put into action their own policies and strategies for managing information.

When a first draft was ready, an editorial consultant was commissioned to make a critical analysis in relation to the project objectives and users as defined by the originators, with specific attention to such matters as structure, the sequence in which information is presented, the treatment of information elements, consistency in the use of terminology, navigation aids, and presentation and language in relation to the intended users.

This extract from the resulting report sets out the criteria used in the analysis:

The objectives of the model 'off-the-shelf' Information Management Policy are:
1 To raise awareness within local government of the issues of information management policy, in the context of the National CRM Programme
2 To make the case for having an information management policy, and to outline what such a policy should cover
3 To provide a starting-point for local authorities to develop and implement their own IMPs.

The intended users of the document are local authority professional staff with responsibility for: information management, corporate policy, website and Intranet management.

To meet the objectives successfully, the IM Policy document must help the intended users to act on it in the required way, that is, to:
- Understand the essential ideas
- Make the business case to senior management for LA information management policies
- Sell the concept within their local authority and gain understanding and support from staff
- Act effectively to develop and implement an IMP for their own authority.

Given that not many of them are likely to be acquainted with the concept of information management policies (though all will bring useful knowledge and experience to them), what content, structure and sequence are going to be most helpful to them?

The answers to that question, based on personal experience, form the criteria against which the quality of the present draft has been assessed.

Criteria for content, structure and sequence

If they are to act on the document in the required way, users need:
- At the very beginning, before anything else, clear definitions of all the key concepts as used in the document
  Purpose: To help them orient themselves before they start reading the document, to make it easy to refer back in the course of reading.

- Background and contextual information about the present document:
- Why it has been produced
- By whom
- For whom
- How it is meant to be used, and with what outcomes
  Purpose: Again, to help users orient themselves before beginning to read the main content.

- Coherent and comprehensive argument for why local authorities need a policy for managing information; the value it can add; the costs and dangers of being without a policy
  Purpose: To help users grasp the main arguments which they will need to deploy in introducing and selling the ideas.

- What an IM Policy should cover: the main elements of the basic model policy, set out briefly and clearly
  Purpose: To provide a single clear statement of IM policy at the level of principles, with guidance on the points at which individual LAs will need to develop and complement it further in the light of their own situation; and examples of topics which will need to be covered.

- The process of developing an IM Policy; essential key stages of the process
- Winning support from the top, and around the LA for the model policy and the ideas underlying it
- Laying the foundations: for the LA's own IM Policy – making an information audit
- Developing the policy in the light of the audit findings
- Putting it into effect – phases for implementing
- Monitoring the policy
- Integrating it into the LA's business strategy

    Purpose: To give practical usable help on starting to do something effective.
If this isn't given, the model policy doesn't stand much chance of being used in the intended way.

These criteria were applied, and the report noted some shortcomings in the draft in respect of structure; the sequence of presentation in relation to the users and the way they were intended use the document; and content. The report suggested revisions to overcome the shortcomings, and meet the criteria; and offered suggestions for an alternative structure.

In the outcome, the client appreciated that more time was needed to produce a document that would give the necessary help to intended users; the original author wrote a revised draft; the consultant made a further QA review; and the final version went forward.

Suppliers and the managers of relations with them

An important category of stakeholders consists of all those from whom the organization purchases products and services that contribute to the creation of IPs – from hardware and software vendors, to typesetters, printers, consultants of various kinds, outside researchers, web designers, writers, typographers, graphic designers – together with the staff who manage the purchasing process and relations with the vendors.

    This, as many organizations have found to their cost, can be a quite a minefield. The risks have often been examined in relation to investment in large IT projects, but less light has been shed on the less dramatic, but still damaging, results of ignorant management of supplier relations in respect of information products.

Troubles with printers

 I got my first lessons in that respect a long time ago, when I became the editor of the magazine of a teachers' association, with the brief to make it fit for an organization that was energetically bringing itself up to date. The association had been founded in the early years of the 20th century and its magazine had been printed for most of its existence by a firm rejoicing in the name of the Bootle Steam Press. This may have been a cutting edge printing establishment in 1904, but it had certainly not moved with the times. The association had recently parted company with the venerable Steam Press, and had moved the contract to another printer – but had left most decisions to them. My task was now to take it in hand and create a better presented product.

I did not realize till a year or so later that I had set about it in a naive and ill-informed way, without adequate criteria. We were not too badly served by the new printer and relations with them were good; at least it was possible to start making

Making knowledge visible

noticeable editorial improvements. But it was only when we took the step of launching a competition for redesign among the organization's members, that by good fortune we found a typographic designer with a sound background in print-buying and deep production knowledge, who was able to produce a proper specification[3] and set standards for the production of the magazine, and willing to stand over the printer to ensure that they were more or less observed.

That experience came in useful when I moved to the next job, with the industrial training board mentioned earlier (*see* p85), which again involved editorial responsibility for printed products – this time a new publishing programme of reports from the board's research department. The practice for the board's existing publications turned out to be a cosy arrangement between a general-purpose purchasing department which bought everything from stationery to computers, as well as print (in which there was no expertise) and a local printing firm. The firm enjoyed a comfortable monopoly, which the quality of its output did not justify, and received contracts for all kinds of jobs that it was not equipped to produce. Again with knowledgeable design support, and with the backing of a strong-minded senior manager, it was possible to save the new research report programme from the clutches of the existing arrangement, and to seek quotations from appropriate firms who could handle quite complex jobs and provide the required quality.

The next example is rather more recent; it comes from the report commissioned a few years ago by the Department of Trade and Industry on its publishing procedures, described in Chapter 3 (*see* pp47–50). The authors commented that a variety of practices was in operation for the production of publications destined for external readership. While many were being handled through an information division, which took a brief from the originators of publications and commissioned design, typesetting and printing from a range of appropriate providers, this was not the case for a lot of others. The investigating team reported examples of staff 'with limited experience' who undertook design and layout themselves, and selected printers and put work out to them. Such staff 'tended to make wrong assumptions about the cost of different methods of production because they lacked knowledge.' It is hardly surprising that some of the products were judged inappropriate for their purpose, failed to meet the needs of the intended readers, and even operated against the aims of the department.

'Cultural' differences between client and supplier

 Some of the problems encountered by the V&A and the mda in their initiatives which were discussed earlier (*see* pp52–53 and 38–40) lay in reaching understanding with the suppliers of the technology they required for the enterprise. In these instances it was not a matter of going to inappropriate vendors; the quality and expertise on offer were high. The difficulty was 'cultural' and interdisciplinary, as exemplified in the observation from the V&A on p52 about the reluctance of people from the technical side to work on paper while developing ideas. The people involved at the V&A found the effort of coming to a mutual understanding was well worth

3 The creation of specifications and briefs for
suppliers is discussed further in Chapter 8

the time and effort it took, while mda commented that their portal project has made them realize the importance of communication, and 'how easily misunderstandings between different disciplines can arise, even when talking face to face.'

This is an important lesson, not only in dealing with technology vendors, but for management of relations with all kinds of suppliers – if you are purchasing or commissioning work from specialists, you owe it to them and to yourself to understand not only what they offer, but also the things that they value most in their specialism, and their 'culture' as it affects their approach to their work – and how it may conflict with that of your own organization. It takes time to achieve a mutual understanding, but it is time well and ultimately profitably spent.

Rethinking the implications of technology change

 Premier Farnell (*see* pp37–38) has devoted a lot of thought to what its policy of integrating web-based technology and print means for what it requires of suppliers. As mentioned earlier, they realize that all content now needs to be created at a very 'granular' level; web technology demands much smaller data elements than the modules created for pages of printed catalogue – for example all parameters for tables are stored in a 'global product database', which had to be created as a bespoke product from scratch. They acknowledge that the gap is not yet bridged between this approach and that of large print firms, and as paper is still a very important medium they are working with paper publishers, and supplementing with an electronic system – a problem specific to very large-scale catalogue publishing, where manual reformatting is not economically feasible. It is interesting to note that the current processes are described as being in some ways more cumbersome than the traditional one of negotiations with supplier, paper processing, filling in a Word template keyed in from various sources, and passing to the publishing department, because no suitable content management system is yet available.

Benefits of long-term relationships with suppliers

 The Co-operative Bank is outstanding for the emphasis it places on building understanding and maintaining long-term relationships with suppliers. This is related to its insistence on briefing and in-house consultation with stakeholders in the Bank over its information products (up to 65 parts of Bank may be involved in planning for some products) which is complemented by what is described as 'intensive interaction' with outside writers. The Bank has a long-term association with its main copy writers; their in-house contacts provide a learning process for them, so that over time they have acquired the benefits of inside knowledge.

The *Partnership Reports* referred to earlier (*see* Chapter 3, p55) are a cooperative effort between the Partnership Management Team, who collect data, copywriters with whom the Bank has a long-term relationship, the staff member who prepares the design brief and the design group commissioned, as well as the independent auditors who are involved in assessing the Bank's performance in achieving its policies.

Users, and how they need to use the products

At last, we come to the USERS – the people on the receiving end, whom the information products are meant to inform. It's very odd: IPs wouldn't be created if there weren't some idea that there are people who need them and will actually use them. Yet even organizations which otherwise manage their information products admirably, like many of those described in this book, acknowledge that relations with the users of the IPs are something they are not so good at, or have neglected in the past, and are aiming to improve (this is the case with the mda and the DTI, for example).4 For the rest, I have come to suspect that the more organizations talk about how their customers/clients/users come first, the less thought they give to the IPs they offer them, and the less they invest in understanding how they want and need to use them.

US Inland Revenue form

 The US designer Karen Schriver (Schriver, 2004) tells the story of how, in response to a challenge from a journalist, she re-designed the notorious form which the United States Inland Revenue Service requires citizens to fill in (it consists of 72 questions crammed into two pages, with a 78-page instruction book to 'help' readers under- stand them). The content of the revision was vetted by the IRS, tax law specialists, and financial experts for legal accuracy and passed their scrutiny. Then it went to the IRS for consideration as a replacement of the existing form. In her own words, this is what happened: 'Within several hours after I turned in the revision, the IRS had a list of reasons why it couldn't be implemented. Most had to do with the need to 'keep things the same'. As the government official responsible for the existing form said to the reporter who had issued the original challenge: 'Agency employees are trained to look for the information where it now appears when putting the information into IRS computers ... Retraining IRS workers to use new forms and reprogramming computers to accept them would run to millions.' And that obviously weighed more heavily than Schriver's argument that citizens are the primary and most important stakeholders for the form – so they will just have to go on carrying the costs of dealing with it.

As another designer commented (K van der Waarde, InfoD-Cafe posting 18 04 04), this is an instance of 'one of the fundamental problems of information design. The person who has to look at/understand/apply the information is not counted as a main stakeholder.' His simple suggestion is that users refuse to fill in forms that are

4 A report (Grant, 2002) on users of the informa- tion products provided by Historic Environment Information Resource (HEIR) organizations shows that while there is a large and increasing demand for such products, very little is known about the users, or the way they use them – and the deficiency is most marked in relation to on-line products, the preferred medium. The report recommends that research of target users, actual users, and use should form an integral part of developing and managing any HEIR, and that HEIR organizations should make increasing efforts to understand their users and how they integ- rate the content from HEIR products into their research and learning activities. A far cry from 'User Experience Strategy' and the 'tools ... for user experience design' which are on offer in other quarters...

ambiguous – 'when people don't use these documents, whole systems fall down.'
It's probably not a feasible one; explaining what's wrong with them and dealing with
the consequences would demand even more time and effort – and the people who
originate the forms know where the balance of power lies and rest comfortably in the
knowledge. (E-Government and e-commerce have the potential, as we shall see later,
to tip the balance still further away from the users – though it need not be that way.)

Too often seen as passive recipients of whatever the originating organization
chooses to give them, in reality users should have a recognized role in initiating and
specifying products in the light of how they need to use them, and active support in
using them. If IPs actually hinder their users from doing what they need to do in their
work, and if users don't get appropriate training and management support in using
them, the products are not helping the organization to achieve its objectives, and they
are probably an unidentified loss.

It is only in rare instances that a direct connection is obvious between the quality of
the users' interaction with information products and its economic effects (the existence
of such a direct relation is certainly acknowledged by Premier Farnell – 'can't find it in
the catalogue, can't buy it' is a readily appreciated truth, and a great stimulus to
thought about the IPs in question).[5] But, as we have seen from stories in Chapter 4,
poor quality of certain critical kinds of information product, combined with lack of
support for the users, can have the most tragic of human consequences (*see* pp70–73).

The scarcity of chances for the originators and users of information products to
meet and tell one another about their requirements is not surprising; few forums
exist, because the need for them is seldom recognized. That being so, it seems that the
most helpful thing to do here is to outline some relevant research findings, and to cite
some convincing arguments. I like the two pieces of research outlined below because
they look directly at actual users of IPs, and at the things they need to do in using
the products.

Research on users of NHS Direct website

 Nicholas et al. (2002) took an unusual line in their research. Observing that, although
health information was one of the most often sought topics on the Internet,
'... research into Internet sites with a health content has almost exclusively centred
around examinations of the quality of information itself, and how this can be assured,
rather than about the needs and attitudes of the people accessing this information',
they decided to rectify the omission, which is not exclusive to electronic sources.
It is also true of the bodies which provide printed information for patients; other
researchers have found that very few of them had 'researched patients' information
needs before they started producing information content'. (Coulter et al., 1999).

The original NHS Direct website too had received minimum user input – in this case
because of a wish to develop it quickly. Nicholas and his colleagues found that
the more than 3000 users who responded to their online questionnaire on the site
had a lot to tell the NHS about what they needed, and how the site as it stood
frustrated their efforts to get it:

5 A recent Delphi survey (Addison, 2003) of the experience of e-commerce development managers shows that they considered the top risk to e-commerce projects was misunderstanding of user/customer requirements.

- The search system on the original site was fragmented and confusing and resulted in poor or misleading searches
- The modular architecture meant that information on a single topic could be spread across several modules, making it difficult to find but also risking duplication of information
- The lack of cross-referencing between information on the same topic maintained by different organizations meant that users could have the impression of partial coverage of the topic.' (Nicholas et al., p312)

This example of the necessity of information-management inputs to IPs, in order to provide users with helpful structure, navigation aids and indexing had a happy outcome. The site has been redesigned 'away from the modular approach of the original towards a much simpler structure focused on the reasons people might visit the site', in terms of what users need to do.

Why users prefer paper – research at the IMF

 We hear rather less about the paperless office these days, presumably because it hasn't happened and shows little likelihood of happening. Sellem and Harper (2001) had the simple idea of finding out the occasions on which a set of users well supplied with modern technology chose to use paper as the medium for work with IPs (*see* also Harper, 2000).

The organization where they made the study was the International Monetary Fund, but the findings could apply to the way people need to work in many contexts. Diaries kept by representative individuals showed that 'paper supports at least five important aspects of knowledge work:'

1 Authoring – when creating documents, paper is a key part of the process alongside the computer. 'They may draft documents in the electronic world, but they show an overwhelming need to refer to paper as they do so.' – which is just what I'm doing at the present moment: drafting on a laptop, while referring to hand-written notes and photocopies of articles.

2 Reviewing documents, especially colleagues' work; reading on paper, annotating, commenting – all things which are easier to do on paper than on computer.

3 Using 'pen and paper as the primary medium' for planning and thinking about projects and activities.

4 Paper supports collaborative activities – 'they sit at conference tables, and go through hardcopy of the reports they are working on. They juxtapose sheets of paper and make marks on their documents in the course of discussions.'

5 Paper 'greases the wheels of organisational communication.' Whenever knowledge workers need to share an important document they will 'print out a hardcopy and hand deliver it themselves to their colleagues rather than send it electronically.' 6

6 Holtham (2005) comments that since this work was done, such developments as much-improved electronic annotation, and electronic sketching, may change the balance of advantage on the first three of these 'affordances' – though not on the last two, which involve interactions between humans.

Paper is also more helpful than electronic presentation for the activity that users carry out with all information products: reading. It was the hope of the paperless office myth that 'Reading too would be altered with computer screens replacing paper and "virtual scrolls" replacing bound books.' Indeed, so excited were some by the prospect of there no longer being a need for books that there was talk of 'book-less libraries', libraries in which readers could simply ask for a text which would be electronically delivered and displayed on a screen. (Not just a 1970s vision, as Harper suggests here; part of the brief prepared for the new Norwich Millennium Library in the late 1990s was that it could in future substitute electronic for printed materials.) The research found three main reasons why paper supports reading so successfully; it:

1 Helps us navigate flexibly through documents
2 Makes it easier to refer across from one document to others
3 Allows interleaving reading and writing.[7]

Yet as Harper points out, this was something that research into reading didn't take into account until very recently. Instead it looked at such things as comparing read-ability of text on screen versus paper, while designers of technologies were more interested in getting the best performance from hardware and software than in what users actually wanted to do with what they read.

This is alas paralleled by the 'plastic dummy' approach to users that some, though happily not all, information designers take – both from the software engineering end of the spectrum, and those with a graphic/typographic background.

Co-designing with the users

 Happily a very different approach is taken by at least one information design organi-zation, the Communication Research Institute of Australia (CRIA, www.communica-tion.org.au/). Its director, David Sless (2000), describes the approach as 'co-designing', and the aim of CRIA as. 'to help people communicate with one another'. Much of CRIA's work is for the corporate sector and large commercial and financial organiza-tions, whose communication practices, 'both internally and with their publics, are performed desperately badly.' Few companies really know what is going on with their IPs (they probably call on consultancies like CRIA because they obscurely sus-pect they may be losing money through them, or occasionally because of a costly disaster that can be traced to an IP). They are not aware of the difficulties and errors their IPs cause, because such monitoring as they do, for example through customer satisfaction surveys, is often a waste of time.

While the clients want to do better in this respect mainly for economic reasons, the concern of CRIA 'is very much with the people who work in those organizations and the people they communicate with.' Co-designing requires the active participation of

7 I have come to wonder if our need to 'get our hands on' the product embodying information we want to interact with is related to the fact that we've had about 6000 years experience (in itself no great period of time) of handling tangible information products on a real substrate, as against a bare half century with intangible elect-ronic ones. The transformation processes involved are difficult ones in any circumstances, so it is unwise to throw away anything helpful from earlier human experience.

Making knowledge visible

users in its projects. Though it has a theoretical basis, in the humanist rather than the behaviourist tradition, in the idea that 'We construct our social realities through communication', its concern is with 'the prosaic, the ordinary, the everyday occurrences that happen between people'. Its focus is on making the information involved in those transactions accessible and usable, and it aims to make the products 'respectful of the people who are going to use it.'

The method of working is to 'ask people what relationship they have with their texts and documents rather than assume it.' At the prototyping stage of designing IPs, CRIA takes them out into the world of 'people who will have to engage with our designs once published or manufactured' and asks them to 'engage with our design. We watch what they do and join them in conversation to find out what is wrong with our designs.' This is not 'usability testing', in which the users are experimental 'subjects'; instead, it is 'a special type of open-ended conversation or dialogue. ... we ask people to help us come up with a solution that they will be able to use in whatever way is appropriate for them. We don't see people as users, as audiences, as targets ... '.

The criteria that should be met in the relation between products and users are expressed in terms of the minimum percentage of people served by an organization who should be satisfied with its communication. For example, 90 per cent of them should find it:
● Respectful
● Attractive
● Usable
● Efficient
● Physically appropriate
● Socially appropriate (eg using appropriate terms to define the organization's relationship with the people it deals with; *see also* Sless, 2002).

Perhaps the most important percentage cited by Sless is the 50 per cent of the time in design projects which 'is spent on the politics ... people's interest, people's power relationships, and so on – are an intrinsic part of any ID project.' Typically (we shall see examples of this from the experience of UK designers in Chapter 8), the boundaries to design briefs are set too narrowly, because the people who will use the end product are not consulted – and that is politics: when those who have been asked to do the designing seek to bring them in, they are saying in effect: 'Those who have exercised power in this area for some time must now give some of that power to someone else.' That power, as Sless points out, is not easy to relinquish, which is why to succeed in such projects and achieve real improvements requires spending a lot of time learning about the organizational politics, finding allies, and devising means of circumventing obstacles.[8]

8 This collaborative approach to the design of communication/information products, including the concern with organizational politics, is very similar to the 'collaborative consultancy' I employ in information auditing projects. Part 4 of this book includes a practical example of this approach to finding out the actual situation with an organization's information products.

Summary

- There are many key groups of stakeholders, internal and external, in an organization's information products, starting from the organization itself.
- They are seldom all recognized; and communication among them is poor where it isn't non-existent.
- Where their interests in IPs are recognized and action is taken to bring them together to collaborate, the organization and its IPs benefit.
- The people who have to use the information products should have a recognized role in initiating and specifying products in the light of how they need to use them, and active support in using them. They are the most important stakeholders, and it's dangerous to see them as passive recipients of whatever the organization chooses to offer them.

References

ADDISON, T (2003)
'E-commerce project development risks: evidence from a Delphi survey', *International Journal of Information Management*, 23 (1) 25–40

COULTER, A, ENTWISTLE, V and GILBERT, D. (1999)
Informing patients: an assessment of the quality of patient information materials, London: The King's Fund

GRANT, A (2002)
'Users and their Uses of HEIRS' Historic Environment Information Resources Network
http://www/britarch.ac.uk/HEIRNET/users. PDF

HARPER, R H R (2000)
'Getting to grips with information: using sociological case materials to aid the design of document technologies', *Information design journal*, 9 (2&3) 195–206

HOLTHAM, C (2005)
Personal communication

LORD, J (2003)
'Information to communication', *Library + Information Update*, 2 (12) 03, 37

NICHOLAS, D et al. (2002)
'NHS Direct: its users and their concerns', *Journal of Information Science*, 28 (4) 305–319

ORNA, E (1999)
The role of information products and presentation in organisations. Unpublished PhD thesis. London: City University

SCHRIVER, K (2004)
InfoD-Cafe posting 16 04 04. (archive: http://lists.webtic.nl/pipermail/infodesign-cafe)

SELLEM, A J & HARPER R R (2001)
The Myth of the Paperless Office, Cambridge MA: The MIT Press

SIMPSON, D (2003)
'Implementing the Freedom of Information Act', *Library + Information Update*, 2 (12) 30–32

SLESS, D (2000)
'Experiences in co-designing'. Keynote address at Co-designing conference, Coventry University 2000
www.communication.org.au

... (2002)
Diagnostic Kit to assess the health of your organisation's communication,
www.communication.org.au/http/p-diagnostic.pdf

VAN DER WAARDE, K (2004)
Info D-Cafe posting 18 04 04
(archive: http://lists.webtic/pipermail/infodesign-cafe

In support of information products

'All the visible, discrete products through which information is presented to people for their use, whatever its medium of delivery, should be recognized as information products, and should benefit from the combined application of three kinds of professional activity: information technology, information design and information management.' TAYLOR (1997)

Introduction to Part 3

I said in the last chapter (*see* p81) that I would deal with three groups of knowledge and skills – information and knowledge management, information systems and technology, and information design – in Chapters 6–8, and promised an explanation of why they merited separate but joint treatment. The time has come to honour the promise, and I have been thinking of how best to do it.

When I need to explain ideas that may seem unfamiliar or even eccentric, I try to find a visual metaphor that gives a fair representation of their essence. The one that came spontaneously to mind in this instance is from dances for a trio of dancers, from the repertoire of late 16th-century Italian courts. The dancers meet, challenge one another, change places, circle warily, interweave, and finally come together in a harmonious close, as represented in the figure opposite. They are a witty and playful representation in miniature of human interactions, and you can't dance them properly without a good-humoured understanding among the dancers themselves. That is perhaps why they presented themselves as a metaphor for how the three disciplines we are concerned with here should interact to support the creation of information products.

First, let me describe briefly their roles in relation to IPs, and why I consider they are critical for the success of this aspect of organizations' information activities – not just individually, but interacting in combination.[1] I should make clear before we begin that the points from which I view the three disciplines differ. I see knowledge and information management from the inside, as a practitioner for more than 30 years; information systems and technology I view from the outside, as a long-term user for my own purposes, and as a collaborator on projects with specialists in those disciplines; so far as information design is concerned, I am half inside and half outside, for all my working life a practitioner as a writer and editor, and for many decades a fascinated collaborator and observer of practitioners of the visually-based specialisms of typographic and graphic design.

The outline below of how I believe the three specialisms should act together, is amplified, with examples from real organizations, in the chapters which follow.

[1] Readers of the book by Marchand and colleagues (2001) on 'Information Orientation' will recall that their research established that it was the combined operation of a similar trio (in their case IT, Information management, and Information behaviour) which was essential for high business performance and added value from information.

Making knowledge visible

Knowledge and information management

The role of KM and IM in relation to the organization and its information products should be to link, on the one hand:

● Organizational objectives and strategy, and their implications for what the organization needs to know and the information it needs to feed its knowledge with, on the other:

● The organization's resources of knowledge and information, and their use in information products (which in turn come to form part of its information resources).

Their unique contribution to IPs is through the 'tools of the mind' which they can offer for thinking about and using information: they can provide content that can be used in multiple ways for IPs, consistent structure and standards to help people access and use them, and links between IPs and the organization's information architecture and information strategy.

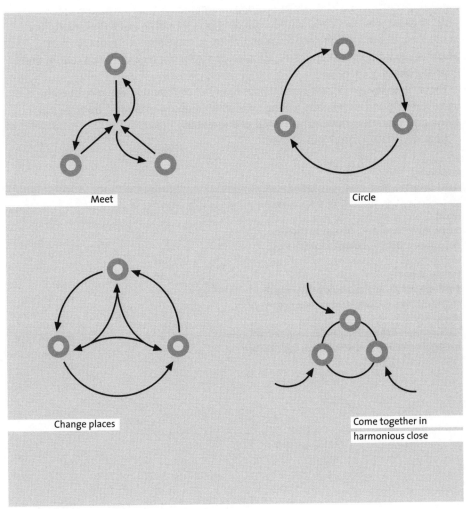

Meet

Circle

Change places

Come together in harmonious close

How information management, information technology and information design should support information products

Information systems and IT

In relation to organizational information products, IS and IT should have the role of providing an infrastructure of technological tools that complements the tools of the mind, and supports people: in managing the resources of knowledge and information that are used in IPs; in the transformations of knowledge to information and information to knowledge that are essential for creating and using IPs; in the actual production processes for IPs; and in accessing and using an increasing proportion of them by electronic means.

Information design

The role of information design should be to make easily traversed bridges between KM/IM and IS/IT and between them and all the stakeholders in IPs, and to reconcile conflicting constraints and needs, by creating information products that give optimum value to all stakeholders. Good information designers should be given the opportunity to use their special kinds of knowledge and vision to make products that take best advantage of both KM/IM and IS/IT, are appropriate for the organizational culture, and meet the needs of users.

These three key specialisms cannot make their full contribution without mutual understanding and cooperation among themselves, and understanding from the top of the organization of their real potential in this respect.

Now let us take a closer look at them.

References

MARCHAND, D, KETTINGER, W & ROLLINS, J (2001),
Information Orientation. The link to business performance, Oxford: Oxford University Press

TAYLOR, C (1997)
'Getting a handle on it: achieving efficiency by improving the structure, management and design of information'
Paper presented at the Popular Communication Training Conference 19–20 November 1997, Slussen

Knowledge and information management in support of IPs

In this chapter

What knowledge and information management should do for information products

Here we are concerned with the domains of KM and IM, the managers with respons-ibility for them, and the resources they manage – all in relation to the organization's information products. It does not appear to have occurred to many writers that such a relationship can or should exist. As in other respects, R S Taylor (1982) is an honourable and far-sighted exception, with his concept of organizational 'information environ-ments', made up of variables which affect the movement of information messages into, within and out of organizations, and which determine the criteria by which their value will be judged in the organizational context. Some of the variables have to do with the organization's information flow patterns and channels, the context in which it operates, and what it seeks to do; others are concerned with the people in the organization and their 'responsibilities, tasks, and problems as reflected in information terms'; and others again with its systems and technologies for generating, storing, organizing and deliver-ing messages. Taylor defines information products – books, monthly accounting reports, or online displays, for example – as tangible outputs of information systems, on the same continuum as information services.

Equally innovative, and apparently equally isolated, is the approach of Meyer and Zack (1996) who bring information products fully into the field of organizational strat-egy for managing information. Their argument is that we should think about informa-tion products in the same way as physical ones, that is, in terms of 'architecture' (an overall design concept covering a whole range of products) and 'platform' (an integrated set of common subsystems for creating families of products that can evolve over time, together with a set of technical processes to support them). With information products, the product platform is the organization's 'repository' of information (its information resources) consisting of both information content and information 'containers' such as files, databases, or documents. How useful and usable the repository is will depend on its architecture – the way information is structured, the elements into which it is broken down, the ways in which it can be accessed, and how it is managed.

Meyer and Zack see the manufacture of information products as consisting of these stages: acquiring raw materials; refining them (a range of activities to make products accessible to users, from indexing to analysing trends by means of appropriate software); storage and retrieval; distribution; and presentation – 'ensuring ease of use and sufficient functionality is part and parcel of the information product itself' (p48). To manage its information products successfully, an organization needs an appropriate infrastructure of hardware, software and telecommunications; internal knowledge about its own business; external knowledge about its current and emerging markets; and understanding of how it organizes and manages itself (p49). If it can keep its technological infrastructure, its repository and refinery, and its knowledge up to date, and make quick use of it, it can create new information products very cheaply compared with the costs for physical products. And the authors consider that the greatest potential lies in the acquisition and refinement stages, rather than in the use of output-end technology such as the Worldwide Web (p50).

Again, this innovative thinking, which may have been a few years ahead of its time, seems to have been followed by silence. However, Meyer and Zack's concern with architecture, and Taylor's early vision of information environments, may have a chance today of coming into their own, as these topics are again to the fore (nicely combined indeed in the title of a recent work: *Information Architecture: designing information environments for purpose* (Gilchrist and Mahon, 2004). And the trouble that websites can cause would-be users has, as shown by the research quoted in the last chapter (Nicholas et al., 2002), begun to make us aware of the need for the special skills of information professionals in creating web-based IPs. A related need for these skills has arisen in the public sector, from the move to e-government, with its requirements for new standards in the description of information products (*see*, for example, O'Neill, 2002).

The link with what information professionals do, however, is still seldom made explicit; and the only instances I know of higher education courses in information studies which contain a significant element devoted to information products, are in Australia (Yerbury et al. 1991, for example, describe an innovative teaching programme covering the marketing of information products, the role of information workers in making it easier to use them, and design as a source of added value for IPs).1

I've written elsewhere (Orna 2004, pp138–145) of how knowledge and information management have distinct but overlapping territories, with a shared common area; and have argued that organizations need both, and get most value from them if they work together rather than in opposition, or in ignorance of one another. It's not necessary to repeat that argument at length here; it is sufficient for present purposes to say that KM and IM professionals have joint responsibility when it comes to information products.

1 In that connection, UK Government librarians have expressed their concern (Griffiths, 2004) at the possibility that schools of information science will not submit for accreditation by CILIP courses whose main content lies beyond 'what has generally been considered the remit of library and information professional work'. They themselves are, as they say, already engaged in work beyond that remit, 'in areas such as intranet and website management, information architecture, records management, departmental publishing, knowledge management and research.' Their anxiety is that lack of CILIP accreditation for courses preparing students for such 'emerging areas' will lead to lost opportunities for library and information professionals in the future.

Knowledge of	Its application to support IPs
The organization's resources of information and knowledge	To supply content for them, or locate the right people to do it
The organization's information architecture	To ensure that it takes account of the users of the organization's IPs, and the ways in which they need to use the information content
How to give structure to information content	To create a consistent structure for IPs that supports users in transforming the information in them into knowledge that belongs to them, which they can apply in action
Creating meaningful categories of information related to what is most important for the organization	To ensure that IPs match the organization's standards as embodied in its information architecture or its taxonomy
Providing metadata and terminology standards	To ensure that IPs have appropriate labelling and indexes, which will give users 'keys' for locating them and for finding their way about in them
Ethical principles and professional codes of practice for using knowledge and information	To ensure that the organization's IPs meet appropriate ethical standards in their content and the uses to which they are put (see CILIP, 2004)

Table 6.1 KM and IM responsibilities for IPs

That responsibility lies in applying their knowledge of specific things in particular ways, as shown in Table 6.1, above.

The case for bringing IPs within information architecture

The currently fashionable term 'information architecture'[2] has been mentioned above in connection with information products. So far as I know, nobody has as yet made an explicit case for applying IA to organizational IPs; so I shall now remedy what seems to me a deficiency.

First, IPs have the defining 'architectural' features described by MacLachlan in her lucid case study of DTI (in Gilchrist and Mahon, 2004, pp199–204)[3], of (my propositions about IPs in italics):

2 A reasonable application of a term from one discipline to another, though I don't care to mention some of the things that have happened to it in the process of transfer, such as the verb 'to architect' and its gerund 'architecting' – as in 'The process of information architecting is usually conducted by an information specialist'.

3 It also, as Misera (2003) defines it, has the same concerns as information design: 'IA is not graphic design, software development or usability engineering but it does touch on all of these and many other areas. IA takes a holistic view of web sites by simultaneously concentrating on users, content and context'.

1 Structure, in terms of such central information-science concepts as taxonomy and classification
IPs consist of parts in relationship to one another; they have distinctive elements whose specific functions are made clear to the user in various ways

2 Navigation, to guide users to information and maintain security of access
IPs have particular elements whose role is to help users get around: showing their structure and the sequence in which its elements appear (contents lists, sitemaps, cross references), helping them to locate the content they desire (indexes, search engines)

3 Content, which requires identifying the information resources the organization needs to support its business
IPs, as combinations of content and container, are (as defined in Chapter 1, p12) the main means by which content is made visible and usable. It always amazes me that people can talk about 'information content' or 'content management' without apparently perceiving that the word 'content' implies a container – it is that which is selected for a purpose and put within a container; no container, no content.

If we accept these propositions, and the role which the third of them implies for IPs, then information products merit being within the scope of information management, and, by extension of that, deserve to be taken into account in developing information architecture. And reciprocally, the standards embodied in an organization's information architecture should be applied to IPs. This should surely be part of what Gilchrist and Mahon, in their introduction to the book cited above, describe as 'the LIS [Libray and information service] view of IA' , which underlies their approach, because there are 'skill sets in LIS that lend themselves efficiently to IA' and which can fit with other technical and skill requirements to 'achieve the overall objective: the efficient use of information.'

Making the link between information management, IPs and communications

Links of this kind are still something of a rarity, but here are two cases where they have come into existence through the initiative of information managers.

Essex County Council

 The account of Essex County Council's Education Service publications in Chapter 3 (*see* pp43–44) referred to the fact that the initiative for what is now a well-managed publishing service was taken by an information professional. Her background and experience allowed her to see the potential for integrating the IPs for the education community, with which the project originated, into the County Council's overall management and use of information resources. (The long-standing formal link between information management and the Council's information products has recently ended, with the initiator's transfer to work on coordinating knowledge management. It is to be hoped that the value of professional information-management input to information products will go on being recognized, and that a formal link will be re-established if Essex moves towards creating a Council-wide publishing unit.)

Making knowledge visible

It also contributed to a very successful information audit, in collaboration with other information professionals concerned with the Council's services for School Governors. This focused on governors' needs for information, the information products currently offered to them, and the possibilities for establishing a 'Community of Practice' through which new and effective IPs could be delivered, and created through interaction among governors and between them and the other stakeholders. Work is now in progress to develop this, and representative governors are taking a leading part in it (Chapters 11 and 12 give a detailed account of the audit and the follow-up).

The contribution of other experienced information professionals to the Council's approach to meeting the requirements of the FoIA has already been mentioned (*see* Chapter 5, pp85–87).

Royal College of Nursing

 An example of information managers winning the lead role in developing a communnications strategy comes from the Royal College of Nursing (Lord, 2003). That role was gained on the basis of the RCN Library and Information Service's earlier work on creating and implementing an organizational information strategy. The communications working group brought together RCN experts in member communications and marketing, external communications, information systems, web management, learning, and financial, administrative and legal systems. Its aim was to recommend an 'integrated, holistic way of working' to provide effective communications between: RCN staff within the organization; staff and members; members themselves; the RCN as an organization and its outside world of government, public, other organizations and the media. Its remit covered all communications among these partners, in all media.

In workshops, the group considered 'What Should Be' – a possible model of how communications should work; 'What Is' – the existing evidence for actual barriers; and methods for auditing communication systems. They found that internal communication systems had not been sufficiently thought of (a not uncommon situation in organizations); and this became one of the main strategy recommendations, with particular emphasis on the intranet as the lifeblood of inter-departmental communication.

Information professionals as creators of and contributors to IPs

The first three examples here are all – perhaps significantly – from organizations whose main business offering consists of information products. In all of them, information professionals play a leading role as creators of or contributors to the products on which their organizations depend.

FreePint

 As described in Chapter 3 (*see* p42) this is a product created by and for information and knowledge professionals whose work depends on using the Worldwide Web.

Here, the original initiative came from an information manager, the product is created and managed by information and IT professionals, and the users are also contributors, some as feature writers, and many as providers of conversational 'notes and queries' and answers in the FreePint Bar. The complete product is a model for electronic IPs in its clear structure, its aids to finding and navigation, its presentation formats, and its editorial management which maintains the interchanges in a business-like, professional and friendly atmosphere. It succeeds in embodying one of the best characteristics of the traditional culture of information professionals – their readiness to exchange ideas and help one another.

The next two examples come from the research mentioned earlier (*see* pp7, 76–77, 83) on how organizations manage their information products. Both are concerned with evidence-based health care, and in both information managers play an unusual and central role.

The Cochrane Collaboration [4]

 The Cochrane Collaboration takes its name and its mission from the work of Archie Cochrane, a doctor who first drew attention to the medical profession's ignorance about the effects of health care, and explained how evidence from randomized controlled trials (RCTs) could help towards the more rational use of resources. In his book *Effectiveness and efficiency: random reflections on health services* (1972), he suggested that, because resources would always be limited, they should be used to provide equitably those forms of health care which had been shown in properly designed evaluations to be effective. He stressed the importance of RCTs because they were likely to provide much more reliable information than other sources of evidence.

The first action to set up a register of controlled trials was in perinatal medicine, with funding in 1978 from the World Health Organization and the Department of Health. This led on to international collaboration in preparing systematic reviews of controlled trials in pregnancy and childbirth and the neonatal period, and the first information products, in the form of publications and a database (The Oxford Database of Perinatal Trials), appeared in 1988.

The response they received led in 1992 to NHS funding for a 'Cochrane Centre' in Oxford to extend the work to other fields of health care. Within a year, Cochrane Centres had been set up in other countries, and an international 'Cochrane Collaboration' was formally established in 1993. The Collaboration has two unique features: it is true to its name as a collaborative organization, which indeed owes its establishment and its continuing existence to its uncharacteristic lack of emphasis on individuals; and its information products were from the start designed to use electronic media to allow its systematic reviews to be updated and corrected as new evidence and other ways of improving the reviews became available (for detailed discussion of this aspect, *see* pp130–131).

In 1995, the major information product, The Cochrane Database of Systematic Reviews, was launched in the UK; in 1996 the database became part of The Cochrane Library, along with The Database of Abstracts of Reviews of Effectiveness,

4 http://www.cochrane.org

Making knowledge visible

The Cochrane Controlled Trials Register and The Cochrane Review Methodology Database; initially on CD-ROM and disk, and then on the Worldwide Web. Since then, there has been constant growth in the range of specialist groups for specific diseases, medical conditions and methods, and in the number of national Cochrane Centres. A 'sibling' organization – The Campbell Collaboration – was set up in 1999, to apply the same methods in the area of social and educational interventions. (More recently, Booth and Brice, 2004, have argued for the extension of evidence-based practice to information work.)

The essence of The Cochrane Collaboration's work consists of finding sources of information of a specific kind in the medical and related literature, subjecting them to highly sophisticated critical analysis, and preparing the structured reviews which make up the final electronic information product. This means that all the information resources it draws on are concentrated towards feeding this process, and that there is a very particular role for information specialists in its work. As well as searching for sources, they have an active and initiating role in helping review groups to identify working strategies, and they continue to collaborate with them as they move into the review process (they help with question definition, turning questions into searchable strategies and then adapting strategies for effective searching in a range of databases). They are therefore regarded not so much as providers of information support, but as an integral part of the review process.

The Centre for Reviews and Dissemination at York University

 Founded in 1994 as a sister organization of the UK Cochrane Centre, the CRD is particularly concerned with the 'outward-facing' aspects of managing and making use of the reviews produced by the Collaboration within the NHS: the people who are the target users of the reviews, the ways in which they need and wish to use them, how to reach the intended audience, what helps them to make good use of the product and what hinders them.

The Centre also carries out systematic reviews, scoping reviews, and reviews of reviews. These are commissioned on behalf of the NHS, and focus mainly on effectiveness, cost effectiveness, management and organization of health services. The Centre disseminates the results in the NHS to inform effective decision making. It concentrates specially on the development of evidence-based clinical practice and service development. Both functions are supported by research on methods of conducting systematic reviews and effective dissemination. The Centre develops and maintains databases of published reviews and studies of economic evaluation of health care and offers an inquiry service about reviews and economic evaluations.

Just as in the Cochrane Collaboration, the role of information and information professionals is both extensive and more intensive than is usual in organizations. The CRD's information service occupies a central position, and the Information Service Manager is a member of the management team and Associate Director. While the information service performs some of the traditional functions, the role of the information professionals has been greatly extended, and they themselves comment on the sense of being valued for the contribution they make. They form an integral part of the teams preparing systematic reviews, for which they carry out literature searches, are involved in primary research, including the development of highly sensitive search strategies, make an increasing contribution to dissemination, market the Centre's databases, give training on the use of the Cochrane Library databases, and give presentations about CRD databases.

Premier Farnell: taxonomy from first principles

 This is an interesting example of thinking from first principles on the part of the company's e-business development manager, who is strongly aware of the need for taxonomy and terminology control in managing the business's catalogues, and has thought effectively about it.

The company originally created its own classification, based upon catalogue chapters, and it worked adequately until the advent of electronic-based IPs. More recently, however, they commissioned a structure for an internal taxonomy (the Premier Farnell Commodity Code) to the brief that the classification of products must be according to the features of them that it is necessary to measure. This was an essential step in creating the company's Global Product database, which holds an average of 15 parametric values per product.

The code maps to other leading taxonomies – UNSPSC (United Nations Standard Products and Services Code), eCl@ss, and RUS (Requisite Unified Structure). There are some problems in this: Farnell's traditional strength in the area of electronic components is reflected in its internal taxonomy code which classifies this product area to a very detailed level, whereas the other classifications are less detailed in this respect. The company is therefore taking a lead in trying to steer the existing classification standards towards more detailed classification and taxonomy in this area. In product areas which are more peripheral for it, such as Office Equipment, the Premier Farnell internal taxonomy is not nearly as well developed as would be that of a dedicated Office Equipment supplier. The relative sparsity of detail in the classification of peripheral product areas can make it dfficult to compete with specialist suppliers dedicated to a single product area, who classify their goods in detail. Standards such as those mentioned above can play a vital role in this respect as they provide non-specialist suppliers with the opportunity to describe goods and services to at least a 'reasonable' level without the need to create their own taxonomies.

Information managers involved by accident: the Department of Health

 The DoH's Comprehensive Health Information Portfolio (*see* Chapter 3, p42–43) began its career without any participation by information managers. The circumstances of its introduction meant that special advisers were the key people involved. By a fortunate chance, however, an information professional who was working in the Secretary of State's Private Office transferred to the information management division, and was asked to advise on its development and then became responsible for managing and coordinating CHIP. Today information professionals lead in development planning for it, as they do for all the other DoH corporate information products including the Directory of who does what. Here, although the content is straightforward, the multitude of ways into it that are needed means that navigation aids and terminology support for users are necessary.

Making knowledge visible

Information products in a context of KM and document management

 The large provincial law firm described in Chapter 5 (*see* pp93–94), has benefited from initiatives taken by its original one information professional, who was responsible for setting up its library and information service in 1988. Since 2000, she has concentrated on developing knowledge management, and the outcome of that forms the context for the work described earlier on standards for the firm's internal IPs. To start with, pilot attempts at working with teams to establish ways of determining their know-how didn't work very well, because it became evident both that a formal structure for any overall knowledge base was essential, and that people had to be encouraged to become aware of the value of the knowledge they have, and of how it should be used.

In 2002, at a time when she had begun making the case that information and documents needed information management if KM was be successfully introduced, a new IT director was appointed. Seeing the force of the argument, he put his weight behind it, and top-level agreement was obtained for investment in a document-management system to support development of both document management and KM.

New approaches to IM in the context of portal development: mda

 mda (*see* Chapter 3, pp38–40) has found that the interactive development of new processes, IPs and the technology to make them accessible has had considerable effects also on its information resources and how they are managed. The development of the portal led to thinking and action on information content and making it accessible.

Creating a catalogue of its own information resources has led to new ideas, not only for using its existing information resources as the source of content for IPs accessible through the portal, but also for treating users' contributions as the source for new products. At the same time, there is recognition that the rights and responsibilities of information management have to be defined in the new context. An initial content management[5] policy for the integration of content across the site has been worked out, and is seen as a contribution both to future publishing policy and to developing an information strategy.

Information resources to support IPs

To end this discussion of information management in relation to information products, we need to consider briefly the resources of information which organizations need to have accessible and properly managed to support their IPs. If IPs are to do a good job in helping them achieve their key objectives, whatever they may be, organizations need information resources to keep their knowledge current about:

5 There are many definitions of content management systems around; this is a useful one from Lander (2003) 'CMS is a software system which helps collect/author content, store/manage it and then publish it. And these three tasks are controlled by an integrated workflow tool.'

1 The people to whom its 'offerings' (whether in themselves information products, or other products/services with which information products are associated) are addressed, as customers or users, external or internal

2 Appropriate content for the information products – current, accurate, related to the needs/interests of the users; and the context or environment in which the organization operates

3 How target markets have responded to past and current products, and the lessons to be learned

4 Their own products, including their information products

5 Competitors and their products

6 Their own objectives, policies, and activities

7 Suppliers of appropriate skills and services

8 Relevant developments in technologies for presenting and delivering information products.

These are resources of various kinds, and if they exist in any given organization are likely to be located in different areas, and managed by staff with a variety of job titles and backgrounds. Some, but by no means all, fall within the scope of jobs usually done by information professionals – those concerned with content context and competition, for instance – though that is no guarantee that they will be so managed in any given organization.

It should be part of the responsibility of information managers to know where all such resources are, who manages them, and how. And the people responsible for them should, as suggested earlier, be aware of their significance for the organization's IPs, and be recognized and supported as stakeholders.

The research on which this book is partly based suggested that this area of information resources was not particularly well provided for in organizations, though it found examples of organizations with some appropriate resources of knowledge and information for doing what they are in business to do, and which managed them effectively to support their IPs. The case studies made for the present book provide other examples. The areas best covered are resources of appropriate content; of objectives, policies and activities; and of relevant developments in technologies. It is less easy to find evidence of other kinds of resources listed above.

Perhaps the most serious lack, as suggested earlier (*see* Chapter 5, pp99–103) is information about those who need to use products, and evidence from interactions with them – as both codevelopers and reviewers of IPs. If this resource were better provided for and managed, organizations could save themselves a lot by taking heed of the lessons of experience.

Summary

Information and knowledge management should support IPs by
- Providing content for them
- Linking them with the organization's information architecture
- Giving them a consistent structure, to support people in accessing and using them
- Ensuring that they match standards embodied in organizational taxonomies
- Providing metadata for them
- Linking them with communications management
- Bringing them within the organization's information strategy
- Ensuring that the organization has appropriate information resources to support them.

References

BOOTH, A & BRICE, A (2004)
Evidence-based Practice for Information Professionals. A handbook, London: Facet Publishing

CILIP (2004)
Ethical Principles and codes of Professional Practice for Library and Infomation Professionals, London: CILIB

COCHRANE, A (1972)
Effectiveness and efficiency: random reflections on health services, London: Nuffield Provincial Hospitals Trust

GILCHRIST, A & MAHON, B (eds) (2004)
Information Architecture: designing information environments for purpose, London: Facet Publishing

GRIFFITHS, P (2004)
'Course accreditation vital to profession', *Library + Information Update*, 3 (1) 22

LANDER, B (2003)
'And the winner is... Our experience with selecting a CMS'
http://www.freepint.com/issues/060303. htm#tips>

LORD, J (2003)
'Information to communication', *Library + Information Update*, 2 (12) 37

MACLACHLAN, L (2004)
'From architecture to construction. The electronic records management programme at the DTI', in A Gilchrist and B Mahon (eds), *Information Architecture: designing information environments for purpose*, London: Facet Publishing

MEYER, M H & ZACK, H Z (1996)
'The design and development of information products', *Sloan Management Review*, Spring, 43–59

MISERA, T (2003)
'Why Information Architecture should be involved from the start of the website development process', *Managing Information*, 10 (10) 48

O'Neill, S (2002)
'DOIs – the key to interoperability', *Library + Information Update*, 1 (9) 44–45

ORNA, E (2004)
Information Strategy in Practice, Aldershot: Gower

TAYLOR, R S (1982)
'Organizational information environments', In G P Sweeney (ed) *Information and the transformation of society*, Amsterdam, Oxford: North-Holland

YERBURY, H, COOMBS, M & McGRATH, R (1991)
'Making the transparent visible: an activity to demonstrate some of the concepts of information service and product design', *Education for information*, 9 (2) 129–137

Other Reading

Material that has been part of the incidental reading around the subject of this chapter, which hasn't been quoted from or directly referred to. It's grouped under headings which relate to the topics covered in the chapter.

'Common Information Environment' (CIE)

POTHEN, P (2003)
'Building a common information environment', *Library + Information Update*, 2 (12) 46–47

The concept of a 'CIE' among related organizations to give access to the complete range of the IPs of all of them, and allow for using it to create new products.

Intranets as IPs in need of information management

DALE, A (2002)
Letters from the Corporanian War Zone. Letter 9 – 'Intranets everywhere but not a drop to drink', *Journal of Information Science*, 28 (3) 253–256

Advocates an 'information products' approach, starting from an information audit to determine 'what information is needed on the intranet to meet the goals of the organization.'

Metadata

BATER, B (2004)
'Topic maps; indexing in 3-D', in A Gilchrist and B Mahon (eds) *Information Architecture*, London: Facet Publishing

Topic maps are in effect sophisticated information products for giving access to meta-information products. Bater's excellent introduction to the concept raises the interesting point of 'whether the topic map paradigm might actually provide the hitherto elusive bridge between technology and human organizational, cultural and cognitive structures.' It certainly requires the combined skills of information management, information systems/IT, and information design.

CHILVERS, A (2002)
'The super-metadata framework for managing long-term access to digital data objects' *Journal of Documentation*, 58 (2)146–174

'The evanescent nature of DDOs and the insidious way that data can become corrupted means that it is even more important in the digital environment to create an effective framework to ensure preservation.' Research by case studies, using soft systems methodology.

DUBLIN CORE
http://www.dublincore.org

TSO (2004)
'Free Digital Object Identifiers pave way to linking public information'
http://services.tso.co.uk/cgi-bin2/DM/y/eLOGoDBl16oEiHoMYroAi

DOI = identifier for digital objects with links to physical manifestation or other metadata; maintained by registration agencies, agreed among community of interest, and mapped to other standards.

Action by Stationery Office to resolve problems of interoperability, and offer free access in the UK public sector.

Content management

CM PROFESSIONALS
http://www.cmprofessionals.org

International Content Management Community of Practice, established autumn 2004; President, Bob Boiko, author of the *Content Management Bible*, Director of University of Washington iSchool CMS Evaluation Lab.

TSO (2003)
'Getting best value from content management' Briefing Notes and Papers
http://www.tso.co.uk/

GREEN, D (2005)
'Content management systems: getting it right!', *Library + Information update*, 4 (1–2) 58–59

Making knowledge visible

TRIPPE, B (2001)
Content Management Technology
www.econntentmag.com Feb/March 22–27

Common features among systems: Broad division
into 1) delivery platforms for dynamic personalized
content delivery over web 2) Editorial-facing systems for capturing content and routing it through
workflow and approval.

WHITE, M (2001)
'Content management systems for intranets',
Vine, 124, 46–50

Advice on developing specifications for vendors
of content management systems. Importance of
version control, authorization and security, search
engine functionality (few CMS vendors develop
their own search engines, and many have licences
from Autonomy & Verity – not necessarily for
latest version). Importance of metadata tags.
Problems of being able to search across internal
and external resources. Acceptance criteria.

... (2002)
'Content management', *Library + Information
Update*, 1 (6) 36–37

Principles for managing intranet and website
content. Choosing content-management software.

... (2004)
'Resources for information architects',
Library + Information Update, 3 (2) 35

Infrastructure for IPs: information systems, technology tools

This chapter has the specific, and modest, though unusual, aim of proposing how the IS/IT infrastructure of organizations, and the technology tools it provides, should work strategically to support all the activities concerned with IPs, by integrating the whole range of IPs, and uniting the stakeholders in them. The stakeholders, as indicated in Chapter 5, need all the help they can get in order to know of one another's existence, understand each other's business, and appreciate how their various kinds of knowledge and expertise are related and how they can support each other in creating information products that do a good job for everyone. Here we consider the nature of the help they should get from systems and technology.

Information systems and IT, as shown in Figure 7.1, (*see* p124), provide the infrastructure of technological tools that should complement the tools of the mind; they should support people in:

- Managing the resources of knowledge and information that are used in IPs
- The transformations of knowledge to information and information to knowledge that are essential for creating and using IPs
- The actual production processes for IPs
- Accessing and using an increasing proportion of them.

Explicit consideration of these matters implies a wider view than is normally taken; it means that the IS/IT strategy of organizations should take account of what systems and technology tools should do for IPs to enable them to support overall organizational strategy. That involves three kinds of help, in:

1 Managing appropriate information resources for IPs (as discussed in Chapter 6, *see* p117–118)
2 Carrying out all the tasks people engage in to create and use IPs
3 Initiating and maintaining all the communications and interactions among stakeholders that are needed for IP strategy.

Managing information resources for IPs

Gilchrist and Mahon (2004), who have been quoted earlier on information architecture (*see* pp18–19), identify as 'the driving force behind the move to information architecture' the fact that 'all, or almost all, the information in an organization is now digital in creation and use', which means that the all diverse kinds of material which people in an organization use for various purposes, applying their own specific skills, 'can be handled in a common fashion through IT facilities.'

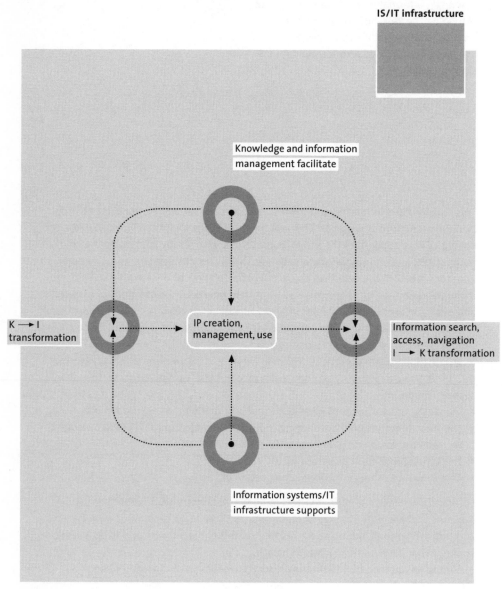

Figure 7.1 IS/IT provides an infrastructure of technological tools to complement KM/IM in supporting the creation and use of IPs

If, as I have already argued (in Chapter 6), information products should come within the scope of information management, then the IS/IT infrastructure should support all the activities and people concerned with the creation and use of information products.

Ciborra (2002) wisely reminds us that infrastructures 'can expand and grow in directions and to an extent that is largely outside the control of any individual stakeholder' (p61), and that, in the interaction between humans and infrastructure, the humans can find productive ways of making use of the technology that go beyond the kind of support which it was originally designed to provide. However, it seems reasonable to say that, so far as IPs are concerned, facilities on the following lines should be offered as a start, with freedom and encouragement for human users to develop ways of using them:

- An overview of all existing products in all media – their history, the people responsible for them, their objectives, intended users, distribution, testing undertaken, evaluation
- Authoritative master of the current version of all products
- The status of products currently in production and planned; responsibility for them; people involved in their creation
- A database of suppliers of goods and services, including specialist skills, with a history of relations, contracts, products they have been used for.

Managing the tasks associated with IPs

The multitude of tasks involved in creating, project-managing, and using IPs need support from such tools as:
- Document-management systems
- Content-management systems
- Electronic records management
- Software to support appropriate applications of single-source multi-channel publishing
- Systems for accessing, navigating, and finding information
- Systems that can help the transformations of knowledge to information and information to knowledge, which human beings have to make in order to create and use information products
- Tools to support collaborative working in ways that the people concerned find most helpful (which may not be those which spring most readily to the mind of system designers – see, for example, the discussion of the 'paperless office' and user preferences in Chapter 5, pp101–102)
- Tools to help maintain the permanence and preservation of electronic IPs.[1]
Some examples of the use of these tools for this purpose are given below.

1 The Legal Deposit Libraries Act 2003, which came into force in 2004, makes the issue even more pressing. The Act provides for extending the scope of compulsory deposit to electronic documents, and the means of accessing them in the form of computer progams etc.

Tate's content-management system

 Proposals for integrated development and use of Tate's Collections information resources in the context of the institution's overall strategic objectives, have already been referred to (*see* Chapter 3, p41). A recently completed CMS project is making a contribution to the aspects which are concerned with information products.

The project's aims, many of which were achieved within a few months of the system coming into operation early in 2004, were to:
- Automate the publishing process, and streamline communication
- Make content publication more manageable and less costly
- Standardize content structures and design control
- Reduce the costs and time spent on updating content
- Provide an integrated authoring, editing and production environment which could be used across geographically remote work places
- Separate the creation of content from its presentation, so that authors are free of formatting constraints [2]
- Free authors from being required to use HTML or other technical knowledge when creating content
- Permit multiple uses of content from a single source in a variety of contexts, and in different media
- Make creation and maintenance of content easy and efficient.

The priority products for which the system was used were *Tate Magazine* and the new *Tate Guide*, together with automated updating of certain areas of the website (for more about the Tate website, *see* pp128–129).

The PRONOM project

 The power of computers in generating information products can blind us to the insubstantial and ephemeral nature of what they create; as Darlington (2003) says, 'It is ironic that the primitive technology of ancient times has produced records lasting hundreds of years, while today's advanced electronic world is creating records that may become unreadable in a few years' time.' because it makes access to them 'dependent on hardware and software environments whose own longevity is doubtful.' While ignored by most vendors, and by many organizations, this problem has presented itself especially sharply to those who are responsible for managing and sustaining access to electronic records; and increased urgency was added by the Government target for all records to be digital by 2005. The account below of the PRONOM project is an example of positive action by the body responsible for the UK's National Archives.

The UK Public Record Office (which joined with the Historic Manuscripts Commission to form The National Archives in April 2003), faced with the necessity of preserving historic electronic records indefinitely, set up a project to create a

2 It is right that CMS systems should separate these activities, but that should not be understood as meaning that the relationship between content and container should be left to take care of itself. Using content-management systems in this kind of context makes it even more critical to bring information design into the early stages of developing briefs for the IPs the system is meant to support.

database of file formats and a supporting library of software products – the PRONOM program – as part of its Digital Archive system. The aim of PRONOM is to hold reliable technical information about the software used to create the records stored in the archive.

The project provides for both of the alternative strategies for dealing with the situation:

1 Keeping copies of the relevant software, and of relevant operating systems
2 'Migrating' records from the obsolete formats in which they were created into current ones.

For the first approach, content has been collected by research and liaison with software developers, and a library of software products is being built up. On the migration side the aim is to design an objective methodology to measure how much the original intrinsic information content of a record is modified by migration paths using specific software products.

Another component of the PRONOM program is a 'technology watch' process to identify developments in the technology that require preservation action.

PRONOM was designed from the start with a Web-based user interface, and was launched on the Web in 2004 (http://www.records.pro.gov.uk/pronom) to make it available to the whole preservation community. It won the 2004 Pilgrim Trust Preservation Award for innovation in the preservation of digital material.

An IS/IT strategy for IPs

Technology tools should be used to integrate the organization's IPs into its business strategy, so that they make their maximum contribution to its success. In particular they should help to bring the stakeholders together at the right times so that they can contribute their knowledge fully and cooperatively.

If that is to happen, there has to be a clear and explicit statement of what the IPs are intended to do for the organization and of what that requires from IS/IT. That in turn requires identifying the people who need to cooperate and whose views have to be taken into account, and bringing them together, because the only people who can produce a valid statement are representatives of the stakeholder groups. They need to be put under obligation to talk together, question each other, explain their professional concerns and expertise, demand explanations of each other's language, until they establish common ground and respect for each other's specialism.

Unfortunately it is still rare for such groupings to be called upon to develop an IS/IT strategy in general terms, let alone one for IPs – with the result that the technology is nearly always less creatively used for the products than its potential. Some encouraging examples have been quoted in this chapter of good collaboration between information managers and IS/IT managers over information products, and such collaborations should form the nucleus for interactions and negotiations among the whole range of stakeholders for that purpose.

The integrating role of web technology

Web technology has a particular significance as a catalyst for change in this respect, that has, I think, not yet been fully appreciated. It allows the creation of those 'meta-IPs' that we call websites, with their great potential for navigation and management of IPs; and above all it can be a powerful means of changing the organizational culture around IPs, integrating the products, and bringing the stakeholders together, and, especially, gaining the attention of TOTO (the top of the organization) for hitherto unregarded IPs.

The growth in web technology, and its significance for organizations' IPs, was the most striking finding from the research which I carried out over the period 1994–1999. At the start of the case studies nearly all the information products encountered were print on paper. But over the five years all the case-study organizations set up websites, and nearly all developed intranets, and so, by the end, print-on-paper products were coexisting in various ways with electronic products contained in websites and intranets. In a number of cases, this turned out to have powerful and significant effects on the way the organizations concerned thought about their information products.

In some instances, the process was a very creative one, like a kaleidoscope, shaking up the elements of the current situation to produce a wholly new pattern with potential for significant progress. In others, web technology was absorbed to good effect into existing practice, enriched thinking about information products, and led to creative new developments which fed back into thinking about the organizations' whole range of information products.

City University, London

 Here, as described earlier (*see* Chapter 5, pp83–84) the website became the means of bringing stakeholders together in a way that had probably never happened before, helping on the way to overcome some of the cultural obstacles characteristic of seats of learning. The University's professionals concerned with information products and presentation cooperated with systems professionals to play a key role in achieving this, with support from the top level. They set up a ground-breaking 'consultation day' for staff users – academics, librarians and administrators – which led to recommendations for a Web Strategy; the strategy was accepted, and given the resources requested. Its objectives include integrating electronic and paper-based publishing to improve efficiency and quality assurance; regular monitoring of use and satisfaction; and performance criteria.

Tate, (ex- Tate Gallery)

 I have found some of the most encouraging examples of this kind in the museum community. A notable one is the Tate Gallery, London (or 'Tate' as it is now known), whose progress towards integrated management of its information products I have been privileged to observe over the past decade, as mentioned in Chapter 3.

It was the Gallery's website (the first major international gallery site to allow direct access to its collection image base and associated research) which brought about a remarkable change in what appeared a decidedly static situation. Set up in 1998,

Making knowledge visible

after a business case had been presented by an alliance of communication and information systems managers, it quickly exceeded the very modest expectations of senior management (today it receives 3.5 million individual visits annually). Its success turned out to be the key to major progress in the Gallery's strategic use of information. The process of setting it up demonstrated effectively that there were multiple stakeholders, and spread understanding of the importance of a high-quality well-managed database as the foundation for a site that added value.

The website helped to underline the relevance and significance of a new Information Systems Strategy, introduced in 1999. Development of the strategy is the responsibility of Information Systems. It has four key aspects: Collections Management, core business systems (such as financial management, ticketing, fundraising, etc), internal communications and information sharing; and over the period since its inception it has brought new thinking about the whole range of information products, as well as playing a key enabling role in their creation (*see* p41 for more about this aspect of the work).

The Department of Trade and Industry, London

 The DTI's story has been told in part in this book (*see* Chapters 3 and 5, pp47–50 and 90). Its background too lies in a five-year research case study. Intranet development[3] was the focal point for changes in the Department's strategic approach to information products. The project board was headed by a senior information manager with long experience of the DTI. Content became the combined responsibility of information professionals and IT staff, and an Intranet Strategy Management Board took responsibility for strategic development. Potential was seen for a new approach to information products, focused on how people want to use information in their work, and supported by new roles for information managers which are largely concerned with promoting information interactions among people. As related in Chapter 3 (*see* p50), since then new lessons have been learned about how it is necessary to involve every user of information in information management in order to achieve the desired situation.

In other instances, web technology has been readily absorbed into the existing practice of organizations, has enhanced thinking about information products, and is leading to creative new developments.

The Co-operative Bank (*see* Chapter 3, pp54–56)

 The Bank used the strengths of the approach it had developed on printed publications to set up an excellent website, designed by an innovative small company, which won the 1998 Financial Times Business Website of the year award. Internal

---

3 Dale (2002) advocates an 'information products' approach to intranets, starting from an information audit to determine 'what information is needed on the intranet to meet the goals of the organization.' 'It is much more effective to take the "information product" approach. Here, the objective is to take each information need and package it into something recognizable as a distinct entity – an "information product" that can be designed, built, tested, marketed, launched, monitored and tuned on the intranet. Many of the products will build on the same raw information sources but each will be presented or packaged in a different way to suit different audiences.'

management of site content is the responsibility of a marketing staff member, working as an active interface between bank and company.

The experience of developing the site brought changes in thinking about the relative roles of printed products and the web as vehicles for information. What the Bank describes as a 'whole new approach to content' resulted, taking advantage of the facility the web provides for creating links to other existing material, instead of repeating it in a number of individual contexts. The next step envisaged is looking at how printed and web versions of information products can complement one another, to meet the various needs of users.

Organizations whose main products were already electronic ones were well prepared to take web technology into existing good practice, and this has led to new developments which feed back into thinking about the whole range of products.

The Cochrane Collaboration

 The way The Cochrane Collaboration and the Centre for Reviews and Dissemination have integrated information management into the core of creating their information products has been mentioned in Chapter 6 (see pp114–116). The Cochrane Collaboration also offers a remarkable example of a far-sighted approach to electronic IPs, based on an unusually close integration of software designers into the organization's work, which has made it possible to take full advantage of the currently available technologies, up to and including web technology. (Despite this prescience, the Collaboration admits to surprise at the rate of growth of the Internet, which has meant that its importance for making its output accessible is now even higher than anticipated, and that it has largely overtaken CD-ROM distribution – though this is still available.)

Starr and Chalmers (2003) document the evolution of The Cochrane Library – a 'compendium' electronic publication bringing together a range of related information products.[4] The authors show how The Cochrane Library and the Cochrane Database of Systematic Reviews were designed from the outset 'to take advantage of features unique to electronic publishing'.

In this they built on the foundations laid by the Oxford Database of Perinatal Trials, which used software based on the dBase file specification. Data from reviews were stored in a relational database in structured form; the systematic reviews were thus also highly structured and all in the same format. Therefore once readers had mastered how to read the graphs and interpret the statistics they could apply that understanding to all reviews in the database, and the process which researchers had followed to analyse data and reach their conclusions was clearly and consistently presented. The raw data used in meta-analyses were stored with the review, and as new studies were added to the database, the new data were automatically incorporated into analyses.

4 The Cochrane Database of Systematic Reviews; the Database of Abstracts of Reviews of Effectiveness produced by the York Centre for Reviews and Dissemination; the Cochrane Central Register of Controlled Trials, assembled from registers from national Cochrane Centres and from Cochrane Review Groups; the Cochrane Database of Methodology Reviews; and a register of articles on the science of reviewing evidence.

The Cochrane Collaboration continued and developed this approach, with its 1994 CD-ROM publication of the Cochrane Database of Systematic Reviews, designed by Update Software. Update Software also worked with The Cochrane Collaboration to develop authoring and information management tools to support the electronic publications – RevMan to help review authors produce highly structured reviews, and ModMan to help the editorial work of Collaborative Review Groups in creating modules of reviews, which were then assembled by Update Software into the Parent Database from which the publications were derived.[5] The authoring tool allowed different parts of documents to be identified and independently manipulated, which permitted them to be transformed into different formats for different publishing systems. Thus, over the years, Cochrane Reviews have appeared as ASCII text, in MARC formats, using SGML, HTML, and XML.

A novel approach was taken in presenting figures and graphs in the Cochrane reviews. The raw data, rather than images, were stored, and the software generated figures and graphs at the time they were displayed, using the MetaView program in the authoring tool. The saving on storage space thus achieved allowed the database of systematic reviews to be published on CD-ROM.

A variety of forms of electronic dissemination was developed in line with the strategy of making The Cochrane Library available directly to subscribers, and preparing the reviews and other resources for those wishing to disseminate the material on other platforms. Thus The Cochrane Database of Systematic Reviews was made available in 1996 on the Worldwide Web through a partnership arrangement with Synapse Publishing Inc., and by 2003 the reviews were available from most major information providers, including Dialog and DataStar, EVSCO, SilverPlatter and Ovid. Open access over the Internet was provided in the UK and in a number of other countries, including Australia, Finland, Ireland, Spain and Norway, while The Cochrane Library was made available throughout Latin America and the Caribbean through the BIREME system, and to all the countries defined by the World Bank as low- and low-middle income, under various programmes.

Electronic publication has also been actively used from the start to encourage readers to engage in both pre- and post-publication discussion with reviewers. A formal 'Comments and Criticism' system for Cochrane Reviews, launched in 1996, allows readers to post comments to a website from links in the reviews, from abstracts of reviews, or directly.

5 The Cochrane Library (http://www.cochrane. org/review/clibintro.htm) is now published by Wiley Interscience (http://www.wileyeurope. com/go/cochrane) – Update Software continues its involvement with the product, under a contractual arrangement with Wiley. The international site of The Cochrane Collaboration, which provides access to a full range of information products, is maintained by the German Cochrane Centre (http:/ /www.cochrane.org/indexo.htm; and the Nordic Cochrane Centre, which has continued the development of RevMan and ModMan tools, maintains an Information Management System website (www.cc-ims.net).

Figure 7.2 summarizes how web technology can act as a catalyst for change, and the factors that can prevent organizations taking full advantage.

As Tiamiyu (1993) expressed it: 'In the interplay of these technology-driven forces and the flexibility of the human mind to dream up new ideas for viable information products lie the opportunities for innovators.'

Looking back over this chapter, what I've been arguing is that information systems and technology tools should let humans take the lead in their relationship, incorporating only those constraints on their creators that will help them deliver products which will help the final users (as exemplified in the IPs of the Cochrane Collaboration). They should encourage them in using their minds and feelings in specifically human ways rather than trying to constrain them from doing so. (We should by now know better than to believe that we can leave our human nature behind when we enter the workplace, so instead, let us try to make the best rather than the worst of it.)

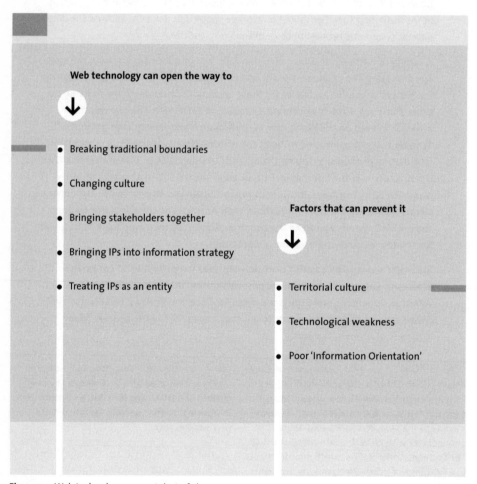

Web technology can open the way to

↓

- Breaking traditional boundaries

- Changing culture

- Bringing stakeholders together

- Bringing IPs into information strategy

- Treating IPs as an entity

Factors that can prevent it

↓

- Territorial culture

- Technological weakness

- Poor 'Information Orientation'

Figure 7.2 Web technology as a catalyst of change

That should be the principle in all applications, and especially in those that support people in activities which are so important to the exchange and creation of knowledge for action, and which are also so difficult. I am encouraged in this argument by Ciborra (2002) – particularly as he makes the case from a background (organization theory and systems) far removed from my own. Contemplating the failures of conventional systems methodology to deal with the issues of decision making, knowledge management or resource planning which organizations face, he asks: 'How to get closer to practice, then, and the real life of systems in use in a fresher way?' and answers:

> ... a different perspective on information systems should be anchored to the unfolding of the human process of encountering the everyday world. Indeed, one way to get closer to the obvious which permeates the everyday chores is first to put aside all our concerns for methods and scientific modelling and encounter the multiple apparitions through which strategizing, knowing, organizing and implementing offer themselves ... (p8)

Ciborra's words incidentally remind us of David Sless's explanation, quoted in Chapter 5 (*see* pp102–103) of the 'co-design' approach, with its concern for 'the prosaic, the ordinary, the everyday occurrences that happen between people' in the design of information products. That makes a satisfying transition to our consideration of information design, the specialism that is probably the most unfamiliar of the three to many readers. So let us try to improve the acquaintance.

Summary

The information systems/IT infrastructure should support IPs by providing technological tools to help in:
- Managing all the information resources the organization needs for creating IPs
- Carrying out all the tasks associated with creating, project-managing and using IPs, and the interactions among the people involved
- Ensuring the permanence and preservation of electronic IPs
- Integrating the organization's IPs into its business strategy
- Using web technology effectively and creatively to develop and integrate the organization's information products.

References

CIBORRA, C (2002)
The Labyrinths of Information. Challenging the wisdom of systems, Oxford: Oxford University Press

DALE, A (2002)
Letters from the Corporanian War Zone. Letter 9 – 'Intranets everywhere but not a drop to drink', *Journal of Information Science,* 28 (3) 253–256

DARLINGTON, J (2003)
'PRONOM – A Practical Online Compendium of File Formats', *RLG DigiNews,* October 15 2003, 7 (5)

GILCHRIST, A & MAHON, B (2004)
Information Architecture: designing information environments for purpose, London: Facet Publishing

STARR, M & CHALMERS, I (2003)
'The evolution of The Cochrane Library, 1988–2003' Available at: www.update-software.com/history/clibhist.htm

TIAMIYU, M A (1993)
'Analysis of components for designing information products', *Aslib Proceedings,* 45 (7/8) 209–214

Information design, reconciler of conflicting needs

In this chapter

The meaning and scope of information design

To begin, a reminder of the definition of information design offered in the first chapter.

> **Information design**
> **Can be broadly defined as everything we do to make visible knowledge and ideas (which by the definition used here live invisible inside individual human minds, and have to be put into the outside world before others can gain access to them), so that those who need them can enter into them and use what they learn from them for their own purposes.**

And as that definition makes clear, what the users want to do must come first; they have an active rather than a passive role. So the information designer's first responsibility is to them – to ensure that products match the users and the ways in which they need to use the information content, and that presentation supports their access to the content.[1] It should be emphasized that responsibility to the users includes taking into account the problems experienced by the large percentage of the population whose vision is affected by age.

The scope of information design therefore includes:
- The conceptual structure of information products
- Sequence of presentation

1 The role is like that which Macdonald-Ross and Waller (1976/2000) described for the person whom they called the 'Transformer', who '...starts with what to say, and then resolves how to say it...' and goes on to discover 'what effect the message has on the reader.'

- Choice of medium and format
- Decisions about how the content is expressed (eg text, graphics, numbers, and combinations of all these)
- Management of the relevant technologies and specialist software
- Writing
- Editing
- Illustration
- Typography.

The definition in itself indicates the points where the territory of information design intersects with that of information management and information systems/technological tools (*see* Figure 8.1 below). It also points to what is unique and special to the discipline, and how it complements what the other two bring.

Information design should help KM/IM and IS/IT to harmonize and integrate their contributions to IPs in the areas where they intersect with its own, as shown in Figure 8.1. And organizations should help information designers to be aware of the multiple

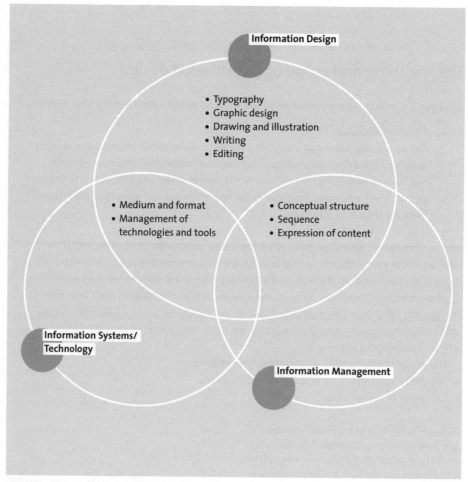

Figure 8.1 The scope of information design and intersections with information managent and IS/IT

Making knowledge visible

and sometimes conflicting requirements and constraints that information products have to meet, so that they can use their special kinds of knowledge and vision to reconcile them as far as possible, to create products which give optimum value to all stakeholders (see Figure 8.2).

The term 'design' needs unpacking to show the range of valid meanings it has – all of them relevant to information products. For people concerned with systems it implies system design to allow 'consistent and clear delivery' across all channels; while for information managers, 'design' means consistent structure of integrated information resources to allow users to find what they need and use what they find easily, and to contribute to the stores of information. These are appropriate uses of the word; but what most systems professionals and information managers are not familiar with is

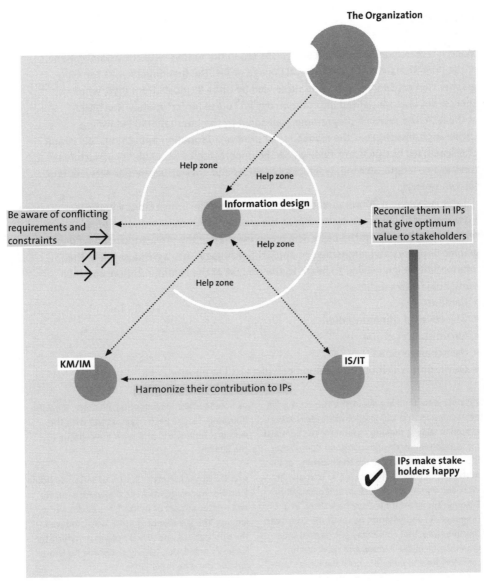

Figure 8.2 Information design, the reconciler of needs and constraints in the creation of IPs

the aspect of design that's concerned with making the results of their work visible to users, ie information design: the aspects of information products which users actually see when they meet them; how words and graphics are arranged on page or screen, the use of typefaces, spacing, colour, in order to make the structure of the content clear and easy to get around.

The education of information professionals does not usually introduce them to this interpretation of 'design'. (There are honourable exceptions; the ones of which I have personal knowledge are, as mentioned earlier, in Australia, where what is now the Department of Information Studies at the University of Technology Sydney introduced an information design module into its first degree courses in the mid-1980s, and other colleges followed the lead.)

Some history

Modern research on information design started in the 1960s[2] with the establishment of the Print Research Unit at the Royal College of Art. The first director was the typographer Herbert Spencer, who was succeeded by Linda Reynolds from 1976, when Spencer set up a specialized information design course (unfortunately shortlived) at the RCA. The research programme, sponsored by the International Publishing Corporation, investigated the readability of print in information publishing. This strand of research led to significant findings on the importance for accessibility of such features as line length, spacing, typefaces, type sizes and page structure (*see* Stevens, 1995, for a summary).

Later research on information design, sponsored by the British Library in the late 1970s, extended the scope by looking at the context in which information products are read, and particularly at the users. The group involved in the project included typographic designers and researchers in applied psychology. They agreed, sensibly, that information design needed to relate to the context of the communication, and their contextual factors included:

- Content
- Objectives of communication
- Circumstances of use
- User characteristics
- Constraints which the information providers had to observe.

2 People were thinking about the subject a good deal earlier than that. Here for example is Joseph Moxon in 1683–4 making a claim for the compositor as information designer: 'A good Compositer is ambitious as well to make the meaning of his Author intelligent to the Reader, as to make his Work shew graceful to the Eye, and pleasant in Reading: Therefore if his Copy be written in a Language he understands, he reads his Copy with consideration; that so he may get himself into the meaning of the Author, and consequently considers how to order his work the better both in the Title Page, and in the matter of the Book: as how to make his Indenting, Pointing, Breaking, Italicking, &c the better sympathize with the Authors Genius, and also with the capacity of the Reader.'

And the Royal Society's Charter of 1664, as Jardine (2000) reminds us, made provision for a 'graver' and printer as part of its staff, thus acknowledging 'the key role of ... those who produced the publications and visual images on which the Society's reputation largely depended for those outside the elite inner circle.'

While their report (Wright, 1979) commented that organizations were 'content to ignore' research findings on how to present information effectively, the only solution it suggested was 'user education' to increase typographic awareness. What organizations actually do in the process of creating information products, and how that might be influenced, was apparently not considered.

Although the British Library did not take the research further, it did lead on to the establishment in 1979 of the *Information Design Journal*. The majority of the contributions to the *Journal* are in such areas as labelling and instructions for use of products, form design, signs and signing systems, typography and information graphics; there are also less frequent but valuable excursions into topics with a bearing on how organizations behave – for example the presentation of financial graphs in company annual reports, and the implications of form redesign for power structures in businesses. More recently established forums such as the InfoD-Cafe (infodesign-cafe@list.informationdesign.org) and international information design conferences, cover a similar range, with an increasing focus on web-based design.

The ideal contribution of information design

My own involvement with information design over the past 30 years or so has covered:
• Commissioning and working with information designers on the design of new information products or the redesign of existing ones
• Working, as an information consultant/writer, with an information designer colleague, on projects to create new information products for particular purposes
• Research on how organizations of various kinds manage their information products, and their approach to design
• Working, as the author of books, with an information designer, and arriving interactively at decisions on structure and visual presentation, as the writing proceeds.

On the basis of that experience, I define the unique contribution that good information design can bring to information products as:
• Integrating content with its container to create a harmonious unity that is fit for the purposes of those who use it,[3] and visually inviting to the users
• Understanding those purposes, and choosing media and forms of presentation that match the users and how they need to use the products

3 Design should save organizations and users from grossly inappropriate containers that do more to conceal and lose content than help people get at and use it. Dyson (1999) reminds us how Erasmus Darwin, whose ideas on evolution were worthy to stand with those of his grandson, misguidedly hid them in such containers as *Zoonomia, The Loves of Plants,* or *The Temple of Nature*. 'Erasmus failed to develop a concise packaging for his argument. He either published his observations as lengthy footnotes to his unwieldy poems or concealed them within his *Zoonomia,* expanded to fourteen hundred pages

- Finding clear but unobtrusive ways of making the inherent structure plain, and guiding the users through it
- Making appropriate use of specialist technology tools in creating the products
- Reconciling the often conflicting needs of the various stakeholders[4] in the products, to give as good a deal as possible to as many of them as possible
- Respecting the culture of the organization, and giving it visual expression with integrity
- Working within external constraints and getting the best rather than the worst solutions from it (this is a self-abnegating job, yet I am constantly surprised at how good designers find new freedoms in meeting fairly preposterous constraints imposed by clients).

As Taylor (1999) expresses it, 'a useful information product models the world in a way that users can handle', so that, in the words of Krull and colleagues (1993) they can 'get in, out, and on with their work' (p326). Quine (2004) links this kind of respect for what users want to do with 19th-century pragmatic philosophy: 'Applying this approach to information design means our starting point is the practical intentions of our audience: what do they want to do. Not what information do we or our clients want to give them, but what they wand to DO with any such information is our starting point, effective information design then requires that we build an information delivery system that serves their intentions.'

Information design which allows users to do that lives up to Stevens' (1995, p134) claim that information design is 'an actual part of the visible information into which knowledge is transformed and from which knowledge is reconstituted.'; as Macdonald-Ross and Waller (1976) expressed it, 'one cannot regard design as just external decoration applied to an existing message. ... design is an integral part of the communication process.'

So ideally, information design can and should bring the work of all the stakeholders involved in the creation of IPs to a focal point, in products that do justice to their contributions and allow them to be used to the best advantage. That requires that it should be able to go, in Sless's words (1995), 'to the heart of the functional information needs of an organization, creating powerful systems that simultaneously shape whole classes of information for workers, consumers and citizens.' It also requires, incidentally, that designers should not throw the baby of aesthetics out with the bathwater of exclusive concentration on the artefact. They should retain what MacKenzie-Taylor (1993/1999) calls a sense of 'the rich and ancient tradition of paper and print' and understand the

4 For example, as between what users themselves want to do and what the originating organization wants them to do; between the needs of people who are asked to give information in forms or questionnaires, and of those who have to input or interpret it; between the needs of different groups of users who want to use the same product in different ways – eg as a reference tool, or as a source of instructions on how to do things; between users who can only make use of printed products, those who will want to print out material provided in electronic form, and those who will use it on screen.

'meticulousness of the craft – the care and sensibility expressed in a piece of visual communication.' It may be that for many it is already too late to wish that; I hope not. That's how it can and should be, and, as we shall see, how it sometimes is, BUT NOT OFTEN ENOUGH.

The reality:
1 Good practice and hopeful developments

There are some encouraging stories to tell, and we shall look at them first, but also evidence on all sides of interested parties not knowing what they should know, and of valuable knowledge in danger of being lost.

These stories of an approach to information design that matches what is advocated in this chapter, are all based on direct experience, gained through working with the organizations quoted, or through making case studies of them.

Essex County Council – integrated in-house design

 The story has been told in Chapter 3 (*see* pp43–44) of how an information professional took an initiative which led to a well-managed publishing service for the County Council's Education Service. Here, it's useful to look at the design aspects of the situation.

It began several years ago when the information professional was asked to provide some information for a book on economics for schools which the Council's Education Service was to publish. She did so, and when she saw the finished product she observed that 'the design treatment was a disaster which didn't do justice to the text', and that the text had not received appropriate editing or proof reading.

The in-house design group, which serves the whole of the local authority, had a key part in the changes described in Chapter 3. At first, the designers were not in the habit of reading the copy of the texts they worked on, and good practice in providing and taking briefs for jobs had not been established. With strong personalities in the long-established design group, relations were 'bumpy at first', but, through a 'mutual education process', understanding and excellent cooperation developed over time, to the benefit of both sides in a working relationship that now extends over more than 15 years (another example of the benefits of continuity).

In this instance, in-house information design is able to make a full contribution as part of a network of mutual understanding and good working relations which brings together managers in the Education Service, authors, editors, Information Services, the Publishing Unit, and Communications. That in turn has ensured the consistent success of the Service's publishing projects, and recognition of the value of its publishing service.

The Co-operative Bank – cooperation in design

 The Bank's excellent website has been mentioned in Chapter 7 (*see* pp129–130), and the account of its background and culture in Chapter 3 referred to the long-standing good relations between its staff and the external design groups and writers it uses, and to the attention it pays to briefing them. Here we look more closely at the design aspects.

All typographic and graphic design is externally commissioned: one agency has done a great deal of design work for the Bank for several years, including the ethical policy and related materials.

The writing of most of the Bank's information products is also commissioned from outside, to briefs prepared by the product managers concerned. There is a strong emphasis on briefing and on in-house consultation with stakeholders in the Bank (up to 65 parts of the Bank may be involved in planning for some products), and intensive interaction with outside writers during their work on jobs. Here too the Bank has a long-standing association with its main copy writers; their in-house contacts provide them with a learning process that over time gives them the benefits of in-house knowledge.

The highly regarded annual *Partnership Reports* have from the start been a co-operative effort between the Partnership Management Team, who collect the information content and the copy writers, and between the staff member who prepares the design brief and the external design group.

The Bank has also taken an unusual approach to its corporate identity, which is the product of in-house thinking over a long period, rather than the more usual process of relying on outside consultants to 'identify the identity' – which probably accounts for its unusual strength and power. The first step was taken in the mid-1980s, to overcome the associations of the words 'Co-operative Bank' with the image of old-fashioned Co-op stores. A revision process started in 1991 on the basis of in-house thinking. The staff concerned worked with the design group who have been responsible for the Bank's most distinctive products. The resultant corporate identity has unusually high information content, which supports the underlying aim of setting the Bank apart from the competition, using ethical policy as the differen-tiator. It has certainly contributed to the high recognition rate the Bank enjoys, and most probably to its consistently rising prosperity.

The quality of the Bank's website has been mentioned earlier. It is achieved by close collaboration among the in-house content manager, the product managers who provide and update information for their web-based IPs, and the web master from the company which set up the site. Rich in content, well structured, and easy to navigate, the site makes the full text of such key documents as the *Partnership Reports* available, together with key sections of others, and other content which complements printed products.

Premier Farnell – 'central creation and design'

As observed earlier, this company takes an integrated approach to all aspects of creating and managing the information products on which it depends (*see* pp37–38, 75, 88 and 116). This carries through to their thinking about the visual design of the products. What the users see and interact with is of a piece with the initial planning and the systems for delivering the products, and is a consistent visual expression of them. Underlying the holistic approach is the fact that, in the words of the e-business development manager, the company recognizes 'information products ... for what they are', and manages the resources available for them as a whole – not a very common proceeding.

The aim throughout is to combine 'central creation and design with channel-specific customization' so as to present consistent and clear delivery. Content is created with multiple channel use in mind; so the elements of information are broken down to a very 'granular' level to allow for use in various contexts for different purposes.

The initial designers are the 'Product Authors', who have specialist market knowledge of the physical products sold through the catalogues. They gather data for inclusion on the decision of the Product Managers, and use their experience in the first place to determine the appropriate forms of information product for delivery. For example, if market demand for a particular product is high, it will be made available via printed catalogues, a direct mail piece, an email feature, a shortform specialist catalogue (mini-logue) and the website. That initial decision sets in train a template-based process in which the content-management system calls for relevant content elements. The detail of what is required is established by how the product in question is defined in the internal taxonomy (the Premier Farnell Class Codes) described earlier (*see* p116).

Because so much is 'pre-designed' into the system, the role of the publishing section in the design of what the users actually see is a comparatively limited one. Publishing is responsible for final layout of the paper-based information products (mainly direct mail and catalogues), and, jointly with marketing and product specialists, for the design of formal style guidelines for electronic ones (mostly websites). The ultimate aim of the guidelines is to define a consistent look and feel for all information products in all media, to match the marketing concept of a 'family' or 'club' brand uniting all the trading companies which belong to Premier Farnell plc.

At the moment there is a noticeable difference between the design of the website for the electronic catalogue (http://www.farnell.com) and that for Premier Farnell plc (http://www.premierfarnell.com). Though the catalogue site is clear and well organized, the typography, particularly the presentation of the tables, has the look of an earlier generation of design; the Premier Farnell site, on the other hand, is more characteristic of contemporary information design in this respect, and in typography and layout. It is acknowledged that in this area staff without specific information-design education have had to learn by experience. The perception is that it needs to be handled in-house, and that there is no externally available training support that would meet the company's specific needs.

This is an illuminating example of the high quality in terms of structure, access-ibility and readability that can be achieved in-house without the intervention of professional information design. While elsewhere in this chapter I argue strongly for such professional inputs, this specific case is an example of the main argument that organizations should treat their IPs as an entity, and that collaborative thinking about information management, information systems and information design are essential for effective information products. The success of the Premier Farnell end products derives from the fact that what can justly be called design thinking permeates all stages and aspects of the process of creating information products, and that deep knowledge of products, markets and users is employed to build the main design elements into the system. The nature of the business makes the absence of professional graphic and typographic design inputs feasible; it would not be universally practicable, but there is plenty to learn from the overall approach.

Premier Farnell is also an example of an excellent application of the 'Multi-format, single-source' approach advocated by TSO (2004a,and b). If that approach is to do right by users in the way that Farnell products do, the more design thinking goes into the front end, the better the match will be between what users require and what they actually encounter in the various formats.

The reality:
2 Failures of understanding; dangerous changes

What follows is the result of asking professional information designers who have spent many years in their occupation to speak for themselves, from their own experi-ence. Their observations fall under the headings of

- What client organizations need to understand about design and designers
- What designers themselves need to understand
- Changes in the approach of both clients and designers over recent years, and their causes and effects.

What clients need to understand about design and designers

First, observations from a typographer who has worked in information design since the 1960s, as practitioner and teacher, and has a deep understanding of the subject.

> At their best, designers are people educated to solve problems. They have the skill and knowledge and intelligence to go beyond the ini-tial brief, which is often excessively product-orientated and narrow in its concept. When you have an enlightened client, who fully under-stands the complexity of the design process, and provides time and resources to those commissioned, the final design answer will be less predictable, but the products will usually be more successful in communicating to their audience.
>
> In actuality, designers frequently find themselves having to work with a brief which imposes the client's preconceived view of the end result. This fixed viewpoint and predetermination of the end product

Making knowledge visible

places the designer in a situation where flexibility to explore all facets of the problem is severely curtailed, and so prevents the asking of open-ended questions or exploration of alternatives.

This sort of client attitude is far from uncommon, and has become more prevalent of late, as the powerbase in organizations shifts yet further away from innovation and towards marketing and financial control. When the values of an organization don't recognize the skills of designers as problem-solvers, and they are seen as minions or tradesmen rather than as professionals of equal standing, the information products created will often be second rate.

These comments are corroborated by another designer colleague, who has a particularly shrewd understanding of how organizations work, combined with the capacity to grasp all kinds of detail of what they do, including the highly technical. She confirms that the skills of designers are usually poorly understood at the top end of the organization,[5] and supervision of their work – particularly when they are external suppliers – is often entrusted to people whose job is at such a level that they either lack appropriate understanding, or have the necessary understanding but lack the authority to act on it.

66 It depends on how much senior management understands about design, but even if they have good understanding, direct responsibility for dealing with designers can be lower down, with people who don't know enough about the company, or who think they know all about design but don't, and who don't know how to assess design. When it gets to the lower orders who can't see why you want to do particular things, and who at worst try to boss designers and thwart them to show their power, that's when you meet obstacles that don't arise when dealing with people higher up.

Other problems are caused by firms choosing to commission inappropriate people, such as advertising agencies, to undertake information design.

66 This story is an example; it concerns a washing machine.

The manufacturers found they were receiving an unusual number of call-outs from purchasers of a new model who had failed to carry out the preliminary steps necessary before operating the machine. These entailed putting the machine on its back and removing fixings and retaining straps which held in place the concrete blocks which stabilise the machine when in operation. If they were not removed, when

5 Gorb (1983) concluded, from experience as a manager in the textile industry, 'that the most important skills available to managers were the skills of designers; and that a preoccupation with design was central to business success.' He observed, however, that neither side recognized this, and the gap was 'sustained by misunderstanding of each other's roles – widened by their respective and mistaken attitudes towards management and design.' Hung up on misapprehensions about the 'creative' nature of design, they failed to see its 'critical and important place between the creative and inventive activities of business on the one hand, and its making and selling activities on the other'. (Another take, in fact, on the 'reconciling' role of design.)

the machine was started, it either damaged itself mechanically by trying to free itself to rotate the drum, or fused the electrics.

Assuming that the problems arose because customers failed to read the instructions for this preliminary 'dis-assembly', the manufacturers commissioned a revision of the existing instructions (which had been produced by the advertising agency responsible for the company's publicity).

On investigation, it turned out that:
1 Instructions for unpacking the machine and removing the inner packaging and restraints were partly on the outside of the outer cardboard box in which the machine was packed – and so were liable to be discarded without being fully read before they were needed.
2 A repeat of instructions for dis-assembly before installing and operating formed part of the operating instructions booklet, which was in a plastic bag inside the drum.

So it was hardly surprising that the essential pre-operating instructions were not found or understood, and the likelihood of failure was compounded by the fact that the retaining devices were highly finished and permanent-looking.

It was evident that the people responsible for designing the machine and the retaining packaging had not anticipated the difficulties. After some resistance, it was possible to get them together in the factory, with a machine in its box, and to go through the required process in order to demonstrate what could happen in the course of setting it up (including an unscheduled severely cut hand). The demonstration made it clear that the problem arose partly from the design of the machine, and partly from the way the instructions were presented. As a result there was some redesign so that the retaining straps etc could be removed from the front, without manhandling the machine, and a thorough revision of the instructions and their location, to make clear what purchasers who were unpacking and installing the machine themselves had to do first.

Briefing is indeed a critical art, and one at which many organizations are not much good. As this designer finds.

66 The initial brief can benefit from being quite loose and general, provided designers are then allowed to explore and are given access to people and things that appear relevant to meeting it, and are able to develop and present their own refinement of the brief.

Designers can find they become the link between different departments, interpreting between different functions and jobs. They need recognition for this role and its value, but the necessary kind of access to permit this is frequently not offered.

Making knowledge visible

And at the end of jobs, there's no opportunity to get feedback about the result of the design work that's been done, and so clients fail to get the best return on their investment, and both parties miss the chance of learning from projects.

The desire to 'save' costs on designers' time can lead clients to require templates into which new and different products can be fitted, in the belief that 'Now we can do it ourselves; we don't need a designer any more.' Not being designers, however, they don't know what to do with the templates when they've got them, and often finish up going to other designers to get them out of the mess they've landed in, which costs them more in the end.

Clients' ideas of the deliverables from design commissions differ from those of designers. They want descriptions of 'concrete' deliverables for accounting purposes, and the intangibles which designers also deliver, such as their capabilities for lateral thinking and visualizing relationships among elements in situations, don't fit into that framework. They think anyone can do the thinking, but that's the unique thing you buy from designers.

Clients can also be unaware of the full capacities of their in-house technology and of what their systems can't do, for example the fact that you need a Postscript printer to be able to print images from Word. So designers need to be able to draw on their knowledge of the in-house IS/IT (and sometimes of the people responsible for it) to protect clients from their own ignorance.

(This is a mature response to a situation that causes a lot of hair-tearing and anti-client exasperation among designers. One has to ask how much ignorance of the technology that designers deal with is excusable in clients, on the grounds that their business is something quite different and that's why they employ designers? And is it not part of the job to ascertain what the level is at the start, and take steps to do the necessary explaining to the right people?)

What designers themselves need to understand

In pursuit of other real-life stories from designers, I posted a message about this book in the 'InfoD-Cafe' – a very lively email discussion list. Here are some responses. This one, from the United States, is a salutary reminder of how designers can stand in their own light, with no apparent sense of self-preservation.

 I'm sure a lot of people will provide you with their ideas of what designers can do to help clients understand the value that communicators bring.

But one thing that I have observed are the thousands of ways that communicators sabotage their own chances for success. …

Examples range from the obvious, like missing deadlines, to the less obvious:

- Responding to requests for proposals with detailed designs. This is considered an unethical practice by the AIGA (American Institute of Graphic Artists), because clients are supposed to pay for real design work. But in these tough economic times, many designers are providing sample designs on spec (writers do the same thing) in hopes that they'll win a client over. It usually doesn't work — and gives the impression that design work does NOT have to be paid for.
- Completely ignoring a client's wishes when preparing designs
- Heard a web designer comment that 'I won't work with a client that won't require broadband because they're obviously not committed to quality.' That's awful short-sighted. Large companies, like IBM, Coke, and Pearson (to name a few) must design sites that people can access over standard phone lines, because that's all that's available to some of their customers and employees.
- Failing to conduct even a rudimentary up-front analysis — merely diving in and trying to write or design (usually disastrously).

Another response told of attempts to keep stakeholders, including designers, in separate compartments:

> In my masters research, I looked at how public relations practitioners (primarily consultants), graphic designers, and writers work together to produce printed materials for clients… Some of the interesting things to come out of the research were:
> - The importance of the briefing process, and the difficulties that many people have with this
> - The tendency of public relations practitioners to keep the client separated from the writers and from the designers (and, in fact, to keep separate everyone involved in the project)
> - The frustration of designers who often get treated as technicians, not specialists/strategists
> 1 The tendency of consultants to work through a traditional model which separates writing, design, production, and distribution roles.

Exchanges in the InfoD-Cafe have highlighted other aspects of this kind of professional pecking order – in this instance involving scientists and the 'also-rans':

> In my distant past, I worked for a number of Australia's public science agencies. Within them… there was (and still is) a sharp hierarchy between (1) the scientists and (2) the in-house science communicators, PR experts, journalists, graphic designers and the like. The latter are very much second-class citizens. Most scientists still implicitly believe that the writer or designer adds nothing to the communication process: the scientist provides the facts, the writer merely 'packages' them nicely, the designer gets called in at the last minute to 'pretty up' some tables or a diagram, rather than early on when they can develop an effective strategy, or rework how scientists explain things, or select what to present or explain.

A scientist who is also a designer responded on the problem of the 'conceptual and skills difference between scientists and information designers' which sets a gap between them that neither is eager to bridge.

> Also quite often members of both these communities are not only shy about making attempts to understand the other one, but are actually fighting suggestions to become involved with the other field.

Change over recent years; causes and effects

The first designer quoted in this section draws on long experience of the changes that underlie some of the situations described above.

> First, the organizational view of what design is for seems in danger of losing sight of the selling/telling distinction. More often than not – particularly in today's working environment – design and designers are in the service of financial management. Graphic design and information design have been brought closer to the philosophy of branding and advertising, where the emphasis is not on objective information, but on sales.

(Recent exchanges in the InfoD-Cafe exemplify this situation. Members have been responding to a young designer who sought advice on brand management, having been made responsible for that by the charity for which she works. Their replies make it clear that they are familiar with this area being seen as part of the information designer's remit.)

Design education, too, at any rate in the UK, has changed considerably, partly in response to financial and other pressures on the whole higher education system, in ways that put recently qualified designers at a disadvantage.

> Information design as a specialist subject in the UK has become smaller in size, and this has coincided with a massive increase in the staff: student ratio and a corresponding decline in individual tuition – from 1:8 in the 1970s to 1:23 today. Today there is very little teaching time, very little interaction between teachers and students.
>
> And subjects that were central to the Information Design curriculum in the past are no longer so today. Young designers, who have been through the design educational process in the last 10 years or so, will probably be unaware that visual design should be serious in purpose, and that their work relates to a social context. They will, also, most likely be unaware of the basic language of graphic design which was developed to help solve individual projects, particularly if no serious consideration is given in their courses to 20th-century design history.
>
> Deprivation of this kind of basic design knowledge has put them at a disadvantage of which they are unlikely to be aware. Without the balance such knowledge could provide, their designs will be heavily influenced by machine technology and the way that visual answers are driven by individual software packages.

MacKenzie-Taylor, in the article quoted earlier (*see* p141) gives a pertinent warning that such designers are likely to overlook the essential role that the aesthetic of information products plays in users' response to them, even when they are designing for organizations which aim to measure the performance of the products.

The education of today's young designers also fails to tell them much about human vision and what happens to it – a strange omission, given that it is mainly through the eye that we meet information, and seek to apprehend it. We are critically dependent on vision for starting the process of transforming external information into internal knowledge that belongs to us, and yet, as this designer observes from his own experience:

> They will most certainly be unaware of the problems that their work gives to a great number of the population over the age of 50. Most designers are young and it is very difficult to get them to work in an environment that would project them into the shoes of an older age group.

Many client organizations – without the excuse of youth – also seem unaware of the problems;[6] and yet many of their staff, as well as a growing proportion of their customers, are in the age group where some degree of visual impairment is common. As the Disability Rights Commission report on a study of web accessibility for disabled people put it, 'Although many of those commissioning websites state that they are alert to the needs of disabled people, there is very little evidence of such awareness being translated into effective usability for disabled people.'

The report (http://www.drc-gb.org/publicationsandreports/report.asp) revealed that fewer than 1 per cent of website home pages comply with reasonable accessibility. User testing shows that disabled people as a whole can complete only 76 per cent of simple web tasks; this falls to 53 per cent for blind people. Most websites (81 per cent) fail to satisfy the most basic Web Accessibility Initiative category.

Finally, an observation from my own experience as a writer – the only aspect of information design in which I can claim to be a professional. In working with typographers specializing in information design for many years, I have often been struck by the difference in the respect accorded to writers and designers, and made angry on behalf of my designer colleagues. The writer's skills are more highly regarded; the people who commission them are in no doubt that they are necessary, and that they can't do the job themselves. They usually know from experience how hard it is to get ideas into the right order, and to find the proper words for them. So the writer generally has an appreciative client who understands what he/she is getting for the fee. Not so the designer, in most cases. And that can only be because clients have no conception or experience of what they actually do, and the skills involved. As the President – a mechanical engineer – of the teachers' union I once worked for said of a proposal to commission a designer to redesign its magazine: 'Why do we have to pay this chap to draw a few indian-ink lines on paper?' (They did pay him, nevertheless, and were pleased with the results and the response of members.)

6 For accessibility standards of web design in respect of visual and other handicap, *see* the websites of Worldwide Web Consortium (Web Content Accessibility Guidelines: www.3.org/TR/ WAI-WEBCONTENT, Royal National Institute for the Blind (Better Web Design Campaign: www.rnib.org.uk/digital), and Office of the e-Envoy (www.e-envoy.gov.uk/webguidelines.htm).

Making knowledge visible

Information design and the web[7]

Web technology has had as strong and dramatic an effect on information design as on the other two professions discussed in these chapters. I cannot escape the feeling, however, that as a discipline it has had to deal with the web from a weaker position than either information management or information systems/IT, and that it has been less able to integrate the new into a strong basis of existing theory and practice.

There are, indeed, a number of established working designers whose career began in the pre-web era, who have made the transition successfully, are at home with the technology, but not exclusively dependent on it, still design for print as well as screen, and are able to apply earlier knowledge successfully to work in the current environment. They were students at the time when the two older designers quoted earlier were already teaching design. Many of them contribute energetically and thoughtfully to such forums as the InfoD-Cafe. However, their position is weakened on two fronts.

We have already seen (*see* p149) how various pressures on higher education have contributed to the discarding of earlier, but still valid and relevant, design knowledge, in favour of almost exclusive reliance on the newer technology to support the work of design. The young designers emerging from this environment lack the strengths and the resources available to their predecessors, and look ill-equipped to make the best of the situation in which they find themselves, or to maintain the values of the discipline.

In addition, they are not the only ones in the field. Web design is also the province of many practitioners without any design background, and many big organizations which employ large teams to create and maintain their websites do not necessarily look for people qualified in design to join them.

Important evidence on how and by whom websites of an international sample of large businesses are managed was presented in 2000 by Van der Walt and Van Brakel.

They got a 63 per cent response rate from a random sample of 100 webmasters from firms on Fortune Magazine's Global 500 list. The majority, as might be expected, were young, between the ages of 31 and 35, and had been in their post for a comparatively short time. Their place in the company's structure was of two broad types: either within a technical Information Systems division, or in marketing/corporate communications. A third were at technical or IT level, 27 per cent in middle management; and 29 per cent in 'other' categories. Overall, 38 per cent were in middle and top management levels – an indication that large firms now tend to see their websites as mission-critical. More than two thirds of them were responsible for managing a team, in which each individual specialises in a certain area.

---

7 Bawden and Robinson (2000) offer an intriguing reminder of what web technology might learn from the early stages of print. Drawing on Eisenstein's work, they remind us that 'the printing press, far from creating an entirely new form of information product, built on, and extended, what was already present.' That included concepts and techniques going back to scribal times, such as footnotes, cross-references, contents tables, and figure references, which supported readers in moving about in texts – a parallel to the way that the Internet was able to use the idea of hypertext. Another parallel between the history of the two technologies: printing in its first decades was used for products of varying quality, with 'assessment and sorting' in libraries (the beginnings of information management) following later; in the same way quality control has been introduced to the Internet, essentially through development of the basic methods of librarianship. Food for thought about the specialisms whose collaboration is needed before a revolutionary new technology can deliver the quality it is capable of.

Project management and content management were significant tasks for web-masters, though they were not primarily responsible for creating or writing content. They considered graphic design was very important, though webmasters tend to be no longer directly responsible, and in most cases design and layout are the responsibility of a team member specialising in interface design or dtp. Tasks seen as 'laborious' such as the design of graphics or multimedia were left to team members. However, 74 per cent of respondents indicated that creativity was a required skill for webmasters, in that they should understand the principles of 'not only the design of graphical elements, but... also... the spatial layout of visual elements on the website' including text, graphics and multi-media.

Griffiths (2004), presents similar evidence, from a number of other sources, including the World Organization of Webmasters (WOW).

The advice on offer

It's a fair assumption, on the basis of evidence of this kind, that many of the people given overall responsibility for their organization's websites have a background in specialisms other than design. Some of the advice on offer to help them understand the design principles mentioned by Van der Walt and Van Brakel is sensible and useful. Much of it, however, in the words of Taylor (2000) in a critique of the work of the most often cited source, Jakob Nielsen's website (www.useit.com) and his book (Nielsen, 2000), amounts to 'a single simple prescription for usability' recommended 'regardless of the context of application'. Taylor continues:

> **in essence, good information design consists of doing all one can to communicate a message or to make information accessible and useful, for each particular group of readers/users, in a particular circumstance of use or particular technology of information provision. Nielsen's greatest 'heresy', if you like, is neglecting the importance of this analytical stage that asks: who are your readers? what do they want? with what tools can they access your information?**

He is particularly critical of Nielsen's assumption that 'all websites are e-commerce sites and that all websites are offering services for whom there are competitive information providers'. There are in fact 'many alternative kinds of Web information provider for whom better public service, not better sales, is the natural motivational factor – including many medical, academic, non-profit and governmental sites.' And he quotes one unkind but telling comment from another reader of the book, which is probably a fair assumption about how it will be used: 'It's the type of work that makes CEOs feel better by thinking they know what's going on, but largely useless for somebody who actually needs to design a website.'

That observation is applicable to a good deal of the advice on planning websites, and on designing and writing for the web offered on the web and in books intended to 'help you get started'. Well-intentioned generalizations which are pretty useless unless you already know enough not to need to read them, are commoner than real help. A typical piece on writing for the web exhorts readers to 'remember to write with the target audience's needs in mind', and to 'think about the best way to structure and present your information', but gives no real help on how to set about doing these worthy things. One welcome contrast comes from Rachel McAlpine's website, which, instead of generalizations that dump the reader just at the point where help is needed,

Making knowledge visible

provides clear and usable advice about such topics as index pages and how to compile them; the meaning of 'content' in the context of the Web (and what the Web has done to the traditional sequence of content, design and technology); intranet style guides and what they should contain.

There are indeed useful things that need saying about 'Web usability', to help both those who have to do it themselves from a non-design professional basis, and those who have the opportunity to commission web designers, but, as Taylor (2000) puts it, that requires 'subtlety and wisdom, knowledge of what is technically involved, and resistance to simple formulas and sweeping generalisation.' By implication, that also demands the collaboration of the three groups to whom Chapters 6–8 have been devoted.

Some of the most acute thinking on the subject that I have come across is unfortunately as yet unpublished, from a book on 'The Art of Visual Interface Design' by Wolfgang Heidrich, an information designer with deep experience of this area. He sees visual structure as parallel to information structure, and describes the benefits that good design confers in these words:

> **Unity – Visual structure unifies dissimilar design elements and lets them work in unison towards a common communications goal.**
>
> **Comprehension – An effective visual structure communicates the meaning of a design by making the relationship between disparate design elements and their associated meaning clear.**
>
> **Clarity – Visual structure improves the clarity of information displays by creating, separating and arranging its content into manageable and meaningful areas that viewers can process simultaneously or sequentially.**
>
> **Control – By distinguishing areas of importance, structure guides viewers' attention towards areas of interest and significance and so facilitates their navigation through the composition and towards a desired focus.**

And to achieve interface structures which promote that kind of experience for users of web-based information products, designers need to 'understand user goals and tasks and business objectives'.

Summary

Information design should support IPs by
- Integrating their content and the container in appropriate media and forms of presentation, so that they match what users need to do
- Making their structure plain, and guiding users through it
- Reconciling the conflicting needs of stakeholders in them, to give an optimal solution
- Expressing the culture and values of the organization through them
- Respecting the constraints involved, and finding the most effective way of working within them.

References

BAWDEN, D & ROBINSON, LYN (2000)
'A distant mirror? The Internet and the printing press', *Aslib Proceedings*, 52 (2) 51–57

DYSON, G (1999)
Darwin among the machines, London: Penguin Books

GORB, P (1983)
'Design and the manager: bridging the gulf', *Icographic* (Journal of the international Council of Graphic Design Associations), 11 (3) 8–10

GRIFFITHS, P (2004)
Managing your Internet & intranet services; the information professional's guide to strategy, Ed 2. London: Facet Publishing

HEIDRICH, W (2002)
From unpublished work on *The Art of Visual Interface Design*

JARDINE, L (2000)
Ingenious Pursuits. London: Abacus, p83

KRULL, R et al. (1993)
'Balancing visual and verbal modes of pre-senting information: diagnostic tools for making effective choices', *IEEE International Professional Communication Conference*, Philadelphia, PA, 326–331

McALPINE, R
http://www.qwc.co.nz

MACDONALD-ROSS, M & WALLER, R (1976/2000)
'The Transformer', *Penrose Annual*, 141–152 (Reprinted, as 'The transformer revisited', with a postscript, in *Information design journal*, 9 (2&3), 177–193

MACKENZIE-TAYLOR, M (1993/1999)
'Appearance and performance', *Communication News*, 6 (3); reprinted in 11 (3)

MOXON, J (1683–4)
Mechanick exercises on the whole art of printing, Facsimile ed H Davis & H Carter, 1958. Oxford: Oxford University Press

NIELSEN, JAKOB (2000)
Designing Web Usability, NewRiders

QUINE, T (2004)
Posting in InfoD-Cafe (infodesign-cafe@list.infor-mationdesign.org), 02 07 04

ROYAL NATIONAL INSTITUTE FOR THE BLIND
Better Web Design Campaign:
www.rnib.org.uk/digital

SLESS, D (1995)
'Information design for the information age', *Communication News*, 8 (5/6)

STEVENS, G (1995)
'Design is more than cosmetic', Chapter 9 in E Orna and G Stevens, *Managing information for research*, Buckingham: Open University Press

TAYLOR, C (1999)
Personal communication

... (2000)
'Jakob Nielsen's view of usability'
infodesign-cafe@list.design-inst.nl

TSO (2004a)
'The multi-format publishing challenge' (presentation by Terry Blake, TSO Strategies for Publishing seminar)
http://www.tso.co.uk

... (2004b)
'Focus on... Multi-format publishing. Ten facts you need to know about multi-format publishing'
http://www.tso.co.uk/solutions/site.asp?FO=11429 30&DI=521720

VAN DER WALT, P & VAN BRAKEL, P (2000)
'Task analysis of the webmaster: results of an empirical study', *Aslib Proceedings*, 52 (1), 20–38

WRIGHT, P (1979)
Designing informatiom: some approaches, some problems and some suggestions, (BL R&D Report No.5509, London: British Library Research and Development Department

Other Reading

Material that has been part of the incidental reading around the subject of this chapter, which hasn't been quoted from or directly referred to. It's grouped under headings which relate to the topics covered in the chapter.

Information design

DESIGN COUNCIL
About: Information Design,
http://www.designcouncil.info

Useful material on what information designers do. Good sense about importance of collaboration between them and information systems professionals, though apparently not aware that there are other professionals who specialize in knowledge and information management, and in information architecture.

RICHARDS, C (2000)
'Getting the picture: diagram design and the information revolution', *Information design journal*, 9 (2&3) 87–110

Diagrams as elements in electronic user guides for products. graphic metaphors. Taxonomy of design variables. Animated, interactive diagrams. Case study of Dixon's documentation overhaul, leading to 60 per cent reduction in 'no fault found' call-outs economic benefits of good information design.

Writing as a design activity

ARTFIELD, S, BLANDFORD, A & DOWELL, J (2003)
'Information seeking in the context of writing. A design psychology interpretation of the "problematic situation" '. *Journal of Documentation*, 59 (4) 430–453

Writing, like design, involves iterative 'dynamic interplay' between analysis and synthesis; and shares with good design the characteristic of being 'an integrated solution to a whole cluster of constraints.'

ORNA, E & STEVENS, G (1995)
Managing information for research,
Buckingham: Open University Press

Chapter 10: 'Transforming knowledge into written information: designing your writing'

Website accessibility and usability

NATIONAL CANCER INSTITUTE (2003)
Research-Based Web Design and Usability Guidelines
US Department of Health and Human Services, National Institutes of Health, and National Cancer Institute,
http://usability.gov/pdfs/guidelines.html

Developed by Communication Technologies Branch of the NCI, to assist 'those involved in the creation of websites base their decisions on the current and best available evidence.' Each guideline has 'Relative Importance' and 'Strength of Evidence' rating. Primary audience: website designers and managers.

OFFICE OF THE E-ENVOY (2003)
Quality Framework for UK Government Website Design; usability issues for government websites. London: OeE,
www.e-envoy.gov.uk/webguidelines.htm

PALFERY, R (2005)
'Access denied; catalogue accessibility for VIPs' [visually impaired people], *Library + Information update,* 4 (3) 32–33

Survey of UK public library catalogues suggests most libraries aren't meeting requirements of Disability Discrimination Act

STRINGER, R (2000)
'The emergence of a new medium at the edge of chaos', *MDA Information,* 5 (5) 2002

Visionary piece by hypermedia architect with particular interest in navigation. Throws incidental light on how the three disciplines might be brought together to create web-based IPs, and navigation tools which would allow people to move gracefully among them, in pursuit of the information they need.

Action for IP value –
a practical process

'In this business, information products are mostly
recognized for what they are and grouped in
terms of systems and organization. Organizing
resources this way allows for information products
to be developed and evolved commensurate with
the needs of the target audience [and]... to manage
the resources available to information products as
a whole. In my experience most companies do
not make the critical recognition of information
products to allow this evolution.'

COMMENT FROM THE E-COMMERCE MANAGER OF PREMIER FARNELL

Introduction to part 4

In the first three parts of this book, I have told readers what I believe information products should do for organizations, and why, with stories – positive and negative – to illustrate what happens in practice.

This final part is for those who accept the main arguments, and want to take action based on them, in order to get better value from the investment their organizations make in IPs. It's short and practical, though I hope not too prescriptive. I hope it will provide a framework onto which readers can build their own existing knowledge, and round which they can grow new knowledge, which will allow constructive action on information products.

The approach I recommend is based on the well-established methodology of information auditing. Chapter 9 explains the essence of the method very briefly; Chapter 10 suggests ways of winning the 'critical recognition of information products for what they are' referred to in the quotation on page 157, and offers visuals and a commentary which could make the basis for readers' own presentations. An extended real-life example of applying the auditing approach in this kind of context is introduced in Chapter 11. Chapter 12 – the final one – takes the story forward from the com-pletion of the audit and acceptance of its recommendations, to the initiatives based on it; relates the way the audit was conducted to the ideas advanced in Parts 1 to 3; and points to actions related to IPs that have worked well in practice, in this project and in the other organizations whose stories have been told in this book.

The only other thing to say by way of introduction is this:

Don't embark on this process unless and until:
● You yourself are thoroughly convinced of the arguments, and prepared to sell them to others
● You see both good reason and some opportunity for action on your organization's information products
● There is a positive response from the top of the organization, with the prospect of tangible support
● You have found some actual or potential allies among colleagues.

If there's a good chance of meeting those conditions, go on boldly; if not, hold on; don't abandon the idea – but bide your time and watch out for favourable change.

Making knowledge visible

An information auditing approach

In this chapter

A well-founded method

Information auditing is a well-founded method that depends on a) working out what organizations should be doing with information and/or knowledge, in the light of whatever they're in business for, b) finding out what they're actually doing with it, and c) comparing the two. The results give a solid basis for change in order to bring b) closer to a).

Information auditing has been increasingly used over the last two decades or so in a variety of contexts, to look at many aspects of information use. It has seemed to me for a long time that it would be a useful tool for looking at IPs, as suggested by R Taylor's advanced thinking in the early 1980s. This very prescient writer, already quoted on information environments and information products (*see* pp64 and 109) argues for information auditing (one of the earliest uses of the term) as a means of looking ' "backward" at the design of the production or support system, and "forward" to the function and utility of these outputs' (Taylor, 1982, p313), and proposes that, in order to make information systems more cost-effective, criteria for assessing the outputs should be derived from users and their environments. 'The key questions for each type of output are how it is actually used and how well it serves its intended function.'[1] He also says that it is essential to understand what the organization does, its history, the place it occupies in its industry, and its market share; to know about its customers, its clients, and its 'public'; and to be aware of organizational 'dynamics' and 'culture' and how they influence the flow of information.

1 With his usual foresight, Taylor also identified evaluating the role that information 'in any formal form' plays in the success or failure of performance as a problem 'of special importance in the design, management, operation and evaluation of information systems and their products and services.' (p318) and one which should 'concern the professional for at least the next decade'. He was right there!

It was not until 2003 that I had the opportunity of working with an organization on an audit where information products were a major focus (the Essex County Council school governors audit described in Chapters 11 and 12). Since then, I have come across some other organizations that have been kind enough to allow me to relate their experiences of applying information auditing to IPs. All these examples, in particular that of Essex CC, are drawn on in the chapters that follow.

The essence of information auditing

A standard definition of information auditing, developed by the Aslib Information Resources Management Network (now KIMNET) describes the process as:

> **A systematic examination of information use, resources and flows, with a verification by reference to both people and existing documents, in order to establish the extent to which they are contributing to an organization's objectives.**

If we unpack the meaning of this compact definition of information auditing, its essentials are that it is a systematic process, which looks at;
- How people use information
- The resources of information they use
- How information gets around within organizations and between them and the outside world they depend on.

And its purpose is to find out how well what organizations actually do with information matches what they should be doing with it.[2]

So information auditing ought to be: a process of matching What Is against What Should Be. It is dynamic, not static, because it looks at the organization and the people who make it up in action. It seeks as its outcome illumination, understanding how people use information and the results of using it, not just enumeration of such 'information assets' as databases, documents and other containers of information.

Its aim is to bring What Is closer to What Should Be, by ensuring that the organization:
- Gets the information it needs
- Manages it effectively
    with the support of appropriate systems and technology
        so that people can find and use it
            in the ways necessary for doing successfully whatever the organization
                is in business to do.

The outcome of a good information audit is a soundly based understanding of what the organization is currently doing with information, which makes a strong platform for change through better use of information and knowledge.

2 Note that what organizations *should be* doing with information will vary from organization to organization, because what constitutes essential information for any organization depends on the nature of its business, and so too do the criteria for successful use of information.

Making knowledge visible

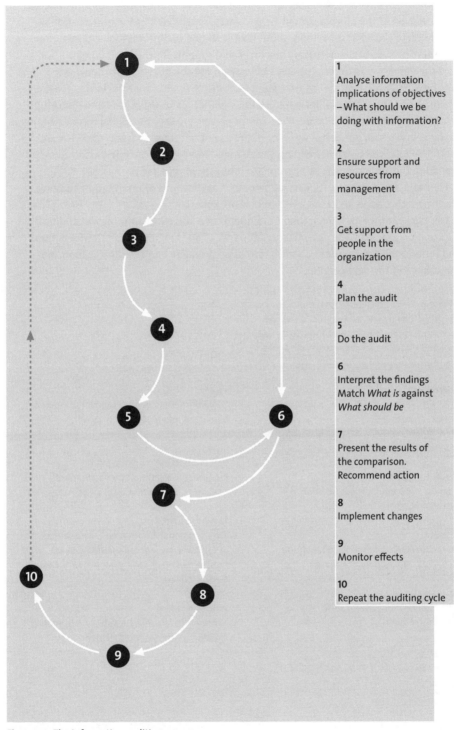

1
Analyse information
implications of objectives
– What should we be
doing with information?

2
Ensure support and
resources from
management

3
Get support from
people in the
organization

4
Plan the audit

5
Do the audit

6
Interpret the findings
Match *What is* against
What should be

7
Present the results of
the comparison.
Recommend action

8
Implement changes

9
Monitor effects

10
Repeat the auditing cycle

Figure 9.1 The information auditing process
Reproduced by permission of the publishers from Orna (2004)

Figure 9.1 on page 161, shows a top-level outline of the information auditing process.

The version of the process set out here[3], starts from analysing the organization's objectives, to see what they imply about how it should use information (stage 1); then, after making sure of the necessary resources and support for the audit (stages 2 and 3), uses the definition to decide the audit objectives and the questions it should ask, and to plan how to do it (stage 4). The next stages consist of finding answers to the questions (stage 5), and then (stage 6) interpreting the significance of the results and matching What Is against What Should Be. Then comes presenting the results and recommending changes in order to get better value from the use of information (stage 7). The audit should be followed by implementing the changes, monitoring the effects, and then repeating the auditing cycle at appropriate intervals (stages 8–10).

For more about the origins, development and applications of information auditing, *see* Orna (1999, 2000 and 2004), Henczel (2001), Robertson (1994, 1997) and Wood (2004).

Let us now move on to preparing the ground for a successful information audit of information products. The essential preliminaries of spotting opportunities for action, and introducing the key ideas about information products into the organization, are the subject of the next chapter.

[3] There is as yet no standard set of procedures, which is probably just as well; this is the one I use in practice – it has evolved through experience and through exchanges with colleagues.

References

HENCZEL, S. (2001)
The Information Audit. A Practical Guide,
Munich: K G Saur

ORNA, E (1999)
Practical Information Policies (Edition 2),
Aldershot: Gower

... (2000)
'The human face of information auditing',
Managing Information, 7 (4) 40–42

... (2004)
Information Strategy in Practice,
Aldershot: Gower

ROBERTSON, G (1994)
'The information audit: a broader perspective',
Managing Information, 1 (4) 34–36

... (1997)
'Information auditing; the information professional as information accountant',
Managing Information, 4 (4) 31–35

TAYLOR, R S (1982)
'Organizational information environments',
In G P Sweeney (ed) *Information and the transformation of society,* Amsterdam, Oxford: North-Holland

WOOD, S (2004)
Information Auditing: a guide for information managers, Ashford, Mdx: FreePint

Making knowledge visible

Making a start

In this chapter

As I said in the introduction to these chapters, before starting any action on information products, there needs to be both good reason, and opportunity.

Good reason for action

Some common situations that reveal all is not well with an organization's IPs, with typical examples:

They give trouble to a large proportion of users, outside the organization and/or inside.

> The confusing communications patients receive from hospitals (like the eye-crossing Asthma Management Card from a local hospital which expects patients to fill in dots to indicate peak respiratory flow readings in cells less than 2mm square – and they want 3 daily readings in 4 cells – and to add numerical codes standing for such events as 'missed work because of asthma'. And they think, 'You may like to join up the dots from day to day across the graph'.)

> Web sites that draw complaints from customers or are singled out in the press as unhelpful; intranets that don't allow staff to find or use the information they need.

Products are created without key stakeholders being given the chance to contribute, stakeholders are brought in too late to make a fully effective contribution, or the need for specialist skills is not recognized.

> Information professionals not involved in developing the structure of websites and intranets.

Content experts asked to provide content for IPs at a point when firm decisions on medium or format have been taken that preclude presenting content appropriately; no provision made for design or editing of important publications.

Errors and failures arise because there are either no IPs to meet important needs, or the existing ones are inadequate for the purpose.

Lack of products that provide training or guidance for essential processes or procedures, or for using software tools; no suitable induction products to help new staff get to grips with their work.

IPs with which customers have to interact give rise to high error rates which are costly to outside users, to inside staff who have to deal with the consequences, and to the organization.

Forms for customer completion which lead to multiple errors, high staff costs in time spent correcting them, and annoyance to customers.

An electronic 'Editorial Review' form which I recently declined to complete, because it required double-working: first to annotate the actual text which I had edited, and then to copy the annotation to the form, adding the details necessary to identify the location. The author on the receiving end had an even worse job – to go from a list identifying the place in the text by a line number, to the actual text, then to consider the changes which the editor had suggested or actually made, make a decision on them, and enter a response on the form.

Making sense of important internal IPs has a high intellectual cost to staff and to the organization, because they make too heavy a demand on time.

Important policy drafts, which require detailed response from high-level staff, are presented in a format that makes it difficult to perceive the structure and navigate through it; and poor legibility caused by inappropriate typefaces, inadequate spacing and overlong lines compounds the difficulty.

Failure to offer information products that the organization has a legal obligation to provide, in a form that meets users' needs.

The poor quality of the products, printed and on websites, which some local authorities offer, in meeting their obligations to inform the public, under the Freedom of Information Act, about their publishing programmes and availability of their publications (see Simpson, 2003 and Pinder, 2005).

Opportunities are missed to develop new IPs that could add value.

Museums which have developed excellent electronic resources of information about their collections, but which don't yet recognize their potential for creating a wide range of IPs for both visitors and staff, or for linkage with their commercial publishing programmes.

Making knowledge visible

The organization's IPs aren't managed as an information resource.

> No single resource of the authoritative version of key policy documents available on the intranet.

> Distribution procedures don't ensure that the library or information service holds a complete set of the organization's publications.

> Staff are embarrassed when customers ask them about IPs they themselves haven't heard of.

Costly muddles happen in development and production.

> Inappropriate choice of medium, format, supplier, or print-run in relation to purpose and audience for information products (*see* the DTI example quoted in Chapter 3, p48); no standards for taking such decisions; no clear allocation of authority for making them.

Products and services are offered without adequate IPs to accompany them.

> Software user manuals which describe the inner workings from a programmer's viewpoint, but don't tell users how to carry out the tasks they want to do. Complaints on this score began shortly after the earliest manuals appeared, and are still going strong today.

Finally, some quotations from experience, for which I am indebted to KIMNET members at an information products workshop:

> 'Lack of understanding of who are our stakeholders and what their needs are.'
> 'Putting organization's needs for economies above employees' needs for IP support.'
> 'Techies take over and lose sight of purpose and users.'
> 'Designers for IPs are not the people in the business process.'
> 'Medium vs message: who controls the budget (info smart or computer smart).'

Anything you encounter of that kind merits investigation to see what's behind the immediate manifestation. Even without such a stimulus, it's worth taking an overview of at least a sample of the range of IPs the organization creates for the outside world and for internal use. Are they self-consistent? Do they live up to what the organization claims about itself? Do they show respect for the users in terms of appropriate content, relevance to the ways in which they need to use them, awareness of their requirements and their feelings?

Taking opportunities

To begin with, two recent examples of incidental findings from information audits which revealed needs and opportunities for action on IPs.

Procedural IPs needed

Members of the KM/IM team in a professional body were asked to carry out an information audit in a department which dealt with complaints casework. It became clear that the nature of the work meant that staff needed guidance through the procedures for various stages, in the form of information products which were accessible, consistent, fully up to date, and capable of being presented in various forms to match the users' needs. The products they were actually using were none of these things; updating was neglected, they were paper-based and so could not benefit from electronic updating from a single source, they lacked standards of labelling, titling, and terminology, and, while the staff were attached to them from long acquaintance, they were poorly served by them in their work.

'Information Riches' at the Inland Revenue

The Inland Revenue 'Information Riches' initiative (Sippings, 2004) revealed that some of the riches could not be strategically used to the full because insufficient attention had been paid to the information products which should give access to them.

The intranet was an important instance; this critical meta-information product was not supporting its users in the manner they needed. It was found to hold 'vast amounts of content published by most of the teams in the Revenue,' some of whom used individual design and navigation styles, duplicated content and generally tended to 'stove-pipe' (ie keep in silos) the material available to users. Some of the authorized publishers 'created new designs for their sites; the lack of governance arrangements meant that they had the freedom to do this. In fact, the intranet felt more like a collection of separate websites for each team.' One of the main problems was that 'to find anything, users had to know which team was responsible for a particular issue or topic in order to drill down from a team site into associated subject knowledge.'

Action was needed:
1 To develop 'a documented and owned strategy, governance standards and style and design guides'
2 To reorganize and consolidate the subject content previously held in team sites into logical groupings, allowing users to find all relevant content in a single search, rather than second-guessing which teams might have some part of it.

The first is being addressed by bringing the intranet within the content management system currrently used for the IR website, and by creating an intranet taxonomy. At the same time a collaboration among Information Resources, Information Delivery (one of the IT teams) and Marketing and Communications is developing the interface and a common approach to structure, standards and presentation. Solving the subject problem is recognized as a long process, which will require a lot of negotiation with individual teams. Information Resources, IT staff and Compliance staff are working together on a pilot site, initially to develop a 'map' to all the other sources which hold relevant information on this subject.

Another collaboration, resulting in an information product that meets a real need, has been between Information Resources and Learning. They jointly created a

Making knowledge visible

well-received learning product on the responsibilities of individuals in relation to the Freedom of Information Act, Data Protection and other areas of information law, such as copyright and the Public Records Act.

Lessons have been learned from experience on the necessity of co-operation between systems managers and information managers in planning and developing IPs. This is recognized as critical, and because it involves different lines of command, achieving it demands both negotiations between different business areas, and good relations between the actual stakeholder groups who have to co-operate – which fortunately exist in the present instance.

Reminders of other examples

The stories quoted in Part 2 of this book provide many examples of opportunities and the constructive action taken in response. Here are reminders of some of them.

Development or re-launch of the organization's portal, website or intranet

> The mda's portal development (*see* Chapter 3, pp38–40.)

Information architecture initiative

> *See* Chapter 6, p111 and MacLachlan's (2004) case study of the Department of Trade and Industry's information architecture project.

Innovative uses of technology that have an impact on IPs.

> Premier Farnell's development of an electronic catalogue for its mail-order business (*see* Chapter 3, pp37–38).

> The Co-operative Bank's move into internet banking, described in Chapter 3 (pp54–56).

> e-government initiatives (*see* Chapter 6, p110).

> The introduction of content-management software to support Premier Farnell's publishing activity (*see* Chapter 8, p143).

> Single-source multi-channel publishing (*see* Chapter 1, p20).

Communications audit being made in the organization

> The initiative at the Royal College of Nursing, described in Chapter 6 (p113).

Knowledge- or information-management initiatives

> For examples of organizations where the implications for information products of a commitment to KM or IM have been followed up, see Chapters 5 (pp93–96) and 6 (p117).

Evidence-based information management projects

> As mentioned in Chapter 6 (p115), the ideas underlying evidence-based healthcare are now being extended to information management. Booth and Brice (2004) make

a convincing case for it, and any such initiatives should obviously include information products in their collection and evaluation of evidence.

Compliance with legislation which requires action on IPs.

> *See* Chapter 5 (pp85–87) for the new kinds of information products which the Freedom of Information Act requires.

> *See* Chapter 7 (p125) for the potential effects of the Legal Deposit Act, 2004, on the management of electronic IPs.

Testing the response, selling the ideas, gaining allies

If you're involved in any developments like this (and even if the fact that you're a stakeholder, have something to contribute, or will be affected by the results, hasn't been recognized, and you haven't been asked to join in) – it's an opportunity to invite the decision-makers responsible for the initiative, and the others involved, to think about the implications for IPs, and their overall place in what the organization does.

How you do it is ultimately for you to judge in the light of your knowledge of your own organization, the alliances you are able to take advantage of, and whatever in-house advice you can get. In case you would like a bit of help, the final part of this chapter consists of a framework for a presentation.

The content and arguments are based on presentations made to various groups here and in Australia. They're presented in graphic form (some of them have appeared earlier in the book as illustrations), with minimal commentary (the bits introduced by **"**) because if you want to introduce people who have other things on their minds to new ideas it's wise not to overload them with words to start with, and fatal to take too long about it. The formal documents come later, when you've sold the essential ideas.

If you do make use of the framework:
- Bring in illustrations and examples from your own organization
- Give your audience a short handout with the reasons why it's important for the organization to think now about its IPs, and definitions of the essential terms.
- And please acknowledge this book as the source!

References

BOOTH, A and BRICE, A (2004)
Evidence-based Practice for Information Professionals; A handbook, London: Facet Publishing

MACLACHLAN, L (2004)
'From architecture to construction', in A Gilchrist and B Mahon (eds) *Information Architecture: designing information environments for purpose*, London: Facet Publishing, 199–214

PINDER, R (2005)
'The art of the possible', *Managing information*, 12 (1), 4–8

SIPPINGS, G (2004)
'Putting information on the map at the Inland Revenue' *Library + Information update*, 3 (4), 28–33

SIMPSON, D (2003)
'Implementing the Freedom of Information Act', *Library + Information Update*, 2 (12) 30–32

No business without Information Products
– a presentation

> The essence of the argument – based on working experience, and on research – made in this presentation.

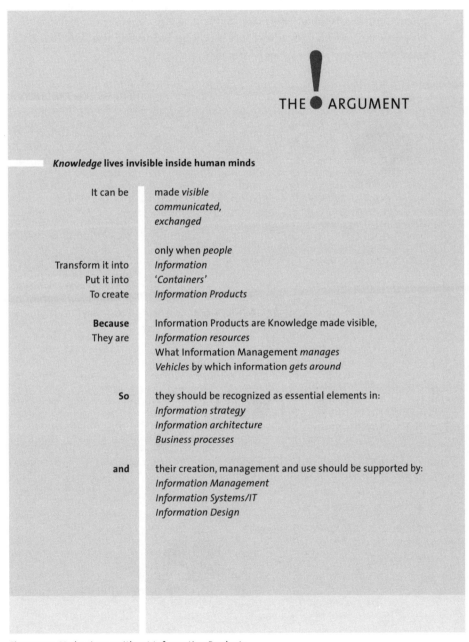

Figure 10.1 No business without Information Products

> Knowledge lives only in human minds; it can't be communicated until it's been transformed into information and put outside into the world in the form of an information product, where others can see and use it.
>
> Examples of the transformation process: creating a page on a website; setting up a record format; writing a report; preparing slides and giving a presentation.
>
> When we find relevant information in IPs, we transform the information we want into knowledge, which enriches what we already know and makes us better able to act succesfully. That's why we look for information!
>
> Information products link knowledge and information; they allow us to communicate what we know, learn from others, exchange knowledge and develop new ideas. They are essential tools in every organization for getting its work done.

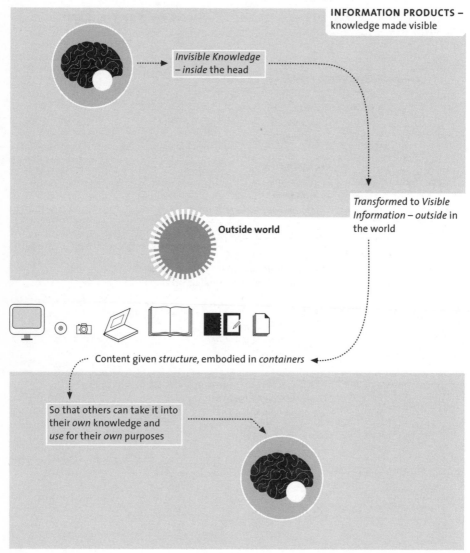

Figure 10.2 Information products make the link between knowledge and information

Making knowledge visible

" So the vital job that information products do is to provide a place where minds can meet and communicate, where we can get access to the knowledge of others made visible in the form of information, and then take away what we need, and transform it into knowledge that we too can use.

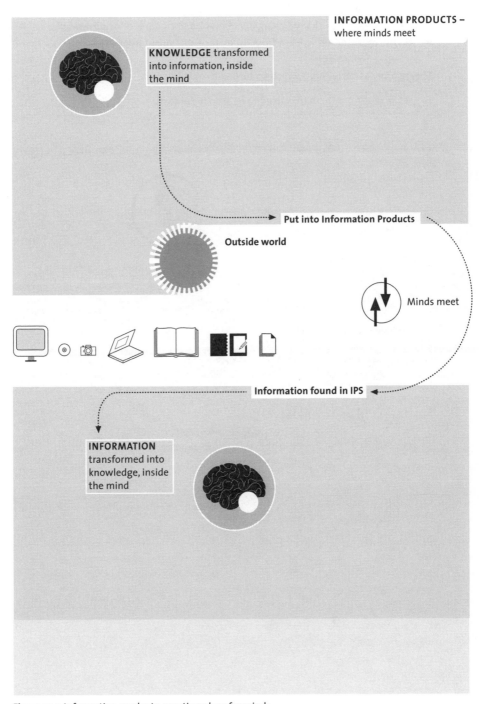

Figure 10.3 Information products: meeting place for minds

> IPs should
> - Show the issues that are important to the organization
> - Convey what it thinks about them
> - Encourage the people to whom they're addressed, inside and in its outside world, to act accordingly
> - Help essential knowledge to get around, encourage its exchange
> - Support response to change, change initiatives, and creation of new knowledge
> - Help the organization to learn from experience, retain and use the lessons, develop self-knowledge
>
> They're a key asset, without which no business could function.
>
> To get the best from them they need to be seen in context.

What IPs should do for the business

Information products should be

Tangible representations	of its values and knowledge
Vehicle	by which they reach outside and inner worlds

Agents	for *transforming*
	    Knowledge into *Information*
	    Information into *Knowledge*
	    diffusing new knowledge

Source	for organizational *Learning*
Embodiment	of business *Memory*

Figure 10.4 What information products should do for the business

Making knowledge visible

> Organizations can't get value from their IPs if they see them as a lot of separate products, without any common context. IPs need to be seen in relation to:
> 1 The organization's objectives, business processes and information culture
> 2 Their tangible and intangible costs and effects
> 3 Their users, and other stakeholders in them
> 4 The support they need from knowledge and information management, information systems/IT, and information design.

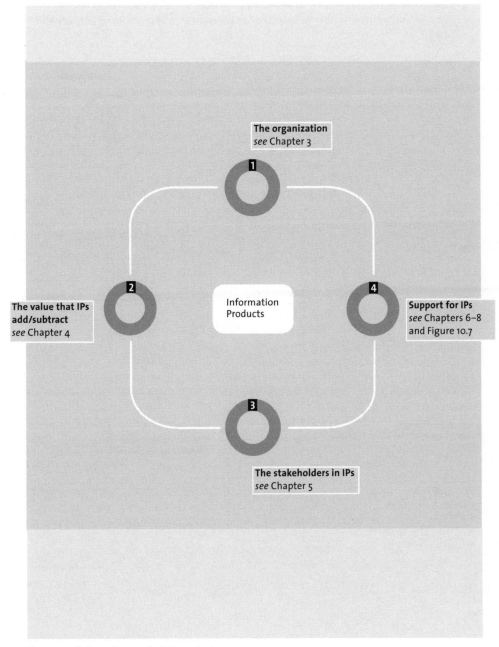

Figure 10.5 Information products in context

> Most organizations don't take into account the full range of stakeholders in their information products, and the products suffer accordingly. Probably the most important of the overlooked stakeholders are:
>
> 1 The business as overall stakeholder. If there's no overall strategic view of IPs from the top, they can't be expected to add much business value.
>
> 2 The people who are meant to use the products. The users and the ways in which they need to use information products are critical for how well IPs fulfil the organization's objectives and support its business processes, but they're too often seen as passive recipients, organizations don't invest much in knowing about what they do and what they need, so they're expected to take what they're given – and they don't like it!

The Stakeholders

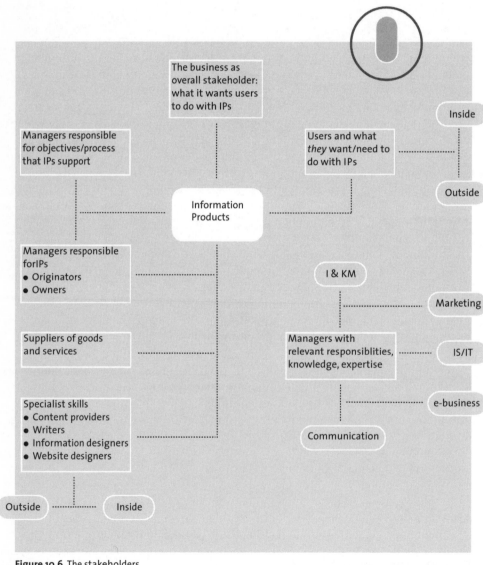

Figure 10.6 The stakeholders

" The 3 essential kinds of support IPs need for full value – and all 3 need to work together

KM/IM should:
  Provide content that can be used in multiple ways
  Link IPs with information architecture/information strategy
  Give consistent structure and standards to help access and use

IS/IT should support:
  Managing information content
  Automating processes to appropriate levels
  Tasks/interactions associated with creating, managing, using IPs
  Using web technology effectively to integrate IPs

Information design should:
  Integrate content and container to match what users need to do
  Help users find their way through IPs
  Reconcile differing needs of stakeholders
  Give visible expression to organizational values

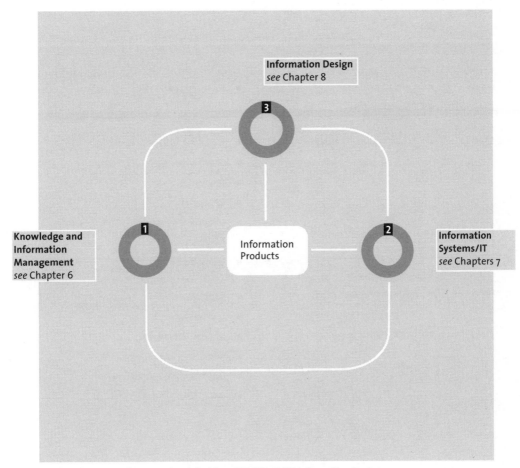

Figure 10.7 Support for IPs and stakeholders: KM/IM, IS/IT, Information Design

" The unique function that information products perform means that
1 The value they add, or subtract, deserves more attention than it gets at present from most organizations
2 They should be taken into account in any attempt to set a value on knowledge and information.

The positive or negative value IPs contribute is always related to the quality of information management, information systems/IT, and information design that supports them, and to the information culture of the organizations that create them. Bad IPs in a poor organizational context can have the most disastrous and tragic consequences in human as well as financial terms (*see* Chapter 4 for examples).

Organizations should take into account both tangible and intangible costs and value in assessing the contribution that their IPs make to business value.

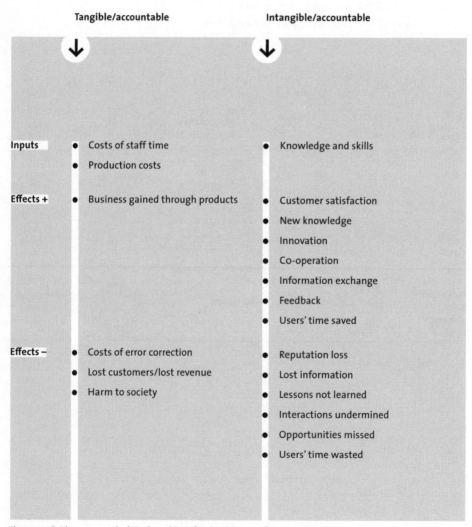

	Tangible/accountable	Intangible/accountable
Inputs	• Costs of staff time • Production costs	• Knowledge and skills
Effects +	• Business gained through products	• Customer satisfaction • New knowledge • Innovation • Co-operation • Information exchange • Feedback • Users' time saved
Effects –	• Costs of error correction • Lost customers/lost revenue • Harm to society	• Reputation loss • Lost information • Lessons not learned • Interactions undermined • Opportunities missed • Users' time wasted

Figure 10.8 The potential of IPs for adding (and subtracting) business value

Making knowledge visible

" There's a long tradition of IPs being 'unseen' from the top of the organization. These are some of the reasons. The arrival of electronic production and distribution hasn't of itself broken the self-perpetuating cycle; in most instances the technology rather than the information products it's used to create has had the lion's share of the attention. Having a website and an intranet doesn't automatically lead to an integrated view of all the organization's IPs.

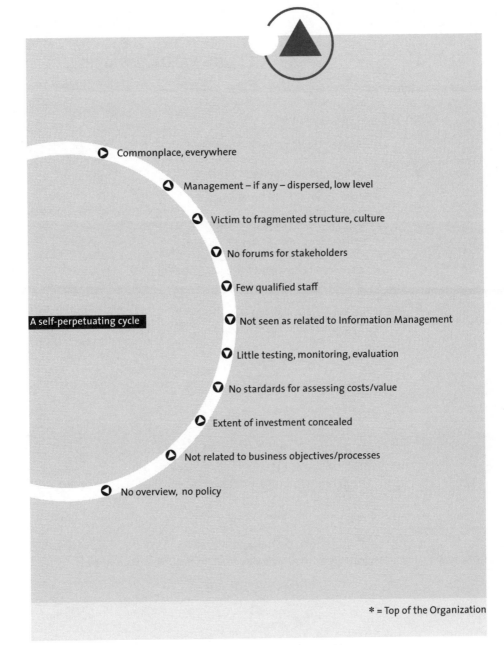

Why traditional IPs are invisible to TOTO＊

- Commonplace, everywhere
- Management – if any – dispersed, low level
- Victim to fragmented structure, culture
- No forums for stakeholders
- Few qualified staff
- Not seen as related to Information Management
- Little testing, monitoring, evaluation
- No stardards for assessing costs/value
- Extent of investment concealed
- Not related to business objectives/processes
- No overview, no policy

A self-perpetuating cycle

＊ = Top of the Organization

Figure 10.9 The self-perpetuating cycle that make IPs invisible to TOTO

"" These conclusions from my own research are supported by the experience of the organizations related in this book. The essential conditions need to coexist, and there has to be understanding and collaboration among all the stakeholder groups. If that happens, investment in IPs pays off for all parties.

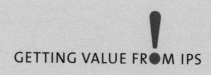

GETTING VALUE FROM IPS

Return on IPs as an information asset

Conditions for getting value from them

Businesses that do well with IPs have ...

- Information-oriented top managers
- *Real* collegial/open culture
- Cross-functional alliances
- Information professionals with authority
- Good understanding between IM and IT
- Overview of all IPs, related to business objectives
- Respect for users
- Stakeholder forums
- Appreciation of specialist skills
- Appropriate information resources

+ Intelligent use of web technology

Figure 10.10 Features of organizations that do well with, and from, their information products

Making knowledge visible

If the ideas presented so far are accepted, and seen as relevant to the organization's situation, the next question is: 'What do we do about it? 'This is the point at which to introduce information auditing as a productive and low-risk way of doing something. The last figure in this presentation outlines the approach and how to use it.

" Information auditing is a well established method for understanding the actual information situation in organizations, amd assessing how close it comes to what they *should* be doing in order to succeed in their aims. It can be successfully applied to information products, as shown in the story of a recent audit told in Chapter 11.

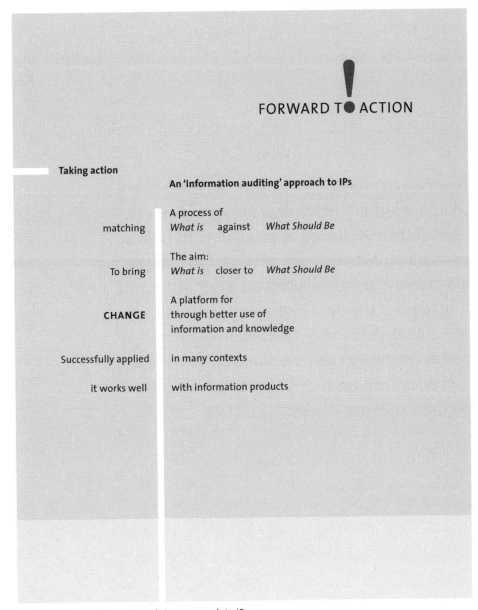

Figure 10.11 An information auditing approach to IPs

'There are in every organizations hundreds if not thousands of information products or services, each of them designed at some time to fulfil a particular function. Many of these have lingered long beyond the time when they fulfilled a function. ... Only by inventorying and auditing present information outputs in an organization and ascertaining their usefulness in benefit and cost terms can we truly begin to get a handle on this expensive process.' TAYLOR (1982)

Auditing information products

In this chapter

Once the organization has accepted that some action on its information products is necessary, and that information auditing is a sound way to start, the next step is to agree objectives for the audit – an essential preliminary which should never be neglected. The agreed objectives form a firm point of reference, and should be understood by all parties, signed up to, and respected.

Objectives for an audit

If it's agreed that it is feasible and desirable to make an audit of the whole range of the organization's information products, the objectives could be formulated on these lines:

Stage 1

- To define the role of our information products in relation to key corporate objectives
- To identify the necessary information content for our information products and the resources of information needed in order to provide it
- To identify the audiences for the products, external and internal
- To define the objectives of the products in relation to: overall corporate objectives and the audiences to whom they are addressed
- To identify the stakeholders in the products
- To define the people who need to interact and work together to create the products
- To define the skills and knowledge they need
- To identify appropriate methods for testing, monitoring and evaluating the products, and assessing their cost-effectiveness.

Stage 2

On the basis of the results of Stage 1
- To investigate the actual situation in respect of these factors
- To identify gaps and areas of unsatisfactory practice or incomplete information; as well as areas where there is a good match between practice and what is desirable in the light of what the organisation seeks to achieve.

Stage 3

- Take action to rectify evident shortcomings
- Learn from good existing practice
- Define and implement a strategy for managing our information products within an overall information strategy.

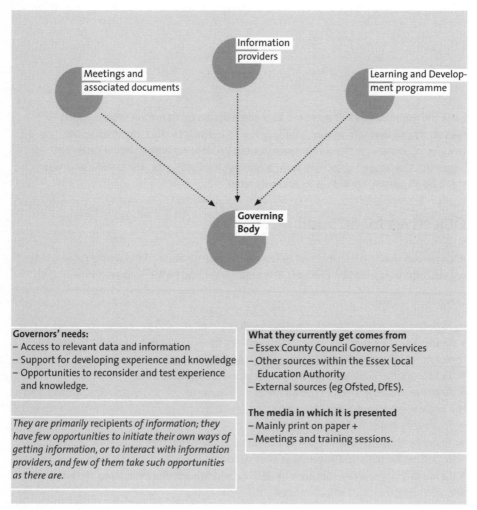

Governors' needs:
- Access to relevant data and information
- Support for developing experience and knowledge
- Opportunities to reconsider and test experience and knowledge.

They are primarily recipients of information; they have few opportunities to initiate their own ways of getting information, or to interact with information providers, and few of them take such opportunities as there are.

What they currently get comes from
- Essex County Council Governor Services
- Other sources within the Essex Local Education Authority
- External sources (eg Ofsted, DfES).

The media in which it is presented
- Mainly print on paper +
- Meetings and training sessions.

Figure 11.1 Background to governors information audit. How governors were getting information at the time when the information audit was proposed. (Based on a 'Process Map' by Heather Leverett, Essex County Council).

Making knowledge visible

Auditing a subset of the organization's IPs

It is probably more likely that the audit will focus on a specific subset of the organization's information products, as it did in the extended example which makes up the rest of this chapter. It is based on Essex County Council's audit of the information needs of school governors. *(see* Chapter 6, p112–113).

 Figures 11.1 and 11.2, (based on 'process maps' presented as part of the proposal which led to the information audit) show the thinking about the current situation in school governance and the aspirations for the future which formed the background to the audit.

The objectives of this audit were defined in these terms, as quoted in the final report of the audit (Essex County Council, 2003):

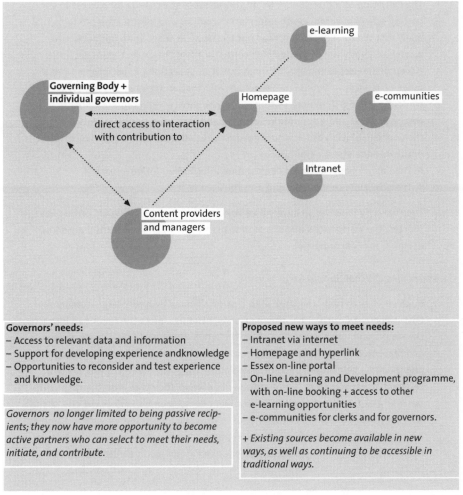

Figure 11.2 Background to governors information audit. Vision of how governors could and should access information, develop experience and knowledge, and try out applying it – supported by 'electronic communities'; presented as part of proposal for the audit. (Based on a 'Process Map' by Heather Leverett, Essex County Council).

In working towards setting up a **Community of Practice** [for school governors]...
ECC decided that in order to understand the functions of these communities, care
should be taken to establish:

- what governors' information needs were;
- the formats through which governors could access information;
- the ways governors wanted information to be presented.

To acquire this it was decided to carry out an audit of governors' information
requirements... [the audit] sought to determine how governors received information; what information they received; and whether this information met their
needs as to content, format and presentation. The audit attempted to establish
areas of good practice, shortcomings and areas for action.

Defining 'What Should Be'

The definition of 'What Should Be', in this instance the criteria for success in supporting school governors with information content and information products that
really met their needs, was worked out by the audit team at an initial two-day
workshop, jointly run by the outside consultant and the project manager – the
Governor Services Manager. The team was a cross-section of specialisms from a
range of services (K and IM professionals; information systems specialists; a
corporate strategist; managers from Governor Services; and representatives of
Data Protection and Information Security), and they used their knowledge of
the Council's objectives for school governance, and their varied experience, to set
out their understanding of how:

- The County Council should be providing information for governors
- The governors should be using it in their work.

They did it by building up a collective 'map' of their answers to questions on key
themes. The instructions and the outline map with which they started are shown
in Figure 11.3, (*see* opposite).

The statement of What Should Be

By the end of an hour, the large map was surrounded by a very large number of
Post-it notes, grouped under the main topic headings. After the team had inspected
the results and had a lively discussion, the whole thing was taken down, rolled up,
and presented to the Governor Services Manager – the overall project manager –
and the Knowledge Management Coordinator. They had the job of producing a
coherent statement from the multitude of answers; they took over the map with
becoming expressions of gratitude, and went off to their labours at the end of the
workshop. After a few days of strenuous endeavour, they emerged with a statement
which grouped the ideas from the team around five key themes, which reflect the
context for information products that has been discussed in earlier chapters of
this book.

Making knowledge visible

▼

3

Information resources and content
the stakeholder groups should have
to sustain their knowledge

3.1 Resources and content they need?

3.2 Forms of presentation they need?

4

Information exchanges and interactions that stakeholder groups
should have

4.1 Who with?

4.2 Purposes/outcomes?

2

What stakeholder groups should
know to work effectively and support
one another

2.1 Governors?

2.2 The education authority?

2.3 School heads?

2.4 Other stakeholders?

5

The support governors and other
stakeholders should have, and how it
should be provided

5.1 For using what they know
effectively?

5.2 For finding information to extend
their knowledge?

5.3 For contributing their knowledge
to information resources?

5.4 For exchanging knowledge
and information?

5.5 For making good use of their time?

1

Stakeholder groups: objectives,
responsibilities, priorities

1.1 School governors

1.2 The education authority

1.3 School heads

1.4 Others

6

Related initiatives

6.1 Any related initiatives that this
project should take into account:
Past?
Current?

Instructions to the audit team

You have a blank 'map' with some questions on
it, and Post-it[1] notes on which you are invited
to put your own brief answers in the light of
your own knowledge and experience.

1 All references to the term 'Post-it' in this book
should be understood as relating to the product
with this trademark.

As you write them, we will put them up around
the large version of the map which is on the
wall, to build a collective picture of the team's
ideas about 'What Should Be' from their
individual answers.

Please put the question number on each Post-it!

Figure 11.3 School governors audit; mapping the issues – what should happen
Reproduced by permission of Essex County Council

Theme 1

The objectives, responsibilities and priorities of governors and other main stakeholder groups (Essex County Council, headteachers, parents, wider community)

What should be: the criteria for success

All stakeholder groups:

- Understand their own responsibilities
- Are aware of other groups' responsibilities
- Realise the differences and potential conflicts between stakeholder groups, and seek to resolve them.

Theme 2

Governors' and ECC knowledge and understanding

What should be: the criteria for success

As well as understanding their own responsibilities and role, and those of other stakeholders, governors have a good working knowledge of:

- Their own school and the community it serves
- ECC education policies
- Relevant legislation
- The education system and how to find information to maintain and extend their knowledge.

ECC knows about:

- The characteristics of individual governing bodies and schools in Essex
- The special knowledge and expertise that individual governors bring to the job
- The information resources available to governors
- How they use the resources
- Changes that will affect governors' responsibilities.

Theme 3

Information resources available to governors: content, presentation, access

What should be: the criteria for success

ECC manages, and provides for the governors' information needs, content and resources relating to:

- The law as it relates to their role
- Relevant education developments
- ECC policies
- People in ECC who can give information on particular topics.

- The resources are accessible to governors
- The information they contain is in appropriate formats and media
- Information is offered to governors in ways that make its meaning and significance clear
- Information distribution is effective and information arrives on time for all governors
- A basic information resources collection for the governing body is kept at schools, and is easily accessible by all governors.

Making knowledge visible

Governing bodies also have easy access to their own information resources on:
- Their meetings, decisions and actions
- Their own school
- Experienced and knowledgeable chairs and clerks act as an information resource
- Clear minuting and agenda make meetings productive.

Theme 4
Information exchanges and interactions

What should be: the criteria for success
Governors understand ECC policies on Information Sharing and Information Security as they apply to school governance:
- They know what information they should give, and receive from other people, as part of the job of being a governor ('Who should tell whom what'), and they act on the knowledge
- They know what is confidential and observe confidentiality
- There are helpful formal and informal arrangements for developing mutual and productive exchanges of information within governing bodies and between governing bodies, schools and the community
- When mistakes related to information happen, lessons are learned from them.

Theme 5
The information environment: support for governors from IT infrastructure and information services

What should be: the criteria for success
ECC training and advice services support the needs of all governors, new and experienced
- There is a single 'way in' for governors to all information resources (including people), and straightforward help in finding information
- The information systems/IT infrastructure is integrated, and there is appropriate training for governors in using it to find information
- The infrastructure supports the Community of Practice by facilitating networks and interest groups and exchanges of information, and by making it easy for governors to contribute to information resources
- There are good standards for presenting information in products that meet the needs and priorities of governors
- ECC information professionals organise, sift, condense and edit information to avoid overload and ensure that essentials are not missed
- Governors have access to training in straightforward ways of managing the information they get, to save time and reduce overload.

Finding out 'What Is': who to talk to, questions to ask, how to find answers

As we have seen, the Essex County Council team started by talking amongst themselves, in order to define 'What Should Be'. They continued the process at the introductory workshop by creating a first picture, from their own experience, of what actually happens, using the same method as before to collect answers to a parallel set of 'What Is' questions. This too was analysed by the project managers; this time, the aim was to identify key topics on which to seek the experience of governors.

Before deciding finally on questions to put to governors, the team carried out individual interviews with a small number of key stakeholders, inside and outside the Council. The purpose was to get their observations on the significant issues identified by the team, and pointers to any other important issues that the audit should cover; to draw on the interviewees' experience of the issues; and to get their judgment of the most serious difficulties and risks in the area of the audit.

The findings from the interviews were used in designing questions for the series of governors workshops which the team ran over the next few weeks, using the same mapping method. Figure 11.4 (*see* opposite) shows the questions that were presented to the governors workshops. The same themes ran through these as were used in the initial workshop, so as to allow comparison of the responses of different groups. The actual phrasing of the questions did vary, however, so as to fit in with the people they were addressed to.

Matching What Is and What Should Be; interpreting the findings

As each workshop for governors was completed, the team analysed the answers for examples of information problems and difficulties, good practice that could be widely applied, and 'action points' – issues that looked as though something needed to be done about them. The lists were consolidated as the audit progressed, and when the series of workshops was completed, the team analysed them critically, bringing their range of specialist knowledge to bear in order to develop ideas about the significance of the issues for successful school governance.

At this stage, the responses about 'What Is' under each of the themes were compared with the 'What Should Be' criteria, to create a table summarizing positive and negative aspects of the actual situation as experienced by governors alongside each criterion for success. As somebody remarked – 'We've got a nice lot of silver linings, most of them with a cloud attached.' Figure 11.5, (*see* p190), shows an extract:
The audit team interpreted the detailed findings on each theme in terms of:
- Costs – in risks incurred, and opportunities missed
- Potential value to be gained by acting on the findings.

They also listed risks and the actions that should be taken to avoid them, and opportunities for adding value.

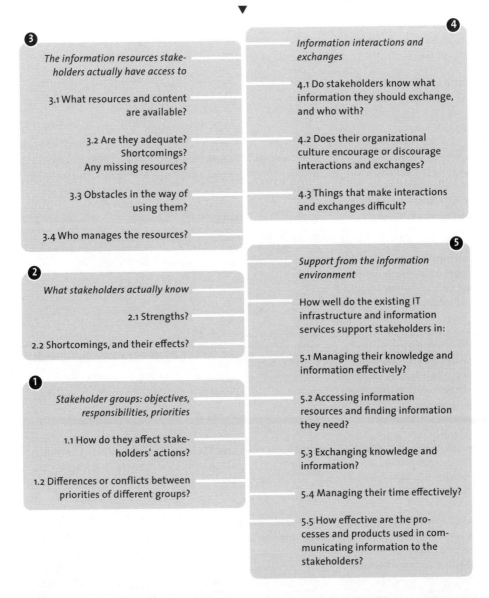

3

The information resources stake-holders actually have access to

3.1 What resources and content are available?

3.2 Are they adequate? Shortcomings? Any missing resources?

3.3 Obstacles in the way of using them?

3.4 Who manages the resources?

4

Information interactions and exchanges

4.1 Do stakeholders know what information they should exchange, and who with?

4.2 Does their organizational culture encourage or discourage interactions and exchanges?

4.3 Things that make interactions and exchanges difficult?

2

What stakeholders actually know

2.1 Strengths?

2.2 Shortcomings, and their effects?

1

Stakeholder groups: objectives, responsibilities, priorities

1.1 How do they affect stake-holders' actions?

1.2 Differences or conflicts between priorities of different groups?

5

Support from the information environment

How well do the existing IT infrastructure and information services support stakeholders in:

5.1 Managing their knowledge and information effectively?

5.2 Accessing information resources and finding information they need?

5.3 Exchanging knowledge and information?

5.4 Managing their time effectively?

5.5 How effective are the processes and products used in communicating information to the stakeholders?

Instructions to the workshop participants

You have a blank 'map' with some questions on it, and Post-it notes on which you are invited to put your own brief answers. in the light of your own knowledge and experience.

As you write them, we will put them up around the large version of the map which is on the wall, to build a collective picture of the group's ideas and experience about the topics from their individual answers.

Please put the question number on each Post-it!

Figure 11.4 School governors audit: mapping the issues – what actually happens in your experience. Reproduced by permission of Essex County Council

Theme 5 The information environment: support for governors from IT infrastructure and information services

What should be: the criteria for success	What is: positive	What is: negative
ECC training and advice services support the needs of all governors, new and experienced:		
• There is a single 'way in' for governors to all information resources (including people), and straightforward help in finding information	The Governors and Clerks Homepage on ECC web site provides a single way in ...	but the Governors and Clerks Homepage needs updating and not all LEA services are known.
• The information systems/IT infrastructure is integrated, and there is appropriate training for governors in using it to find information	Training sessions are provided and more are planned ...	but many governors do not use the internet.
• The infrastructure supports the Community of Practice by facilitating networks and interest groups, and exchanges of information, making it easy for governors to contribute to information resources	Support for a Community of Practice is planned and established cluster groups exist.	
• There are good standards for presenting information in products that meet the needs and priorities of governors	Some publications from ECC are excellent ...	but many documents are too long. Summaries preferred.
• ECC information professionals organise, sift, condense and edit information to avoid overload and brief to ensure that essentials are not missed	Gateways* provides a good executive brief ...	but the quality of information in some publications is sometimes poor.
• Governors have access to training in straightforward ways of managing the information they get to save time and reduce overload		but training in information management not yet available.

*Half-termly LEA publication for School Governors and Clerks in Essex

Figure 11.5 'What Is' compared with 'What Should Be' Reproduced by permission of Essex County Council from the report of the audit (Essex County Council, 2003).

Making knowledge visible

Presenting the results

The numerous action points they identified provided the basis for just four top-level recommendations to the Council (it was a deliberate choice not to deluge the decision-makers with detailed recommendations – experience shows that this is a pretty surefire way of delaying decisions).

1 An ongoing campaign to improve governors' understanding of their objectives, roles and responsibilities, and of services provided by ECC
2 Establish ways, such as face-to-face, written and electronic, through which governors can share information
3 Ensure ECC has strategies for meeting its legal obligations to provide governors with the information they need, in the right format, and at the right time
4 Arrange for a successor group, based on the audit team and governors, to present and initiate a related plan for action.

The understanding that the audit team had gained from the very full and thoughtful responses of governors and other participants led them also to make a separate set of recommendations addressed to school governing bodies, which were designed to help towards mutual support and cooperation between governors and the Council.

Having reached this point, the team presented a draft report for comment to the Steering Group for the project, and to the collaborators in the audit, in separate sessions. This is always a wise move. Steering group members who are in touch with currently sensitive issues and know the 'King Charles' head' phrases of the moment, are able to warn of things liable to cause trouble, and advise on how to avoid negative responses and win agreement. The people who have contributed to the audit appreciate the opportunity to consider what the auditors have made of their responses, and enjoy expressing themselves freely about the way the report should be presented to the audience they represent. In the present instance, the advice received from both presentations led to beneficial modifications; the final report was well received, the recommendations were accepted, and action started forthwith.

This happy conclusion does not happen with all information audits! At the beginning of a research case study in an organization which had excellent information products, but was less advanced in managing information, I was given a recently produced report on what was in effect an information and communications audit. The aim was to get full value from the products and the high-quality content which went into them, by developing the organization's information management capacity. The report presented at the end of it – which included a matrix of all the organization's information products – contained sound recommendations for action.

On a follow-up visit to the organization, a year or so later, I inquired about what action had been taken as a result of the project. I found that the staff member who had taken the lead in it had left, all record of the fact that it had taken place seemed to have disappeared, and it appeared that I had the only copy of the report!

The Essex recommendation for a 'successor group' based on the audit team and key stakeholders, with a remit to get on with the action, was a really useful device. Experience suggests that if key members of the audit team don't go forward to take part in implementing the recommendations, the chance of getting value from an information audit is seriously damaged. Some time ago, I encountered another audit, which went very well up to the point when the recommendations were accepted. Unfortunately in that instance, the audit project leader left for another job outside the organization, the steering group members were dispersed by organizational changes, and new staff members – from elsewhere in the organization – who had had no contact with the audit when it was in progress, were given the job of implementing the agreed actions. A year later, very little of the original intentions had been achieved, and the audit was rapidly disappearing into the limbo of 'organizational oblivion'.

The next chapter brings up to date the story of action to implement the recommendations, and offers suggestions for those who are ready and willing to take action of their own in this little-explored but rich information territory.

References

ESSEX COUNTY COUNCIL (2003)
Governing for success. School governors information audit

TAYLOR, R S (1982)
'Organizational information environments', In G P Sweeney (ed) *Information and the transformation of society*, Amsterdam, Oxford: North-Holland

Other reading

SLESS, D (2000)
Experiences in co-designing. Keynote address at Co-designing conference, Coventry University 2000

Quotes useful criteria which the Communication Research Organization Australia (CRIA@communication.org.au) applies to information products in its co-designing projects with clients. They're expressed in terms of the minimum percentage of people served by an organization who should be satisfied with various aspects of its communication.

See also: http://www/communication. org.au/html/diagnostic.html

Into action for value from IPs

In this chapter

From audit to action: the end of the beginning

To begin this final chapter, here is the rest of the story of the Essex governors audit, and what happened after it.

 The audit was the 'end of the beginning'. What came next had two important and unusual features that gave a good start to the action:

- The 'Successor Group'
- A fortuitous opportunity for evaluation.

The 'Successor Group'
The group responsible for taking forward the recommendations of the audit consisted of five governors and the Governor Services Manager who had led the audit. They proceeded by a pilot exercise. As mentioned in Chapter 11, the final report offered some recommendations to governors, as well as to the County Council. They were grouped under the main audit themes.

Theme 1
Working together
- **Know and understand each other's roles and responsibilities, and plan for these.**
- **Work in co-operation, balancing support and challenge.**
- **Learn from experienced governors.**

Theme 2
Knowledge
- **Find out the skills, experience and knowledge available in the governing body.**
- **Plan to share knowledge and contribute to governing body work.**
- **Attend training and put learning into practice.**

Theme 3

Information

- Have an information strategy and use available information.
- Enable the clerks' learning and development to fully benefit from their skills.
- Establish and maintain a governors' resource collection.
- Make sure all policies are available and have planned review dates.

Theme 4

Learning from each other

- Have a system and process in the school to ensure information is shared.
- Use Communities of Practice.
- Share good examples.
- Work at creating and maintaining good channels of communications.
- Be involved in the community.

Theme 5

Support

- Know whom to contact.
- Plan access to facilities.
- Train on how to use computers and the Internet.
- Encourage sharing ideas for improved ways of working.
- Subscribe to Governor Services.

The report also presented a 'culture check for governing bodies' to help them evaluate how they are doing on meeting the recommendations.

In the school year following the audit, the Successor Group piloted the recommendations with 11 'trailblazing' schools of various types – including Primary, Infant, Special, Grammar, Junior, Church, and Sixth-form college – as a preliminary to inviting all schools in the county to take part in the process at the start of the 2004–2005 school year.

The Group developed a range of self-evaluation IPs on the basis of the audit report to help governors manage knowledge and information: an audit check list, the culture check, a worked example of an action plan, terms of reference for participating schools, and model documents. The response of the 'trailblazing' governing bodies who tested them showed that they met a real need. The majority felt that any time invested in using them would 'reap rewards that far outweighed the commitment'. Several of the governing bodies found these tools were 'exactly what they had been crying out for' when they took part in workshops during the audit (see p188–189). Case studies in the Successor Group's report (Essex County Council, 2004) show that schools found they could use them in a range of ways to suit local situations.

Inspired by the products resulting from the audit, many governing bodies decided to start developing IPs of their own, including handbooks and written governing body development plans. Another recommended initiative already taken up by some is appointing an 'Information Governor', a member with special information management responsibilities, which cover developing a governing-body information strategy, managing information resources, and maintaining such information products as the school governors' page on the Community of Practice site, and the handbook.

During the same period, a pilot Community of Practice website was also tested in preparation for launching. The audit led to a clearer understanding of what form this should take, especially the realization that there are a number of different school-governor communities rather than a single one – for example groups of governors with shared interests in specific subjects, and 'clusters' of school governing bodies who choose to meet as a group. Contributors to the audit made suggestions for a number of products that should be offered through the Community of Practice: they include a database of skills, policies and guidance on education issues; and summaries of important papers with links to the full documents.

The 'eGovernors' website – 'an electronic community of practice for Essex governors' – launched after this process, at the start of the 2004–2005 school year, is very different from the Community of Practice that might have been developed on the basis of the original focus group, and without the audit. It offers users both a common area open to all governors, and one which is reserved for their own governing body. In both areas there are facilities for posting information products created by users, as well as products from other sources; and both also offer a discussion board. There are easily usable search facilities allowing search by title, document text, date, etc, from current and archive material which can readily be accessed.

Research retrospect on the audit

By a fortunate coincidence (though she probably wouldn't have called it that at the time) the Knowledge Co-ordinator who was one of the core members of the audit team was studying part-time for a higher degree during the audit, and she was able to undertake research on its outcomes for her dissertation. After the audit she interviewed members of the audit team, and a sample of the governors who had taken part in the workshops and in the presentations of the interim and final reports.

It's worth looking at the results in some detail because they support both information auditing as a method, and its application to a situation where IPs were central.

 The governors: For the governors, the audit appears to have been a positive experience, from which they learned a good deal. They felt they had been well informed during the process, and involved in it to the end, through the presentation of the interim report, and the final report which embodied changes in response to their comments.

Most of them enjoyed answering the workshop questions; new governors liked doing so 'because it gave them a chance to have an input. They had been worried that in a discussion they wouldn't have much to say.' Their experienced colleagues found 'it provided a focus and gave them a chance to "concentrate the mind"'. Several of them liked the flexibility of the Post-its, and the fact that 'they were whipped away so quickly that they couldn't change their minds'. Asking people to start by getting their own ideas down, rather than beginning with a discussion on the issues, was welcomed as a way of getting at what people really thought, and as allowing participants to see that 'so many people felt the same, and see the whole range of other people's remarks.'

The interviews made it possible to explore more fully three important issues which emerged from the audit: interpersonal relationships on governing bodies; new governors; and the '25/75' split between the governors who do the work and those who contribute little. The significance of these emerged more and more clearly in the discussions at the workshops and in the two presentations of the reports, as governors became readier to talk from experience. The individual interviews allowed them to take this to greater depth, with detailed examples of the problems they faced, which not only confirmed the audit findings about what happens, but also provided an insight into why it happens, and how the issues are inter-related. (These findings are reminiscent of Sless's (2000) report of the proportion of time that has to be devoted to investigating and dealing with organization politics in 'co-designing' – a design process whose approach parallels that of information auditing.)

The auditors: The evaluation interviews with the members of the audit team revealed that most of them considered that, while they had learned a great deal from the process, and gained some knowledge about schools and governing bodies, the findings from the audit provided evidence of 'what we already thought we knew'.

It was possible to check the accuracy of that observation by comparing the 'What Is' map which the team created at their initial workshop with the actual findings from the audit. The researcher did this, and produced an interesting tabulation of the results. It shows that while the findings did indeed confirm much of what the team had anticipated beforehand, they also revealed a number of factors which did not appear in the map on which the team recorded their knowledge and belief about 'What Is' before the audit.

Many of these were of high significance, and required action. For example:
● The team believed before the audit that while some governors might be uncertain about their responsibilities, most knew what was required of them.
In the event, there turned out to be widespread ignorance or lack of understanding of statutory roles and responsibilities, with constant changes to legislation as a major problem.
● They also assumed that the majority of governors knew what information they should/could exchange.
In fact, the audit showed a large degree of ignorance or confusion about the critical issue of confidentiality, and governors complained that no advice had been given.
● The team believed before the audit that information resources in schools were managed by the link governor, the head teacher, or school administrative staff
A different situation, requiring priority attention, became clear from the audit.
In some instances the information resources were 'locked away' by the school head, and getting at them was not easy for governors. Many governors revealed that

they kept personal information collections, and the need for training to help them manage them emerged as a major issue.

● The problems faced by new governors was not anticipated by the audit team were. *In actuality this emerged as a very significant issue.*

Informed judgement

The researcher was able to conclude that 'the audit has contributed significant information on governors' information needs and the problems they face', and that it had been of value in relation to the development of a Community of Practice because it had identified:

● **The specific interests of potential community members**
● **Who the most active participants might be**
● **The types and formats of information required**
● **The functionality required for a virtual community**
● **The cultural willingness to share information and knowledge**
● **The support required by new members.**

This retrospective study, undertaken shortly after the process was over, made possible a uniquely full and well-founded assessment of the value the audit had contributed. It is certainly the first instance of this kind in my experience, and I wish it might become a part of standard practice.

The audit in the light of the ideas advanced in this book

This was acknowledged to be a successful and productive audit. Now let us look at how the practice it followed relates to the ideas that have been put forward in earlier chapters, about the context in which information products should be seen, and how they should be developed and managed.

The organization's objectives, business processes and information culture

● The organization's objectives and its business processes should determine what kinds of IPs it needs, and the appropriate content, medium and form for them.
● Information products should help achieve objectives, and support business processes – and as such should be part of an overall information strategy.
● Information culture and behaviour has a decisive influence on how IPs are created, managed, disseminated and used, and so on how effective they are.
● Organizations should study the culture and its effects and learn from the results; this may lead to action which will modify information behaviour and get better value from information products.

The governors' audit
> *Was based on the ECC's overall objectives, and on the specific objectives relating to school governance. It examined stakeholder conceptions of the objectives of the various groups. It looked at the processes involved in the work of governing bodies, and in the relations between them and the Council.*

It was carried out within the framework of the Council's existing information and knowledge strategy; the audit, together with the earlier work on education publications, has opened the way to including information products within that strategy. The recommendations to governors also include an information strategy for governing bodies.

The audit looked particularly at cultural factors which influence the perceptions of governors, their interactions with the local authority, and relationships within governing bodies and between governors and other stakeholders.

The discoveries in this respect influenced decisions about action to rectify shortcomings, about the form that the Community of Practice should take, and the information products that governors needed.

The stakeholders

- There are many key groups of stakeholders, internal and external, in an organization's information products, starting from the organization itself.
- Organizations seldom recognize them all; and communication among stakeholders is often poor or non-existent.
- Where their interests in IPs are recognized and action is taken to bring them together to collaborate, the organization and its IPs benefit.
- The people who use the information products are the most important stakeholders; it's dangerous to see them as passive recipients of whatever the organization chooses to offer them. They should have a recognized role in initiating and specifying products in the light of how they need to use them.

The governors' audit

Incorporated representatives of key stakeholder groups in the audit team, took advice from other major stakeholders in planning the audit, and investigated the experience of a range of governors and clerks through workshops. Particular emphasis was placed on governing bodies as users of information products, and the implications of the findings for the kind of products they should be offered. The Successor Group which developed and tested the self-evaluation tools and planned the eGovernors Community of Practice was mainly composed of users.

Information management, information systems/IT, and information design

- The three specialisms of information and knowledge management, information systems/IT, and information design should make a critically important contribution to the organization's IPs.
- They can make their full contribution to IPs only if:
they understand one another and cooperate, and if the top of the organization understands their real potential in this respect.

The governors' audit:

The project was managed by information professionals – the Governor Services Manager, and the Knowledge Management Coordinator from Information Services, a department which brings together information management and information systems expertise. The audit team included systems/IT managers.

*The project sponsor was the Head of Information Services, and the other members of
the Steering Group/Project Board were the Information Services Corporate Knowledge
Manager and the Head of Governor Services.*

*The planning of the eGovernors community of practice site was a collaborative
process: the Successor Group and the Council's Governor Services and Information
Services contributed content and specification for structure and navigation facilities;
and a professional from the Council's systems/IT partner designed the website and
technological support that embodied them.*

*The information design component was covered by the fact that the KM Coordinator
had been responsible for developing a publishing system for the Council's Education
Services, and establishing design standards for the work of the in-house design team.
The IPs resulting from the audit were carefully designed to those standards, with
proper regard for what had been learned from the audit about the users and the ways
in which they needed to use information.*

Value added and subtracted

- Since information products are the means by which people access the information
they need, so that they can transform it into knowledge and act on it, any attempt to
value knowledge and information must take them into account.
- Information products can both add and subtract value – tangible and intangible.
- When they subtract value, the consequences can range from direct financial loss and
loss of customers, to appalling human tragedies.
- Well-managed information products benefit from and contribute to a high level of
information orientation in their organizations, and add value to their overall offering in
a range of ways.
- Organizations need appropriate criteria for assessing the contribution their information products make to business value.

The governors' audit

*The final purposes of the audit were to add value to the governors' contribution to
education in the county, by helping all of them to understand, learn, keep up to date,
and act effectively; and to reduce the risks created by the lack of essential information,
and by inappropriate information products. The discoveries made through the audit,
in the view of the audit team as expressed in the final report, significantly increased
the chances that the action taken as a result will achieve these aims. The research
investigation which followed immediately on the audit confirmed the judgment, as did
the views volunteered by governors quoted above from the report on the period
of trial of the various information products created as a result of the audit.*

Approaches that work in practice

To end this journey, and, I hope, send readers on their way well equipped for action on
their own account, a reminder of approaches and ideas which have proved their worth
in relevant situations. First, a summary of things the Essex governors audit team found
worked well for them; then a recapitulation of useful points from some of the stories of

real organizations told earlier; and finally, for those who really enjoy challenges, a note of some of the territories where more exploration is needed.

Essex governors' audit

Actions by the audit team which contributed to the success of the audit, in the judgment of the audit team and of participants in the audit:

- They prepared themselves thoroughly for the job. The initial two-day workshop allowed them time to think and exchange ideas about the issues, to agree on how they would work and allocation of responsibilities, to start planning, and to start understanding one another and working as a team.

- Their thinking was in the framework of the Council's information strategy and its overall 'Essex approach'.

- They contributed in appropriate ways to the audit. While the heaviest load was inevitably carried by the two members responsible for managing the project, the other team members joined in running workshops, analysing responses, advising from specialist knowledge, and report editing.

- They kept stakeholders involved and informed before, during and after the audit, without over-informing them en route.

- They made good use of the Steering Group throughout, particularly in discussions about what the recommendations should be, and received good advice from them.

- They got through the process at a fair speed, and kept it moving so that nobody had time to forget about it. There were just six weeks between the first workshop and the presentation of the final report – a timescale imposed by the nature of the education calendar. The audit managers certainly didn't have time to think about anything else, but judged that the experience and the outcome made the associated wear and tear worth while.

- They asked appropriate questions. The audit team devoted a lot of time to formulating questions for the governors workshops, and it paid off. Governors thought the questions they were asked 'got to the heart of things' and found themselves well able to answer them from their experience.

- They gave respondents a comfortable situation, in which nobody felt at a disadvantage. The workshops allowed people to start by answering questions for themselves, rather than by taking part in a discussion, where some could have felt anxious or unable to contribute. They liked putting short answers on Post-its, and being able, when they'd expressed their own experience, to see the whole range of answers, which made the basis for a relaxed discussion in which all were able to join.

- They gave those who had contributed information the chance of commenting on what the team had made of their contributions, in an interim report; and showed them the results of their comments in a presentation of the final report. The subsequent research interviews showed how much that was appreciated; and it helped to get the Successor Group off to a good start on its work.

- They made sure they got the final report as right as time allowed. Editing the interim report to take account of comments was a collaborative effort among team members (the research interviews showed that they thought there should have been a single editor, and this practice was in fact adopted in the next audit undertaken for the County Council). Writing and visual presentation got proper attention, and the information product delivered was accessible, readable, well-signposted, and attractive.

- They prepared thoroughly for presenting their recommendations, and sold them successfully to the decision makers.

- They provided for an appropriate group to carry forward action on the recommendations, and that Successor Group brought users into the planning of the information products developed on the basis of the recommendations.

The experience of other organizations

The information-product stories from a variety of organizations which have been related in this book embody many useful practical points. They are brought together in summary form below, with cross references to the places where the stories are told in full.

Briefing outside designers with care and building understanding with them over the long-term
– The Co-operative Bank 142

Bringing information products within information strategy
– Tate 40–41
– DTI 47–50
– mda 117

Bringing users into the planning of information products through 'co-designing'
– CRIA 102–103

Building links among key specialisms
– Essex publications 43
– FreePint 42
– mda 88
– RCN 113
– Premier Farnell taxonomy 116
– The Cochrane Collaboration and the Centre for Reviews and Dissemination 114–116

Giving attention to communicating and interacting with people, and to training to support them in this
– Royal College of Nursing 1113

Identifying and bringing together all stakeholders at the start of any major project involving new IPs
– City University website development 83–84
– V&A 50–54
– Co-operative Bank Partnership Reports 54, 56, 142

Identifying the specialist skills and knowledge which are needed for creating IPs, and bringing them together
– FreePint 114
– Premier Farnell 88
– V&A 51

Knowing the strengths of the organizational culture and applying them intelligently to IPs by long-term well supported relations between in-house staff and suppliers of specialist design skills; attention to preparing briefs for them.
– The Co-operative Bank 54–56, 142

Making users into partners in creating IPs
– FreePint 42, 113–114

Meeting change by using technology to complement and support new kinds of interactions with users, new kinds of products, new views of objectives and business processes
– mda 38–40

Recognizing IPs as an business entity and providing for unified and co-ordinated management, with responsibility clearly assigned
– Premier Farnell 37–38, 157

Recognizing the importance of information culture in major projects involving information products, learning about the effects. and observing the changes in culture created by the project, and using the lessons for future projects
– V&A 50–54

Respecting the users learning about how they want/need to use the organization's information products, and the difficulties they meet in doing so.
– NHS Direct 100–101
– IMF 101–102
– CRIA 102–103

Understanding of organizational structure and politics used to alert the organization to the implications of legislation for information products
– Essex County Council 85–87
– DTI 47–50

Using changes in how the organization operates as an opportunity to establish a unified management structure for IPs
– DTI 47–50
– mda 38–40, 117
– Premier Farnell 37

Using web-based development projects
1 to build alliances among stakeholders
– City University 83–84
– Tate 40–41, 128–129
2 as an opportunity to consider the relative roles of printed products and the web, and the potential for integrating the whole range
– The Co-operative Bank 129–130

Little-explored territories

I mentioned in Chapter 1 a number of aspects of information thinking and practice where little if any attention appears to have been given to the place, potential or requirements of information products. There is scope for investigation, discovery and action in these areas:
• Information resources for managing information products
• IPs as part of information architecture
• The explicit inclusion of IPs in information strategies and their development
• What senior managers and information professionals should understand about information design, and what they actually understand
• What information designers should understand about the organizational context of design, and about information management – and what they actually understand
• Recognition of the potential of IPs for adding and subtracting value, and exploring relevant ways of doing it – including applying evidence-based information practice. (Booth and Brice, 2004, Brice and Booth, 2004)
• Working with users in testing draft IPs and monitoring the effectiveness of existing ones.

Making knowledge visible

Outcomes?

I end this book with my hopes for what it may lead to – and what I wish it may not.

I should dislike greatly to find 'Information Products' becoming a new buzz-word, the subject of articles full of cliches in the journals devoted to keeping senior managers up to date, and of energetic takeover bids from quarters that see opportunities for self-advancement and profit there.

The results I should really like to see would be:

● The spread of recognition that the ideas we have been discussing here, and the practical applications of them that we have seen, make common sense for organizations and businesses of all kinds, and are worth their serious attention.

● Instances of stakeholders (especially the three essential groups made up of information managers, systems professionals, and information designers) exercising their existing skills and knowledge in new ways, working together in new alliances, in an equitable and truly collegial way, and enjoying the process, as well as adding value for themselves and their organizations..

References

BOOTH, A & BRICE, A (2004)
Evidence-based Practice for Information Professional; A handbook, London: Facet Publishing

BRICE, A & BOOTH, A (2004)
'Consider the evidence', *Library + Information Update,* 3 (6) 32–33

ESSEX COUNTY COUNCIL (2004)
The next chapter of governing for success, Chelmsford: Essex County Council

SLESS, D (2000)
'Experiences in co-designing.' Keynote address at Co-designing conference, Coventry University 2000
CRIA@communication.org.au

Other reading

DALE, A (2002)
'Dispatches: Letters from the Corporanian War Zone', *Journal of Information Science,* 28 (3) 253–256

Recommends information auditing as a method for dealing with intranet problems, and suggests using the evidence from it to 'take each information need and package it into ... an information product' – many of which will draw on same information sources, but require different presentation.

Index

continued

continued

continued